A sampling of the critics' commendation
for THOMAS MERTON ON MYSTICISM

"To synthesize and put in an ordered system the teachings on mysticism in Merton's more than 50 books was assuredly no easy task, but [Bailey] has accomplished it in an expert manner. . . . Within the framework of a detailed biography, Dr. Bailey describes the successive steps in Merton's spiritual journey. . . . In short, it is one of the best and most authoritative works yet to appear in the rapidly growing library of books on Thomas Merton."
—*The Catholic Review*

"Those who are strongly interested in Merton or mysticism will find a wealth of material in this book to peruse." —*St. Anthony Messenger*

"[Here] is a portrait of Merton's mysticism which is . . . sympathetic, temperate and insightful, and should prove useful to those for whom finding a path through Merton's thought has been a problem." —*Publishers Weekly*

"Bailey gives us some penetrating glimpses into Merton the man. Such glimpses are, for this reader at least, the best feature of this book." —*Spiritual Book News*

"[A] deeply perceptive and thoughtful study of Merton's inner spiritual development. . . . Bailey avoids pedantry and writes lucidly clear prose. His book is a marvelous exploration into how classic mystical experience filters through contemporary man's consciousness, and as such has significance beyond portraying one man's inner experience. Thomas Merton would have been pleased with it."
—*Library Journal*

Thomas Merton
on Mysticism

Thomas Merton
on Mysticism

First Image Books Edition published September 1975. Revised
March 1976 by special arrangement with Doubleday & Company,
Inc.

Thomas Merton on Mysticism

RAYMOND BAILEY

Library of Congress Cataloging in Publication Data
Bailey, Raymond.
    Thomas Merton on mysticism.
    Originally presented as the author's thesis, Southern
Baptist Theological Seminary, Louisville.
    Includes bibliographical references.
    1. Merton, Thomas, 1915-1968.   2. Mysticism—History.

BV5095.M4B34   1975   248'.22'0924
ISBN 0-385-11018-5

IMAGE BOOKS
A Division of Doubleday & Company, Inc.
Garden City, New York
1987

First Image Books Edition published September 1976; Reissued
March 1987; by special arrangement with Doubleday & Company,
Inc.

Library of Congress Cataloging in Publication Data
Bailey, Raymond.
    Thomas Merton on mysticism.
    Originally presented as the author's thesis, Southern
Baptist Theological Seminary, Louisville.
    Includes biographical references.
    1. Merton, Thomas, 1915-1968. 2. Mysticism—History.
I. Title.
BX4705.M542B28 1975 248'.22'0924
ISBN 0-385-24015-5

Contents

CONTENTS

Preface

It is almost unbelievable that a Texas Baptist ignorant of Catholicism for almost thirty years should become a teacher in a Catholic institution. No less incredible is the fact that a person with no knowledge of the mystical tradition prior to 1964, and who had never heard of Thomas Merton until 1967, should write a doctoral dissertation on Merton as a modern expression of that tradition, while holding the position of director of the Thomas Merton Studies Center of Bellarmine College. This work was originally done in partial fulfillment of the requirements for the degree of doctor of theology at the Southern Baptist Theological Seminary in Louisville, Kentucky. Incredible or not, these are the facts. What's more, the principal in this strange turn of events comes out of this experience convinced that the rich reservoir of spiritual riches of this tradition, particularly in the patristic period, has been grossly neglected by his own Baptist tradition, in spite of the fact that it contains the most adequate foundation for Baptist theology, a theology of personal spiritual transformation in Christ. Thomas Merton's discourses on grace and faith delivered from a Baptist pulpit would arouse no hostility—indeed, from many would evoke a hearty "Amen."

The number of people to whom this writer is indebted is legion, but space permits only the mention of a few. First and foremost is Dr. E. Glenn Hinson, chairman of his Graduate Committee and the one who introduced him to patristics, spiritual theology, and Thomas Merton. No supervisor could have been more considerate and help-

ful. Brother Patrick Hart of the Abbey of Gethsemani has
been most generous with his time, tips, inspiration, and
prayers. John Howard Griffin has been completely un-
selfish in his encouragement and generous sharing of information gathered through intense investigation over a period of years. The author of this study came away from his
first meeting with Griffin with the feeling that his immediate uncritical acceptance of a virtual stranger was the
kind of expression of love that characterized Merton. The
Merton Legacy trustees, James Laughlin, Naomi Burton
Stone, and Tommie O'Callaghan, have made every effort
to encourage this work and to make available the needed
materials.

I am grateful to Bellarmine College for providing me
the opportunity to work in the Merton Center and for
bringing me into the realm of Merton influence. Special
thanks are due those who assisted with the preparation of
the actual manuscript: Donna Hagewood, who suffered
through the first draft and the rigorous requirements for
the formal dissertation; Lucille Pickett, my present secretary at the First Baptist Church in Newport, Kentucky,
who worked above and beyond the call of duty; Sue
Rankin and Carol Thompson, for typing a portion of the
final manuscript; Douglas Anderson and Ed Wheeler's
proofreading and helpful comments were most appreciated.

Most importantly, I hope that my wife, Pat, and my
two daughters, Hollie and Sarah, will someday think this
work worth the hours it left them without a husband and
father; not to mention the undeserved displays of a non-
spiritual temper by a tense writer.

Thomas Merton
on Mysticism

Thomas Merton
on Mysticism

CHAPTER I

Introduction

The Age of Aquarius has dawned, and in spite of the continuing existence of war, famine, disease, and death, it may well develop into the golden age of the re-emergence of the spirit. The niagara of technical knowledge and skill that dominated the third quarter of the twentieth century has failed to extinguish the burning desire for the integration of fragmented humanity, an integration that is possible only in the convergence of the elements of the human in the holy. It is ironic, though not surprising to the student of history, that this period of rapid scientific discovery and technological progress should create frustration and crisis sufficient to generate the most intense period of spiritual searching in the modern era. In the front ranks of the new Seekers was an Aquarian who discovered new truth in one of the oldest and most traditional religious life styles. It is he, Thomas Merton, contemplative monk, who is the subject of this book.

Few writers, let alone religious writers, enjoy the literary success that made Merton a public figure and won him unsought acclaim as poet, literary critic, spiritual adviser, and social commentator. His thirty-plus books and hundreds of articles and reviews attracted a curiously diverse audience of the whole religious spectrum, not to mention philosophers, poets, and statesmen. Highly respected in literary circles, he was considered a knowledgeable aesthetician who achieved success in several genres.

Thomas Merton was a rare individual, who encompassed in himself in almost equal degrees the four elements of religion: the institutional, the intellectual, the social, and the mystical. It was the mystical element that

held together the others, but it was the others that gave
form and visibility to the mystical, in a sense preserving it
for others. Merton is a troublesome case study for critics
of mystical religion who charge that mystics withdraw
from society and make no contribution to history. Merton
emerged from a semi-agnostic Protestant background to
commit himself to the most hierarchical of Christian communities and to adopt the rigorous discipline of Cistercian
monasticism. Paradox marked virtually every facet of his
life. A close friend of John Howard Griffin and the Berrigan brothers, and an ardent admirer of Martin Luther
King, Jr., Merton was extremely vocal in his support of
the civil rights and peace movements. He was writing antiwar materials in the 1940s and 1950s and was instru-
mental in the founding of the Catholic Peace Movement. However, an analysis of Merton's writings reveals
that these activities were only peripheral to his primary
concern, the mystical quest for union with God. His social
commentary, as well as his poetic outpourings, were the
fruits of his preoccupation with the quest for the Divine.
The dominant motivation in Merton's life and the primary motif in his work was this mystical quest for union
with God. Throughout his life Merton remained constant
to his contemplative commitment explicit in the poetic
vow recorded in *The Tears of the Blind Lions*: "May my
bones burn and ravens eat my flesh/If I forget thee, contemplation. . . ."[1] Moreover, Merton's thought and meth-
odology were rooted in traditional mystical theology and
framed in the matrix of the symbols and structures of Catholicism. Merton presented little in the way of original
thought. His great contribution was the particularity of his
person and the synthesizing and contemporizing of ancient
and universal truths. In 1949, Merton commented in the
opening pages of *Seeds of Contemplation* that only his expression was new, with the content free of "a line that is
new to Catholic tradition or a single word that would perplex an orthodox theologian."[2] A *Commonweal* article
published six years later noted that Merton's originality

was alloyed with ". . . an intrinsic sense of the orthodox . . ."[3] Glenn Hinson concluded in an essay written in 1972 that Merton had creatively recast the rich legacy of classical Christian mysticism.

> Merton's originality lay, therefore, in the way he fed the whole tradition of contemplation through his own gifted and fertile mind and personality so as to create a profound new synthesis which could speak not only to his monastic confreres but even to the wider circle of humanity.[4]

Merton drank deeply at the springs of the classical mystical tradition. His fertile mind and compulsive spirit would not let him be still. Life and the world converged in a process of continuous unfolding of mysteries. Every resolved mystery kindled new excitement and anticipation because our mortal vision is always "through a glass darkly," and each answer radiated new questions, each new boundary penetrated new wilderness. Merton appears to have carried on within himself a continuing dialectic, keeping his thoughts always in process. His later lectures and writings on spirituality were not the results of some sudden enlightenment but were inevitable stops on the journey. His conclusions were always heuristic ones, subject to change in degree or even in kind by a new synthesis produced by a new experience or the insights of some new intellectual or spiritual influence. Merton's thought and in turn his words changed almost daily, certainly periodically, so that he would often contradict his own earlier conclusions, stages in the evolution of his thought and experience. Growth was a characteristic of his life and thought, and just as there is little resemblance between a bulb and a tulip or an acorn and an oak, so there are striking differences in Merton at various stages of his development. Nonetheless, the seeds of his mystical thought were present germinally even before he entered the monastery, and grew to full bloom in interaction with the historical and personal crises during the period 1941–68. Merton himself provided an archetype for the philosophy stated in his last address, "What we have to be is what we are."[5]

Merton's interest in mysticism and his dialogue with those in other religious traditions with a similar interest cast him in a special if unofficial role in post-Vatican II ecumenics. Merton was only one of many who saw the blind alley of suprarationalism and the pseudosalvation of science. Merton was a part of a spiritual renaissance that continues even today. It is ironic that in this highly technical age there should be a rediscovery of mystical theology, but this seems to be the case. Since the Reformation, certainly in Protestantism, mystical theology has been relegated to the periphery of Christianity. Those who have dared to pursue the mystical way have been treated at best as eccentric charismatics, at worst as freaks. Mysticism is viewed with suspicion by those who see it as a threat to institutional religion because of its subjective and personal nature. It has often taken an anticultural form, which greatly disturbs those who see it as too "other-worldly." Catholics have feared the possible challenge to the authority and sacraments of the Church; if God can be apprehended directly, then the Church can be circumvented. Protestants have associated it with Catholic monasticism and have been apprehensive of the possible challenge to the biblical norm. But ferment and change have characterized religion and religious expression in the twentieth century. One manifestation of this ferment is the increasing social consciousness and active social involvement of the Church.

Almost counterpoint to this hyperactivism that captured the imagination and energy of many Christians emerged a new consciousness of man's need for total integration, the key to which many found in the release of ontological spirituality. In some instances this has resulted in new, bizarre interest in the occult, and dualistic worship of evil powers. But these circumstances have also produced a new appetite for works concerned with transcendence and mystical theology. Books on prayer and the Holy Spirit compete

with works on astrology and Satan worship on the paper-
back racks in drugstores and supermarkets throughout
America. Even before the tremors of the sixties, a conservative Protestant theologian of no less distinction than
Karl Barth, in his great tome *Church Dogmatics* (IV, 2),
had kind words for monastic spirituality and predicted its
continuance. Catholic scholars such as Butler and Bouyer
have sought to recover and legitimatize the mystical tradition in Roman Catholic history.

The rebirth of interest in metaphysics in the West has
stimulated intense dialogue with Eastern religion and philosophy. Bridges cites this phenomenon as an offspring of
the post-World War II era.

> During this period the American people, like those of
> other lands, have shown persistent interest in mys-
> ticism, an interest that may now be rising to an un-
> precedented peak. If the wave is in fact rising to new
> heights, its crest would seem to be the intensified
> popularity of Oriental mysticism that developed in
> America after the second world war and received
> renewed impetus in the fifties and sixties from the
> vogue for psychedelic drugs.[6]

In his last years Merton became engrossed in the commonplaces of Eastern and Western mysticism. He was one
of those for whom "ecumenical" meant "worldwide or
universal in extent and influence." His understanding of
the unity of the world, a panentheistic God, and a cosmic
Christ prohibited a narrowly defined humanity or limited
theater of God's action. The universality of the human
quest for authentic being seemed to hold for him the
potential for establishing a transcultural family of man.
Merton's last works reflected his absorption with a dialogue
with Eastern contemplatives, and his ill-fated journey was
characterized by his conversations with Eastern spiritual
masters. In a 1962 essay for *Catholic World*, Merton exhorted his Christian colleagues to plumb the depths of
Eastern wisdom, admonishing them that the contempla-

tion-oriented oriental tradition proffered "new perspectives" on which "our spiritual and even our physical survival may depend."[7] Merton's exploration of the religious traditions of the East established him as an ecumenist in the fullest sense of that term.

Mysticism

The matter of defining "mysticism" is far more problematic than the assertion that the label "mystic" is an appropriate one for a particular individual. To set the mysticism of Thomas Merton into perspective, some review of the milieu is required. This exposition will necessarily be sketchy and piecemeal, for a complete and altogether satisfactory examination would require a separate volume of no small dimension. The word "mystical" and its various derivatives did not easily find its way into the Christian vocabulary. "Contemplation" was the expression of the Latin Church. "Mystical" was too reminiscent of the pagan mystery cults and their esoteric rites to gain easy acceptance in the primitive Church. It was Pseudo-Dionysius who first applied the term to Christian experience in the treatise *Mystical Theology*, dated around A.D. 500. Even then it was not readily accepted, so that "mystical" did not come into common usage until the late Middle Ages, and "mysticism" not until much later.[8] Some contemporary writers resist its use still, preferring "contemplation" because of the association of the former language with psychophysical concomitants such as visions, ecstasies, and spiritual auditions.[9] A mystic was originally one who had been initiated into certain mysteries. Through the possession of certain formulas or participation in secret rites, he entered into a special status. However, there is a biblical sense in which all Christians enter into a new status, a new relationship, even new knowledge. They are the "stewards of the mysteries of Christ," but here it is not a matter of entering darkness but of illuminating it. Christ is the Revealer of mysteries, and the mystical quest is one to which every disciple is called—he is to be a "learner" and to find himself in God. The Christian transcends himself via the Holy Spirit in and through Christ.

Mysticism presupposes metaphysical reality that cannot be rationally comprehended or expressed. The mystic perceives "an ultimate nonsensuous unity in all things, a oneness or a one to which neither the sense nor the reason can penetrate."[10] Though it is unfathomable for human reason and beyond the expression of human language, the mystic believes that the ineffable can be experienced. Underhill includes the suggestion of process in her definition; mysticism is, according to her, "the name of that organic process which . . . is the art of [man's] establishing his conscious relation with the absolute."[11] The inference of "art" is extended as she describes the process as one of "ordered movement towards even higher levels of reality, ever closer identification with the Infinite."[12] The mystic discerns a spiritual whole in the universe that is not apparent in individual components and not subject to scientific or rational verification. The apprehension of reality comes not from scientific reductionism or dependence on rational analogies but through spiritual intuition.

> When the contemplative concentrates, he doesn't perform a psychological act, but rather condenses ontologically, actually con-centers the most disparate and widespread circles of reality, in such a way that in himself the universe is concentrated and is reflected in a unity which, under the circumstances of the usual dispersion of being in nature, cannot take place.[13]

Underhill's use of the term "art" infers the existence of a body of knowledge that can be acquired by observation and study and then applied in a systematic way to produce a desired effect. But as she comes to state some three hundred pages later, ". . . mysticism is a way of life—an experience of Reality, not a philosophic account of Reality. . . ."[14] It is always then the act of an individual that can never be completely comprehended except by one who has shared a similar experience. A problem encountered by any student of mysticism is the difficulty of translating words into experience. Objective language inevitably transforms the experience. Mystical literature has little appeal to the intellectual or the pragmatic person because of its failure to be either prescriptive or descriptive. It often takes the form of a hymn of joy or a simple outburst of elation. Scientific treatises of mystical theology are nonexistent. Bridges describes mysticism as "selfless, direct, transcendent, unitive experience of God of ultimate reality, and the experient's interpretation of that experience."[15] The mystical writer does not attempt to draw a map for another but only to describe his or her own journey and in the process to offer a model that may help another along the way. Merton wrote to a friend in 1964 that contemplation could not be taught but that it could be awakened in those with an aptitude for it when "made real and creditable by someone who knows by experience what it is . . . it is a question of showing them in a mysterious way by example how to proceed." The mystic's spiritual counsel is most often reflective of the barriers and inhibitors to the experience of authentic spirituality rather than a ladder to a special state of grace. The neophyte is aided in differentiating between the false and true obstacles and may follow the pattern of the spiritual master in creating an environment conducive to mystical experience. As Merton instructed the novices of Gethsemani, such works can be approached only as a "summary of the techniques by which one can dispose himself to ascend the degrees of the spiritual life . . . under the guidance of grace."[16] The commonplaces in mystical literature occur without conscious regard to theories or philosophies as a result of gifted, devout souls sharing common experiences in prayer, contemplation, and union with God. Theory has relevance for the mystic only when it is incarnated in experience.

The intensely personal nature of mysticism is inclined to arouse hostility within religious institutions, structures that see in it a threat to discipline and authority. The mystic strives for a direct experience of the absolute without any intermediary, institutional or otherwise. Within Catholicism the rise of monasticism with its contemplative orientation occurred during the period of greatest organization and hierarchical power in the Church. As Welsh pointed out:

> Mysticism was for many devout spirits a "way out" of the maze of scholastic philosophy and ecclesiastical dissension. While fulfilling all ceremonial duties with appreciation as well as regularity, and accepting the dogmas of the Church, the mystic transcended the organized system, and pursued the "direct way" up to the High and Holy One. He sought immediate awareness of spirit above clear thinking.[17]

The pursuit of direct religious experience as manifested in Church history in the monastic, pietist, and charismatic movements has provided at various times an oasis for the spiritually thirsty who could draw only dust from the structures of organized religion. Underhill notes that interest in mysticism has often erupted in periods of exceptional scientific and social advancement. The circumstances of the 1960s appear to corroborate this opinion, as this period of accelerated scientific and technical progress has engendered experimental forms of worship and religious life. The Church, at least in America, has lost some of its vigor because of its identity with establishment power structures, and many have turned to the inner experience. This is not to suggest that no objective criteria exist for testing the "spirits." Merton often expressed concern about potential delusions with regard to spiritual matters and subscribed by example and admonition to the need for community and discipline. In the last days of his life, at a time when many of his friends and readers believed he was on the threshold of taking leave from formal monasticism, he described the "work" of the contemplative as "suprapersonal." It is transcultural and transpersonal, but is the result of the interrelationship of person, community, and spirit.

> . . . it is usually expected to follow from discipline and initiation into a *traditional religious* "*way*," that is to say a special mode of life and of consciousness which meets certain unwritten, indeed inexpressible, conditions. The special formation required to meet these conditions is imparted by experienced persons, or judged by a community that has shared something of the traditional consciousness we may call mystical, contemplative, enlightened, or spiritually transformed.[18]

Mystical theology then, if such a phrase is not self-contradicting, cannot be judged against the technical apparatus of dogma but can only be studied in the context of an evolving tradition of those who have made a career of contemplation and reflected on it as *professio*. What the students of mystical theology must address themselves to is "the study of the life of prayer and the degrees of prayer and union."[19]

Contemplation can be explored only as it has been incarnated in flesh and blood in others or self. Mysticism is to be scrutinized not in terms of divine "science" but in the form of human life. Inge remarked in the Introduction to his study of the English mystics that Christianity can best be understood in its embodiment in great personalities rather than in the philosophical systems or doctrinal formulas it has spawned.[20] This approach has been the traditional one beginning with Athanasius' *Life of Anthony* and including a wealth of biographical and autobiographical data. Even William James' psychological study was one of mystics rather than of mysticism. Theologians who have difficulty with this approach should ask themselves if there is any difference in the translogical argument of the mystic and their own case against the philosopher who discounts all "revelation."

The cumulative records of mystics, including such notables as Gregory of Nyssa, Augustine, Bernard, John of the Cross, and Teresa of Avila, do seem to identify certain levels or stages in the mystical pilgrimage. In the definition of Underhill included above there was mentioned an "ordered movement." Happold writes of "a movement of consciousness towards a higher level" as powers are cultivated.[21] Gregory the Great set forth a scheme of mystical ascent that has long provided a common language for discussion of the subject. The pilgrimage commences with a moment of insight in which one discerns the nugatory quality of mundane values and the sublime value of the spiritual. The classical prototype for this stage is Moses frozen with awe before the burning bush.[22] This initial glimpse of truth is the aperture through which the bold seeker may pass. "Truth will enlighten us and illuminate our eyes with its rays. And that truth . . . which thus occurs is God."[23] The purpose here is to free the subject from the bonds of materialism. Life must be simplified in order to achieve a proper focus; attention is directed "not on things that are seen, but on things that are unseen" (1 Co. 4:18). Passing through this door, one enters the *via purgativa*, i.e., the process of detachment. Here there is the repudiation of the corrupted self: *contemptus sui*. The penitent is struck with *timor* before the perfect Holy One. Purgation empties and cleanses the vessel for the gift of *amor*, which energizes the new man. Thus for Gregory, "as for Augustine [love is] the motive power of the soul: *machine mentis*, this it is that leads . . . to the mystical contemplation of God."[24] One is then prepared for and motivated to *theoria*, union with God.[25] In modern existential terms, one must escape the inauthentic in order to actualize the authentic. In the Calcutta conference, Merton outlines virtually the identical stages discussed by Gregory, only in twentieth-century terms. The first step is to find an environment where the concerns of secular routine can be unburdened. There follows an absorption with ontological concerns, i.e., personal being and the ground of being. The climax comes as a sense of internal transformation rises to the level of consciousness and with it the discovery of transcendent dimensions of life and impending spiritual metamorphosis.[26] The end of the trek implicit in each step is intimate knowledge of God, knowledge not any degree removed from the object. The experience of knowledge aspired to by the mystic is one in which object and subject become one. "In the advanced stage of the mystical life knowledge transcends the categories of thought; there is direct, unmediated, spiritual intuition; it is modeless, unconditioned. . . ."[27] It is not conceptual knowledge, nor is it abstract; it is a crepuscular vision of absolute reality.

Merton's life and literary work demand that some attention be given to the popular myth that the contemplative life requires not only detachment from the world but also disassociation from it. Those who insist on a dichotomy between the spiritual life and the life of active works of charity demonstrate an ignorance of Church history. The pioneers of the mystical way were not idle dreamers or ivory-tower meditators; they were public men, preachers, administrators, and writers who left their imprint on the history of the Church and the world. Consider Augustine, Gregory, Bernard, and Catherine of Genoa, who utilized their spiritual resources in attacking political, social, and ecclesiastical problems of their respective periods.[28] It appears that the journey inward leads to reservoirs of energy sufficient to face the challenges of the world and to effect change. The writings and the biographies of the giants of the spiritual life suggest that mysticism constitutes a kind of metaphysic for authentic charity. Merton recounts in an article in *Cistercian Studies* an anecdote about Pachomius in which the not-yet mature father sought of a "luminous personage" to know the will of God. The hermit was shocked to hear the thrice-repeated directive, "It is God's will that you serve men in order to bring them to him."[29] In another treatise addressed to contemporary contemplatives, Merton suggested that the monk did not choose between the world and Christ but rather chose the world in Christ. "It is only in assuming full responsibility for our world, for our lives and for ourselves," he wrote, "that we can be said to live really for God. The whole human reality . . . interpenetrates the world of nature . . . and the world of history. . . ."[30] St. Teresa explained the interaction of the spiritual and profane with the simple admonition that "Martha and Mary must work together when they offer the Lord lodging."[31] This is one of those problems that absorb the theoretician rather than the practitioner of the contemplative life.

Underhill delineates four characteristics that seem to occur in five successive stages that may be used as a paradigm for investigation of the mystical ascent. A period of seclusion and struggle results in the realization of a transsensate experience—the potential for a level of knowledge that lies beyond *scientia*. It is, in the words of William James, the sudden "possession of an active subliminal self."[32] This new and deeper level of consciousness exposes the vacuity of his former life, and a determination sets in to press onward through further purgation to higher levels. This second stage of self-analysis, purgation, or even annihilation is the one that seems to be the really difficult one to get past. For some it undoubtedly reveals a perversion and becomes the end rather than the means. A society such as ours, dedicated to self-satisfaction and "fulfillment," is repulsed by self-denial as barbaric, Puritan, or at least anti-American. The third stage is one of joyous detachment from the old social world, but there is not yet the total integration in the One. The fourth stage is one about which much has been written and one about which we will have a great deal to say farther on in our examination of Merton. This is the experience that John of the Cross called "the dark night of the soul." The joy is negated and replaced by a sense of alienation and dread. There is a sense in which this is the travail of birth, for the apogee of the climb is the "unitive life." The fifth level is out of the valley to a plateau, a resting place: Tranquillity and peace are the rewards of having made contact with one's deepest consciousness.[33] A sixth stage not included by Underhill is the active one referred to above. The social world, which was abandoned as the quest was begun, is no longer a threat, and thus the mystic is free to manifest his love in practical involvement in social situations.[34] When one becomes unattached to the world, no longer dependent upon it for definition and affirmation, he is free to serve it, to give himself for it.

The mystic searches for a window through which he may obtain a broader and clearer view of the world. Jesus is said to be the true light by whom darkness is obliterated. The Christian mystic is devoted to uncovering that light of Christ within him. The individual who sets out on the inner journey has intuited an underlying wholeness to himself and his work and seeks to apprehend it and to be properly assimilated into it. The mystic senses a transcendence that is above himself and at the same time of which he is a part, and he struggles to find the connection between that which transcends him and that which he is becoming. The experience of this transcendent reality becomes the goal of his life. In spite of the record of those who have gone before, the way is unmarked, and no system serves as more than a point of embarkation. Tennyson caught the spirit of mysticism in these lines from *In Memoriam:*

> Our little systems have their day;
>   They have their day and cease to be;
>   They are but broken lights of thee,
> And thou, O Lord, are more than they.
> We have but faith: we cannot know,
>   For knowledge is of things we see;
>   And yet we trust it comes from thee,
> A beam in darkness: let it grow.

The mystic strives for the "real" that lies beneath the surface, for experience as opposed to the acquisition of knowledge.

A Historical Approach

The approach of this study is historical rather than topical. Such an approach is dictated by the general nature of the subject matter as well as the particular object of this study. This is true for several reasons. First of all, mystical literature is inevitably autobiographical. As indicated above, mystical theology is neither didactic nor systematic, but tends for the most part to be reflections on personal experience. An analysis of Merton's mystical theology revels that a great deal of his published material was extrapolated from his lengthy and detailed personal journals; thus most of his work constitutes a kind of spiritual autobiography. Another important factor to be considered here is the contention upon which this current study is predicated, namely, that Merton's theology was not new, but only a modern reformulation of traditional mystical theology, which must be interpreted in the context of Church history. Furthermore, even the expression of his thought was in large measure determined by an acute personal historical consciousness. As one writer has observed, "[his] thought is always fragmentary and always 'historical,' in the sense that it was always centered upon that portion of reality which he was confronting even though it still retained, at least in his own mind, a definite relationship with what has gone before and what is yet to come."[35] His friend Jean Leclercq speculated that Merton's "spiritual journey" evolved from "an intense scrutiny of history" in his early monastic life.[36] Merton himself recognized that he was a product of a particular historical period. "That I should have been born in 1915, that I should be the contemporary of Auschwitz, Hiroshima, Viet Nam and the Watts riots, are things about which I was not first consulted. Yet they are also events in which, whether I like it or not, I am deeply and personally involved."[37] His contribution was the examination of contemporary events and life styles against the standards of

Christian humanism that have emerged from historical witness. Merton's life and thought seem to follow the classic dialectic mode, thesis, antithesis, synthesis, with each synthesis becoming a new thesis.

As indicated above, the study will proceed biographically. Merton's works will be analyzed by period. Later reflections will be incorporated into the discussion of the period recalled. An attempt will be made to link Merton's ideas to traditional mystical theology and to identify his modifications or original ideas. The primary sources for all aspects of this study will be Merton's own works, including his lengthy teaching notes and journals.

Merton's life falls naturally into six periods: (1) Premonastic, 1915–41; (2) Novitiate, 1942–44; (3) First Vows to Ordination, 1944–49; (4) Master of Scholastics, 1951–55; (5) Novice Master, 1955–65; and (6) Eremetic Universalism, 1965–68.[38] As indicated above, the development of Merton's thought can best be analyzed chronologically, and these divisions will be utilized for this study.

Merton's personal history is documented in his early autobiography. Chapter II will explore the influence of his family heritage and the confluence of historical events that led him to Gethsemani. Special attention will be given to the development of his poetic vision. His early education will be scrutinized, particularly as it applies to philosophy and theology. Chapter III will examine Merton's "desert" experience in those first years in the monastery, combining the period of the novitiate and the period from first vows to ordination, thus roughly covering his first decade as a monk. Merton withdrew from the world to immerse himself in monastic discipline, theology, and Church history. His works during this period tend to be pietistic and dogmatic. In the womb of the Church he gained the security necessary for some first steps toward creative thought and experience. The effect of fame on a monk who has surrendered "all" will be the first consideration of Chapter IV. The success of his first works of a religious nature forced him into dialogue with the world. Merton's spiritual growth soon freed him from authoritarian crutches and allowed a rapprochement with the world. He became aware of the world and the interrelationship of man with his environment, both natural and personal. Chapter V deals with these developments in the context of his office as master of scholastics and the first years of his tenure as novice master. His role as a spiritual director extended beyond the walls of Gethsemani to the service of a growing number of disciples living in the tensions and pressures of the 1960s. The works of this period reveal a growing awareness of the person and a world of persons. He diagnosed the ills of society that contribute to the illusory life and even went so far as to suggest some antidotes. Unwittingly and unwillingly, he became a world figure, a voice of conscience in a world of violence. The contemplative life was given a new respectability in a secular society and was presented as a viable alternative to the materialism of diverse and opposing political and philosophical systems. Merton became thoroughly *catholic* during his last years. His religious ideas caught up with his social and political views, which transcended particularism. There is a growing eschatological consciousness in his works, but it is increasingly a realized eschatology of the spirit. Persons are to be the terminals for the integration of creation. He became more aware of his own self-transcendence in self-forgetfulness and the memory of the divine image, which made him, in union with God, the center of his world with all its suffering and all its hope. The final chapter will attempt to bring together the major motifs that recur in every period of Merton's life, evolving into mature notions with regard to ultimate reality: man's place in the order of creation, the paradox of immanence and transcendence, freedom, and unity.

CHAPTER II

Birth to Birth: The First Twenty-six Years

Most men spend their lives in a small corner of the world yearning for broader horizons, for open doors through which they may move to become "men of the world." Thomas Merton came as near to being born a cosmopolitan man as is possible, but his longing was for a solitary reservation in an out-of-the-way place where he could put down roots and know the security of a home. In the knob hills of Kentucky he found such a place, a place where he could breathe fresh air, smell aromas untainted by asphalt, sewage, and the like, a place where he could see the sky, hear himself—and God—and as a result become a universal man. Behind walls as drab as those of any prison, with his movement as restricted as that of a convicted felon, he discovered freedom.

Early Life

"Owe no one anything, except to love one another; for he who loves his neighbor has fulfilled the law." These words, which might well be used to characterize Tom Merton's life, were included in the reading from the Epistle on the fourth Sunday of Epiphany, January 31, 1915, when Merton embarked on his life journey at Prades, France. The son of a New Zealand artist and an American Quaker, he was to go through life feeling himself to be without nationality or roots.[1] Owen Merton, Tom's father, was a struggling artist who was to achieve only modest success before a premature death. His father's appreciation for the world of nature extended beyond the delicate dabbling in paints or practice in a narrowly defined area of "fine arts." Owen made the furniture for the new baby's use and earned his livelihood during Tom's childhood as a gardener and house painter. Merton's exhilaration in the menial tasks of Gethsemani was undoubtedly due in part to early impressions of the utilitarian art of his parents. His painter father instilled in him an eye sensitive to the world around him, the ability to perceive the beauty of ordinary, everyday things. Tom's earliest home environment must have contributed to his mystical sense of unity of all, i.e., a sense of himself as a part of nature, and nature as a part of him. The deep respect of his parents for nature prompted them to place him under its tutelage. It was almost inevitable that the time would come when he would proclaim and join the author of Genesis in proclaiming the goodness of all creation. Perhaps it was this vision inherited from his father that was to enable him to be a part of the world and yet be unattached to it. Tom's admiration for his father was indicated in his analysis of his disposition: "The integrity of an artist lifts a man above the level of the world without delivering him from it."[2] His American mother endowed him with a Spartan intellectualism. It was her intention that Tom be guided by his head rather than his heart.

> Mother wanted me to be independent, and not to run with the herd. I was to be original, individual, I was to have a definite character and ideals of my own. I was not to be an article thrown together, on the common bourgeois pattern, on everybody else's assembly line.[3]

Merton's description of his mother's perfectionism suggests a kind of Deistic puritanism. Ruth Jenkins Merton was a strong-willed liberated woman who was determined to be the "captain of her soul," insisting in controlling even the conditions of her death. She was an ardent pacifist who prevailed over her husband's patriotic desire to become a soldier in World War I. She attempted to impose on Tom a respect for work, a Yankee sense of self-sufficiency, and an uncluttered vision of the world.[4] However, in the process, she may have withheld the maternal affection every child needs. This is not to suggest that she did not share in the creation of a positive attitude toward the natural world in Tom. Her early recollections record daily walks without regard to weather, and her Quaker theology left its imprint in an inclination to look for and listen to signs and promptings of inner reality.

Few men have left behind them personal histories as complete as that of Merton. His childhood exploits and growth were recorded in diaries by his mother from his birth to her death.[4] He was a precocious child, able to read in two languages by the age of five. Merton's earliest memories were of a nomadic existence. The unsettled situations in Europe forced the family to the non-aesthetic environs of Flushing, Long Island, where his father earned his livelihood working as a house painter and part-time pianist at the local movie house. In 1918, a brother, John Paul, was born. In his early years, John Paul's life was more settled, and he was, from all appearances, a more stable child. His mother's premature death was not to have the shattering effect on the younger John Paul that it would on Tom. To the grandparents with whom they both lived for a time, John Paul was an ideal lad, while moody Tom was a chronic problem. Merton's personal allusions to his brother suggest that Tom was unsatisfied with their relationship. Tom regretted that they were not closer and that later, in John Paul's adolescence, the older brother was not able to be a surrogate father or counselor-friend. In later years Tom would feel that in some way he had failed his brother, who lost his life in a plane crash during World War II. Merton comments on how as a boy he rejected the younger brother's love[5] and the confused state of "spiritual emptiness"[6] the elder brother detected in their last meeting. The abnormal human relationships in Tom's childhood left their imprint on his life. His notebooks reveal a strong sense of failure that he never developed a really intimate relationship with an individual. He could love the world and God and persons as persons, but he had difficulty giving himself completely to any single person. Only the mystical marriage with love itself could grasp him and demand his all. The love he manifested in his writings and that motivated his involvement in attempts at the spiritual transformation of the world was the *caritas Christi* and subsumed his *contemptus mundi.* Throughout his life Merton worried about his difficulty in establishing intimate personal relationships. His personal notebooks contain recurring questions about his capacity for ordinary responsible love over an extended duration on a one-to-one basis.

It was during his sojourn in New York that Tom came under the influence of his paternal grandmother, who made a postwar visit to the Merton household. She appears to have provided some of the maternal warmth and affection that is noticeably omitted from the list of his mother's attributes.

> My grandmother, Gertrude Grierson, was the best of the lot (she died at a hundred and two). She is one of the people of whom I retain the strongest impression in my childhood. She taught me the Lord's Prayer. She was born in Wales of a Scotch father. But the best that is in us seems to come from her Welsh mother. . . . It is the Welsh in me that counts: that is what does the strange things, and writes the books, and drives me into the woods.[7]

It was this colorful old-world character who taught him the "Our Father" and impressed him by putting salt on her oatmeal. In his biographical notes she is the only one whose recollection suggest familial warmth. The memories of tender moments with his father elicit melancholia rather than happiness.

The year 1921 confronted six-year-old Tom with the reality of separation imposed by death. It was in that year that intestinal cancer was diagnosed in his mother. In her stoical way, she issued an order that Tom's "nice, clear,

optimistic, and well-balanced,"[8] *Weltanschauung* was not
to be disturbed by visits to the hospital. There is no evidence that she ever made any overt display of her feelings
or allowed an opportunity for the boy to ventilate his. The
small boy learned of his mother's impending death
through a farewell note she sent to him shortly before her
death. He never saw her again but seems to have been
haunted by his recollection of her as "thin and pale and
rather severe."[9] He never seems to have learned how to
release his emotions, never feeling free to express emotions. His deepest, most passionate feelings were expressed
in his inward experience of God and in his poetry. The
monastery, with its stress on silence and control, permitted him no more freedom of expression than had his
mother. But words and poetic form were vehicles for his
soaring, sometimes weeping, spirit.

In the following year, Tom accompanied his father to
Bermuda, but, in 1923, much to Tom's disappointment,
he was sent back to Douglaston, New York, to live with
his maternal grandparents while his father pursued his art.
Owen achieved some success as an artist and returned
somewhat triumphantly to New York in 1925, for a showing of his works. He was now financially able to take Tom
with him. It was a real liberation for the boy, who had
been utterly miserable during his father's absence. John
Paul was left with the grandparents, and Tom and his father returned to France, where they were to spend pleasant hours wandering the French countryside and discussing life and beauty.

When he later gave thought to becoming a monk, Tom
recalled these experiences and wanted to enter one of the
French communities. Had it not been for the disruptions
of Hitler's imperialism, he might well have had a quite
different environment and perhaps a quite different career.
It was in spontaneous discussions on these pastoral hikes
with his father that he received the only valuable religious
training he had as a child. When the time came for
school, the boy was enrolled in the Lycée Ingres in Man-

tauban. The living conditions there were a foreshadowing
of what life would be like at Gethsemani in the forties
and fifties. Long hours in classes, physical confinement to
small cubiclelike cells, and a weekly bath in a frigid court-
yard were the joyless routine. Tom was able to maintain
his sanity by devoting his energy to a literary clique, of
which he was the leader, and by writing three novels (at
the age of eight). These romantic swashbucklers were the
beginning of his literary career.[10] His attitude toward the
human environment at the school is reflected in his description of the students as "tough, cynical and precocious,"[11] but he had already learned the meaning of
solitude and was able to survive his loneliness.

In 1928, Tom and his father took up residence in Eng-
land, where the boy continued his education, first at Ripley
Court and then at the Oakham School. It was during
this period that his mind recorded an image of insipid
Kulturprotestantismus that took a long time to erase. The
religion of Oakham was apparently a sterile religion of
chivalry, the empty external trappings of eviscerated liber-
alism. He recorded his impression of the school chap-
lain: ". . . his religious teaching consisted mostly in more
or less vague ethical remarks, an obscure mixture of ideal
of English gentlemanliness and his favorite notions of personal hygiene."[12] Tom's opinion of this brand of religion
was stated in indicting rhetorical questions with regard to
his analysis of the Protestant minister he had encountered
at the school. "What is the good of religion without personal spiritual direction? Without Sacraments, without
any means of grace except a desultory prayer now and
then, at intervals, and an occasional vague sermon?"[13]
When Merton's spiritual struggles began at Columbia, he
gave first thought to the "vague Protestantism" of his
childhood.[14] His discussion of the matter suggests that his
apprehensiveness about the Protestant way was at least in
part due to the distrust of feeling instilled in him by his
mother. There had to be objective norms and greater intellectual content than the faith premise of Protestant
commitment.

> I wanted a solid foundation of doctrinal truth to
> build on, and I could not find any. Protestantism was
> so highly subjective that each individual was isolated
> with his own personal experience, and faith had be-
> come in practice, almost incommunicable.[15]

Tom went through a brief adolescent religious period
but soon became embarrassed by this disposition and
abandoned his clandestine Bible reading and prayer. A flir-
tation with his mother's old Church failed to meet his
need. He could not trust the "inner light" of his mother's
religion or what appeared to him to be a formless faith
upon which the mind could not focus. Merton was
searching for the ultimate; ultimate experience, ultimate
reality. The forms of Protestantism to which he was exposed lacked vigor and were too compromised for Merton
to stake his integrity, his very life on. He was looking for
that pearl of great price for which a man will abandon everything to possess. The honor of God had to demand
more than quiet acquiescence.

Tom was to be deprived of any extended home experience or a full-time father. Death again intervened, and a
brain tumor claimed Owen Merton's life when his son was
but sixteen. To the normal trauma of adolescence was
added the frustration of a parental vacuum with no hope
for its being filled. "The death of my father left me sad
and depressed . . ." he wrote later, "the hard crust of my
dry soul finally squeezed out all the last traces of religion
that had ever been in it."[16] Depression soon gave way to a
desperate search for something to fill the void. He was
officially alone now, with no place to anchor and no navigator to steer him. His interior turmoil surfaced, and, like
so many tormented artists, he tried to find himself by losing himself in a swirl of activity. Like the authors he was
reading during this period, André Gide, James Joyce,
Hemingway, he had a gargantuan appetite, which he fed
on a wide range of human experience. The loss of his father must have affected him in a similar way to the tor-
ment expressed by another Tom, Tom Wolfe, at the loss

of his father. Subconsciously, Merton must have been driven to search for his lost father, with feelings akin to those that inspired Wolfe to write:

> . . . the deepest search in life . . . [is] man's search to find a father—not merely a father of his flesh, not merely the lost father of his youth, but the image of a strength and wisdom external to his need and superior to his hunger . . .[17]

> We are the sons of our father, whose face we have never seen. We are the sons of our father . . . whose life like ours was lived in solitude in the wilderness.[18]

After his father's death, Tom became the ward of a London doctor, his godfather, an old friend of Owen's. His guardian was a sensitive, cultured man who encouraged the boy to read broadly and to avail himself of the cultural opportunities all around him. Tom's inability to cope with independence led to intemperance, a source of great disappointment to his benefactor. Merton's increasing undisciplined escapades concerned his guardian, who sought to modify the young man's behavior through gentle admonition and eventual firm confrontation, but his efforts were futile. In spite of his personal indiscretions and excesses, Merton's intellect bore fruit. His performance at Oakham earned him a scholarship to Clare College, Cambridge. The summer was spent in travel in Italy and the United States, after which he went on to Cambridge for a successful academic year. He was certainly not a model student, drawing numerous reprimands for his failure to attend classes and continually evoking the censure of his guardian. Nevertheless, his resilient mind served him well, and, in spite of his undisciplined behavior, he ranked second in examinations in French and Italian. Thirty years later he would recall those days without enthusiasm. It was, he wrote,

> The world of civilization and books, of ease and humor, of good conversation, art and music, of good

restaurants, at least in London—and of course on the Continent. The world of Cambridge colleges, and rowing, and rugger, and concerts, and audit ale in Hall, and tea at my Italian tutor's. Certainly there was a lot of nonsense in it, a lot of falsity, but one did not take all that seriously.[19]

The next stop was Columbia University. It was a place of ferment in the late thirties, a place where ideas filled the air, giving birth to myriad movements and organizations. Merton was apparently feeling some guilt over his irresponsibilities and was looking for channels of penance. The environs of the campus offered ample opportunity for uniting with organizations and movements to improve the human condition. His European travels had evoked in Merton compassion for the downtrodden masses. The Nazi war drums were sounding in Europe, and he was looking for alternatives to power politics. One alternative that he examined at Columbia was Marxism, and, for a period of about ninety days, he was a member of the Communist Party. Merton's interest in Marxism never completely disappeared, but he was able to distinguish between ideological communism and the practical expressions it took in Russia and other places. Merton understood Marx's Jewish background and the biblical understanding of history that Marx distorted and translated from a spiritual to a material mode. Merton rejected and repudiated the political methods and goals of international communism. This was only one of the movements he dabbled in during this period. With boundless energy he worked on all the school publications, while making the rounds with the "isms." Columbia brought him together with Mark Van Doren, who became an important influence on Merton as a writer and a person. He later credited Van Doren with "salvaging" him and delivering him from the popular intellectual excesses of the day. Van Doren was apparently no less impressed with young Tom Merton.

I for one have never known a mind more brilliant, more beautiful, more serious, more playful. The energy behind it was immeasurable, and the capacity for love. The energy and the love, the passion and the joy —these things, in his case so miraculously and effortlessly mixed, were evident in him when he was student at Columbia more than thirty years ago, and as time went on they grew rather than diminished.[20]

Another teacher who entered his life at this time and became a lifelong friend and an important influence in Merton's life was Dan Walsh, who taught Merton philosophy and introduced him to the Abbey of Gethsemani. It was during this period that Merton wandered into a New York bookstore to purchase a copy of Gilson's *The Spirit of Medieval Philosophy*. The failure of the sensate or rational to satisfy, combined with the opening of new awareness for exploration, made this a *kairos* moment that altered the course of his life.

The Columbian coterie brought Merton together with Bramachari, a Hindu monk who had come to America for the Century of Progress fair at Chicago and remained to move among the eastern intellectual circles. Merton was fascinated by this strange little man he would one day describe as a "perfectly formed" monk.[21] The genuine humility and authentic spirituality of the Asian monk profoundly impressed him. Merton, who had been introduced to Eastern thought in Huxley's *Ends and Means*, inquired about oriental sources of mystical wisdom, only to be directed by Bramachari to Christian mystical literature. "There are many beautiful mystical books," the wise teacher counseled, "written by the Christians. You should read St. Augustine's *Confessions* and *The Imitation of Christ*."[22] This was Merton's first encounter with flesh-and-blood mysticism, and it was to have a lasting effect on his own spiritual formation. Bramachari's asceticism was practical and visual. He was able to survive without financial security or institutional dependence. He accepted persons uncritically as persons and rarely offered advice, even to those who sought it. Merton never forgot Bramachari, whose life revealed his faith. Here was a man who incarnated his belief, whose mysticism was not just something to talk about but a way of life, perhaps life itself. There was now coming together a confluence of ideas and experiences that would determine the direction of Thomas Merton's life. The year 1938 was an eventful one, as he received the bachelor of arts degree, began work on a master's degree, and was baptized into the Catholic faith.

The Road to Conversion

Merton kept changing horses on the collegiate carousel, but each one soon brought him back to the place where he started. He apparently indulged in all the human vanities open to a young man in the realm of the sensate and intellectual modalities. However, no single experience or succession of experiences satiated his appetite for life.[23] These words, penned by his poet friend Ernesto Cardenal, which were included in one of Merton's Gethsemani collections, may express the despair of this period.

> Like empty beer cans, like empty cigarette butts;
> My days have been like that.
> Like figures passing on a TV screen.
> And disappearing, so my life has gone.
> Like cars going by fast on the roads
> With girls laughing and radios playing.
> Beauty got obsolete as fast as car models
> And forgotten radio hits.
> Nothing is left of those days, nothing,
> But empty beer cans, cigarette butts,
> Smiles on faded photos, torn tickets
> And the sawdust with which, in the mornings,
> They swept out the bars.[24]

Merton turned to the spiritual because of the failure of the material and rational to fill the emptiness of his life. Over thirty years later, he would remind the novices at Gethsemani of the experience of estrangement that they had known in the outside world. "In order to be in a place like this a person has to have experienced alienation outside. . . . The experience of alienation is the experience of living a life which is to you meaningless."[25] The absurdity of his existence in those days compelled him to search for a reason to exist.

Merton credited Mark Van Doren with preparing him for an encounter with medieval philosophy and Catholic theology. Merton was impressed with Van Doren's "sober and sincere intellect,"[26] which would not permit sentimental wallowing in emotionalism or Freudian speculation in literary analysis. Van Doren directed his students away from the "naïve errors of those who try to read some favorite private doctrine into every poet,"[27] whether those doctrines were those of fascism, communism, or any of their cousins. His mentor inculcated in Merton a hermeneutical sense for penetrating rather than interpolating.

Even before Dan Walsh's philosophy classes, Merton was introduced to metaphysics by Gilson's *The Spirit of Medieval Philosophy*. On his application forms for admission to Gethsemani, he listed two works that marked turning points in his thinking: Gilson's, and Maritain's *Art and Scholasticism*. Huxley's *Ends and Means* was Merton's introduction to mysticism. In 1941, Merton wrote in his journal that he had "never even heard of the word mysticism" until he read Huxley and that the book had played an important part in his conversion. The same entry noted that Gilson had implanted in him "a healthy respect for Catholicism." Merton's list of influential books in the preconversion days included Underhill's *Mysticism*, Joyce's *A Portrait of the Artist as a Young Man*, and Lahey's *Life of Gerard Manley Hopkins*.[28] His lifelong friend and fellow poet, Bob Lax, encouraged him to read mystical literature and introduced him to the Hindu monk Bramachari, who directed him to Augustine and *The Imitation of Christ*. The personal element in religion intrigued Merton, leading him to investigate oriental mysticism as a possible answer to his own spiritual questions. The seed planted during this period lay dormant for a long time, but it was to grow and bear fruit in his most fertile years as a spiritual writer. There was a universal lesson in mysticism which, while not satisfying his immediate spiritual needs, fascinated him. He came away from his study ". . . with the conviction that man could, by detachment from created things and by a profound interior transformation, enter into direct experimental contact with God."[29] The Catholic Church could provide the discipline and dogma to nurture him until he was ready to seek that "direct" experience of God.

Merton's conversion provides an archetype for Starbuck's portrayal of spiritual awakening. First, there occurs an "unselfing" born of a desperate compulsion to seek "self-preservation and self-enlargement." The plunge into the depths of being results in consciousness of the real world. "Conversion," according to Starbuck, "is the larger world-consciousness . . . pressing in on the individual consciousness . . . the person emerges from a smaller limited world of existence into a larger world of being."[30] In an adolescent novel written in those early days of belief, Merton's sense of an existential leap from nothingness to faith surfaces.

> I know I am in danger, but how can I be afraid of danger? If I remember I am nothing, I will know the danger can take nothing from me. . . . Yes, I am afraid, because I forget that I am nothing. If I remembered that I have nothing called my own that will not be lost anyway, that only what is not mine but God's will ever live, then I would not fear so many false fears.[31]

He found something worthy of allegiance, something demanding genuine and total commitment; with despair on one side and hope on the other, he made the leap. The Roman Catholic Church could meet his every need at this point. It offered to him a faith that had intellectual content and offered an alternative way of life while preserving a dimension of mystery. His intellectual quest satisfied, the experience had to be actualized by an act of the will.

> I found that God existed, and that He was the source of all reality; was, in fact, Reality, Truth, Life itself. He was pure actuality. On the other hand, I found that I had an intellect made to apprehend the highest and most perfect Truth in a supernatural intuition born of love, and that I had a free will that was capable of turning all the powers of my being either toward that Truth or away from it.[32]

Once he had "put his hand to the plow," there is no evidence that he ever looked back.

A Prodigious Child of Faith

Tom plunged into the spiritual quest with the same fervor with which he had sampled secular wards. Immediately he adopted a personal, ascetic regimen. He did not progress fast enough to satisfy himself, and later chastened himself for falling "into the ranks of . . . tepid and dull and sluggish and indifferent Christians . . . who barely put up a struggle to keep the breath of grace alive in their souls."[33] The immediate and complete purgation and transformation that he obviously anticipated did not occur, and it must have quickly become painfully clear that the "ascent to truth" would be an arduous and painful one. He read voraciously the classical spiritual texts that would determine his spiritual formation. His nascent spiritual diet was John of the Cross, Bernard's On the Love of God, Thérèse of Lisieux, and the Spiritual Exercises of Ignatius of Loyola. It was the latter work that he cited as his instructor in prayer. Even before his baptism he had begun to think in terms of the priesthood, and shortly after baptism he sought the counsel of Dan Walsh on the matter. Again, it was his Jewish friend, Bob Lax, who influenced Tom's course; it was he who urged Tom to enroll in Walsh's class, a course that was unrelated to Tom's curriculum and described by him as an "academic bypath." Walsh was a personal acquaintance of both Gilson and Maritain and soon introduced his pupil to Maritain when the French philosopher visited the Columbia campus. Walsh was quick to point out to Merton that he had a predilection for the mystical, voluntaristic Augustinian tradition as opposed to the speculative Scholasticism of Thomas Aquinas. Under Walsh's tutelage, Merton explored the heritage of Anselm, Bernard, Bonaventure, the Victorines, and Duns Scotus, not to mention the stackpole of Catholic theology, Thomas Aquinas. Merton soon realized that Walsh's insight had been a correct one and that his "bent was not so much towards the intellectual, dialectical, speculative character of Thomism, as towards the spiritual, mystical, voluntaristic and practical way of St. Augustine and his followers."[34] It was with rare preparation, insight, and direction that Merton set out on his Christian pilgrimage. Embued by his baptism and first communion, his spirit soared:

> For now I had entered into the everlasting movement of that gravitation . . . God's own gravitation towards the depths of His infinite nature. . . . And God, that center Who is everywhere, and whose circumference if nowhere, finding me, through incorporation with Christ, incorporated into his immense and tremendous gravitational movement which is love . . . loved me.[35]

The language here is that of a mystic searching for words to express the tug felt in his soul toward something or someone, a pull like the magnetic attraction of attracting poles when a field of interference has been cleared. The switch had been opened, and Merton's proleptic conversion experience of God's love initiated a momentum that was to lead him to Gethsemani in the hope that there he would find a vacuum where the force of that Divine love would exert an uninterrupted force uniting him with pure being. Merton's metanoia was complete, and now his boundless energy, incisive intellect, and literary skills were redirected in the service of the Spirit.

A two-year teaching stint at St. Bonaventure's College provided a period of incubation for the nurturing of the sense of vocation, a place where the Truth he had experienced could develop fully into the actual substance of his whole being until his entire existence would become a vision of love and truth. Merton led a thoroughly ascetic, almost monastic life during those years surrounding his baptism. Particularly significant in the development of Merton's thought at this early stage were the writings of John of the Cross. Merton never completely graduated from John's influence, and, in later years, when references to other writers are more prominent, traces of John's teachings are still indentifiable. Merton's daily life became a practicum for mystical purgation, exemplifying the "counsels" of John.

Strive always to choose, not that which is easier, but that which is most difficult;

Not that which is most delectable, but that which is most unpleasing;

Not that which gives most pleasure, but rather that which gives least;

Not that which is restful, but that which is wearisome;

Not that which gives consolation, but rather that which makes disconsolate;

Not that which is greatest, but that which is least;

Not that which is loftiest, and most precious, but that which is lowest and most despised;

Not that which is a desire for anything, but that which is a desire for nothing;

Strive not to go about seeking the best of temporal things, but the worst.

Strive thus to desire to enter into complete detachment
and emptiness and poverty, with respect to that which
is in the world, for Christ's sake.[36]

Merton wrestled with himself to find within himself the
image of God. One of the best-known incidents recorded
in *Seven Storey Mountain* is that of a conversation with
Lax on a stroll down Sixth Avenue in which his friend
abruptly turned and asked young Merton, "What do you
want to be, anyway?" To which he stammered out the
reply, "A good Catholic." Lax pressed him, insisting that
what he wanted to be and could be was a saint. Confirmation of Lax's statement by Mark Van Doren set the idea
in Merton's mind until it became the obsession of his
life.[37] Tom registered the struggles of this period in *The
Secular Journal*, a diary that he kept from October 1939
to November 1941.[38]

Robert McAfee Brown defines theology as "our attempt
to love God with our minds."[39] Such a definition aptly
describes Merton's trauma during this period. He was
struggling to give himself *completely* to God. Excerpts
from *The Imitation of Christ* frequently appear in the entries, and Merton was determined to concretize his love
for God by imitating his life. "We love God on earth," he
echoed, "by imitating Him."[40] As every generation of
Christians, he had no difficulty in finding the word for
God; it was simply "love," but how is that symbol, that
abstraction, to be given substance and form? "Love does
not merely give money, it gives itself."[41] Here it is again;
for him to give love, he must give himself—but how?
Being is becoming; one does because one is. Christianity
was not for him the cessation of certain activities and the
mere abandonment of an undesirable style of life. It was
putting on the "new man," the discovery of a way of life.
"Purity in the Christian sense is not merely . . . the absence of carnal indulgence. It is something positive, con-
structive, and fruitful. . . ."[42] He was still not satisfied
with himself. The encounter with God intensified his

sense of inadequacy and imperfection. The pallor of his own love compared to God's was a source of shame and "the greatest unhappiness . . . the ontological root of all suffering. . . ."[43] His life at this point was a dynamic dialectic emerging out of its own energy, extending out in search of a personal truth, not an objective proposition, but a truth that could be incorporated into his being.

Merton's reading of Pascal and Francis agitated his disenchantment with the burgeoning technocracy of World War II America. He was already repudiating "our modern rat-race civilization," with its "reverence for perfect, sterile cleanliness. . . ."[44] Even then he saw a society ". . . worshipping frustration and barrenness."[45] The world in which he found himself was a hall of mirrors, which reflected not even the true image of self. But how could one cut through the shadow to substance? Where could salvation be found for himself and his generation? As time passed and his interior turmoil continued, he began to read the signs:

> . . . an army of saints . . . from the poorest of the laity, from the depths of the slums, from the concentration camps and the prisons, from the places where people are starving, bombed, machine-gunned and beaten to death. Because, in all these places, Christ suffers most. Maritain adds . . . that they will also be found in religious orders—especially the contemplative ones.[46]

Merton rejected the Greek historicists who advocated ignoring the realities of social injustice and international war and enjoying the moment before it elapsed, and opted instead for discerning one's role in God's historical process. His first concrete move was toward becoming a Franciscan. Embued with the romantic spirit of the old churches and piety of Spanish Catholicism in Cuba, he resolved to follow in the steps of Francis. He was never completely comfortable with this idea, which he finally concluded was his own will and not the will of God, but he was earnestly seeking a way to give himself to God. The life of the Franciscans as he perceived it would be too easy a course for him. It would demand little change from his present secular existence. "The truth of the matter," he decided, "is simply this: becoming a Franciscan especially at that precise moment in history, meant absolutely no sacrifices at all, as far as I was concerned."[47] The doubts ate away at him until, with his emotions in a state of shambles, he turned away from the Friars Minor to find another path.

The year 1941 was to be the one of decision. Holy Week of that year, acting on a suggestion of Dan Walsh, Merton made a retreat at the Abbey of Gethsemani, just a few miles outside Bardstown, Kentucky. Merton was filled with awe and excitement by the experience. His enthusiasm exudes from the pages of his diary. "This is the center of America. I had wondered what was holding the country together, what has been keeping the universe from cracking in pieces and falling apart."[48] It was, he wrote, "the only real city in America."[49] The quiet, rural setting must have stirred memories of the French countryside. The austere sanctuary of the monastery walls closed out the pseudo cities of steel, cement, noise, and hucksterism, where he had lived in exile. For the first time, there was a quiet without and within.

When he returned to New York, he could not forget the smell of the woods and the echoes of the *Salve Regina*. Temporarily, he was distracted by work on his novels[50] and the routine at St. Bonaventure's. During that school term, Catherine de Hueck visited the campus to talk about her work among the poor in Harlem. That evening he wrote in his journal that she was a physically striking person with ". . . a strong sure voice" and "best of all she used the word 'martyrdom' without embarrassment, not like something crazy and 'imprudent' and abstract in some old book."[51] This experience complicated the vocational crisis that was growing more intense within him. Here was a new alternative: He could give himself to God by giving himself to the disadvantaged in New York's black ghetto. He soon visited Harlem and Friendship House and came away with images of a "dark furnace" and a "seething cauldron" and scars of marijuana, gin, hysteria, and venereal disease; and in the midst of it all, "the profound and positive and elemental reality" of love manifested in the workers who lived there with God.[52] Perhaps it was here that he could more profoundly experience the love of God by loving. He wanted to find himself by losing himself in God; perhaps Harlem was the sea of humanity where he could accomplish this. His struggle now began to take a shape that was to occupy him for the rest of his life, the conflict between the real and the illusionary self. From the very beginning, his understanding of love was an incarnational one. Gilson's *Spirit* has a chapter on the nature of love that is an exposition of Bernard's "Degrees of Love." Gilson's commentary suggests that to be in the image of God means to share in God's nature as love. When Merton became novice master, he would instruct his charges that the more they were true to God, the more they would discover their true self that was in God, the common substance being love.[53] The question then was not which virtue was most fundamental or how to respond to God, but how to give form to the only appropriate response, which is love. His journal entry for September 3, 1949, begins with a quotation from Thomas à Kempis: "For as much as each one is in your eyes, he is that much and no more, said St. Francis."[54] Merton was painfully aware that one might genuinely serve God in a number of ways and that the challenge to each individual was to discover his particular talent and medium for its expression, to discern God's specific call to him. In later years, when his parade of visitors—activists, intellectuals, and Protestants—suggested that he was wasting his life at the monastery, he would smile and respond simply that he was where he was because God called him there.

But the will of God is not easily discerned by even the most sincere seeker, and Merton wrestled with the angel struggling to separate his personal desires from the revelation of God. The matter was further complicated by his compulsion to write, an activity that he believed would interfere with either social work or monastic vocations. It was a different kind of anxiety from his pre-Christian alienation, but it was anxiety nonetheless. He ascribed this suffering to the not yet filled vacuum, ". . . we have let go of the goods that can no longer please us . . . so for the time being we have nothing, and only ache with the sense of our own poverty."[55] Merton had swept his interior house clean but longed to fill it before the return of the expelled demon with friends. A second trip to Gethsemani convinced him that this was the environment in which he could best move toward God. The claim of the gospel on him was that he should leave all and follow Christ as Abraham had into a new world. Like Abraham, he must change the whole form of his life, leaving behind all vestiges of security to embrace the unknown.

> Going to live in Harlem does not seem to me to be anything special. It is a good and reasonable way to follow Christ. But going to the Trappists is exciting, it fills me with awe and with desire. I return to the idea again and again; "Give up everything, give up everything!" I shall speak to one of the Friars.[56]

Now Merton was to "work out his salvation" by living the Christian paradox. "Having been set free from sin," he was resolved to become one of those "slaves of righteousness" (Rm. 6:18, RSV). There appeared to him at this time to be only one way by which he could immerse himself more completely in the Body and let the Holy Spirit become totally operative in his life—the way of asceticism. He was grasped by thoughts of union: "Our divine sonship and our inheritance of the joys of the divine life depend on our union with Christ. . . ."[57]

Blake, Mystical Poet

An important link in Merton's thought is the work of
his master's thesis, written in 1938. It was a study of
William Blake, whose ideas influenced both his theology
and his poetry. Blake had been a favorite of Tom's father,
who had brought the poet and his son together as he had
walked the hills of France with the youngster. Tom said
that it was through Blake that he had come to the Church
and to Christ.[58] The thesis was an exposition of Blake's
philosophy; indeed, it was an apologetic for the poet's
Christianity. "As mystic," Merton argued, "Blake belongs
to the Christian tradition of the Augustinians and the
Franciscans. . . ."[59] Already Merton was cognizant of
similarities between Christian and oriental mysticism. He
called attention to Blake's acquaintance with Hindu philosophy. He drew attention to ideas common to Blake and
Meister Eckhart, in whose thought Merton was to develop
a vital interest during the sixties. He mentioned Eckhart's
concept of created things as "ideas" of "forms" in the
mind of God each with an innate, peculiar character of its
own. He struggled to bring this notion into harmony with
Aquinas, as interpreted by Maritain, i.e., that form is the
expression of essence.[60] Sense experience points beyond itself to the metaphysical reality that lies behind it. In later
years he would become critical of Thomism and opt for
the possibility of a direct perception of beauty. Merton
applauded Blake's indictment of secular naturalism: "Everything is Atheism which assumes the reality of the natural and Unspiritual world."[61] He wrote of Blake's emergence from the "dark night" and his discovery of the
personal dimension of knowledge.

> The knower and the thing known actually became
> identified. This identification of being and intelli-
> gence is also made by the Hindu, and it is implicit in
> Blake's remarks, "Every eye sees differently. As the

eye, such the object." St. Thomas says, "The thing known is in the knower according to the mode of the knower."[62]

This idea is one which has been developed by the philosopher Michael Polanyi, who contends that knowledge and the knower are synthetically united. In the act of perception, the knower is affected and infected by that which is known. From this analysis Merton infers a doctrine of "connaturality" of artist and object. Blake is depicted as a religious artist determined to give form to his vision. Both the vision and the artist's creation are the products of the love of God. The gift of an artist like Blake is an "infallible critical judgment" that enables him to discern what is authentic.[63] In Blake, the mystic and the artist appeared to Merton to be inseparably bound together. Both are committed to the passionate search for truth, the real obsession of Blake's life. The problem is an epistemological one: How do we know? Blake's synthesis of mystic graces and aesthetic sensitivity enabled him to transcend the rational and intuit the whole more through prehension than comprehension. "Pure aesthetic experience is theirs in whom knowledge of ideal beauty is innate, and is known intuitively, in intellectual ecstasy, without the accompaniment of ideation, at the highest level of conscious being."[64] This notion of a knowledge that is beyond facts and that is obtained through union with being is crucial to the mystical quest.

Merton's interest in Blake did not end with the completed thesis. In 1968, he wrote a book review essay, "Blake and the New Theology."[65] The apocalyptic experience of the nuclear age and the continuing revolution require a new assessment of Blake, who has come to be accepted as a prophet by a larger audience than campus literati. With obvious reverence, Merton advocates the reading of the poet-mystic as a prophet in the sense of "one who 'utters' and 'announces' news about man's own deepest trouble. . . ." He concurs with the author's critique of the perversion of Christianity in the development of a monolithic organization. Altizer's appraisal of Blake as a visionary is applauded, and the reviewer states his own appreciation for the subject as one who

> . . . substituted for it a Christianity of openness, of total vision, a faith which dialectically embraces both extremes . . . moving freely between dialectical poles in a wild chaos, integrating sacred vision in and through the experience of fallenness as the only locus of creativity and redemption.[66]

Blake's art is interpreted as a manifestation of existential tension between "what is" and "what ought to be" or between the "false" and the "true." He scores Altizer for reading into Blake a concept of pure immanence for the divine, not allowing for the paradox of the creator "in" and yet over against His creation. Merton identifies with what he sees to be a truly tragic vision of the fall and the eschatological tension between what is and what will be.

> Without the fall not only is Christianity itself emptied of meaning, but Blake too becomes incomprehensible. Eschatology is the vision of a totally new and final reality, cosmic reversal that brings ultimate meaning and salvation to the fallen world. That reality is, in effect, the total integration of God and Man in Christ—that is to say in concrete and communal Mankind united not by politics but by mercy.[67]

Man alienated against God is man alienated against himself. Man has posited himself over against being, and his experience of anxiety is the result of his self-dipolarization, which is overcome in the intensity of the transcendence of God, which calls him back into the unity of being. Blake had a profound influence on Merton as a prophet, poet, and mystic. "Merton followed Blake in adopting Blake's prophetic role in writing poetry so that at least one-third of all Merton's poetry is a crying in the wilderness to a doomed world."[68]

Merton, Poet-Mystic

It will be instructive at this point to examine Merton's poetics and their effect upon his evolution as a mystic. Above, it was pointed out that Merton's compulsion to write was a source of personal soul-searching for him, and when he made the decision to become a Cistercian, there was a concomitant decision to abandon writing. Although he was never able to stop writing, it was twenty years before he was free enough to accept himself as a writer and to publish a statement to that effect. He wrote in *The Seven Storey Mountain* that his father had taught him that "the artistic experience, at its highest, was actually a natural analogue of mystical experience."[69] Both the poet and the mystic are concerned with the organic whole of the seen and the unseen. Not every poet is a mystic, nor is every mystic a poet, but the gifts have combined in a significant number of persons: John of the Cross, Dante, Blake, and Hopkins, to name only a few. A certain inner compulsion energizes both, the tune that they hear is not heard by all, but the poet may so orchestrate it that others may share in its experience. Both the artist and the mystic are concerned with giving form to the interiority of things. The artist strives to bring to the level of conscious experience the extraordinary concealed in the ordinary.

> Art teaches man the pleasures of the spirit . . . and from afar off, without thinking, it prepares the human race for contemplation . . . the spiritual joy of which surpasses every other joy and seems to be the end of all human activities.[70]

Poetry uses form to reveal and heighten a segment of human experience that gives meaning to a wider range of experience. Such art may be thought of as "an incarnation of the genius of rhythm, manifesting the living spirit of things with a clearer beauty and intenser power. . . ."[71]

Poetry is a record of experience. The poet sets out to

communicate something that transcends fact or opinion. An obscure intuition is expressed by a combination of words and structures. Dilthey described the function of poetry in this way:

> Thought produces concepts, artistic creation produces types. These . . . embody a heightening (*Steigerung*) of experience, not in the sense of an empty idealization, but in the sense of a representation of the manifold in one image, whose strong, clear structure makes the lesser, confused experiences of life intelligible (*verstandlich*) in accordance with their meaning (*Bedeutung*).[72]

The mystic immerses himself in the spirit to experience the universal unity. Both the poet and the mystic subscribe to a theory that reality lies beneath the surface, the appearance of things. There is a spiritual dimension that invests matter with whatever meaning and value it has. Both the poet and the mystic synthesize the diffused experiences of life into a discernible pattern. The poet appears to create beauty, which may well be, as Hegel concluded, ". . . merely the Spiritual making itself known sensuously."[73] Both art and mysticism attain "directly to the world of pure being in which all symbols and forms have their transcendent justification."[74] The experience dictates the form of its expression. The poet expresses the inexpressible in extraordinary combinations of words, sounds, and structures. Humbert Wolfe expressed in a sonnet the poet's perception and projection of his experience of ultimate reality.

> I will tell you the poet's secret. It is this
> To trap the shadow and leave the light that cast it,
> To set a sound beside those silences
> That give the sound its glory and outlast it.
> There is a net of colour at the edge of the mind
> And the poet beats against it, as a bird
> Against a stained glass window, but, behind
> The window, distance stainless, cold, unstirred.[75]

The poet constructs myths that portray the fundamental problems of the inner man. "Nuances of feeling, subtleties of thought that practical experience keeps us too gross or too busy to observe . . . have in the arts their moment of being."[76] The poet translates abstractions according to their distinctive modality for free formation into representative symbols. Inner experiences are depicted in relation to life. The artist labors to capture in form in a concrete moment the experience of life, which is a flow through time. Artist and priest both try to weave together the segments of human experience that flow through consciousness and achieve a mosaic that gives the total experience lucidity, vividness, intensity, and depth. The mystic poet struggles to make the dream a waking one and to make of life more than what William James called "a big blooming buzzing confusion."[77] It is in a Christian sense the "abundant" life, often marred by tragedy, that concerns the artist. Out of the fog of our often vacuous diurnal life, the poet extrapolates stimuli that clarify, intensify, and interpret life.

Karl Rahner cites the union of priest and poet as among the highest human possibilities and states that "the Perfect Priest and the Perfect Poet" are one.[78] Each is concerned with the concatenation of the interior and exterior elements of life. The thoughts and passions of man are explored as they interrelate with one another and with the natural universe. Merton believed that art can "form and spiritualize man's consciousness."[79] By nature he was a poet who found formal logic stifling and capable of producing only certain kinds of truth. As a poet and as a priest, he was willing to be transcended by his work. Artistic discipline and religious discipline, he believed, can complement one another.

> Religious ascetics have something to learn from the natural asceticism of the artist: it is unself-conscious, organic, integrated in his art. It does not run the risk of becoming an end in itself. But the artist also has

something to gain from religious asceticism. It not only raises him above his subject and his material but above his art itself. He can now control everything, even his art, which usually controls him.[80]

Both the artist and the priest point beyond themselves to something that is greater than they and yet that gives meaning to their existence. Merton wrote of the Christian poet as the successor to the prophets. There can be little doubt that Merton's capacity for mystical experience was enlarged by his poetic instinct. "A genuine aesthetic experience . . . is a suprarational intuition of the latent perfection of things. . . . Its mode of apprehension is that of 'connaturality'—it reaches out to grasp the inner reality . . . by a kind of affective identification with it."[81]

One does not choose to be a poet but is one by accident of his individuality. The greatest obstacle to the realization of this vocation is the same as that which obstructs spirituality: the false self. It took Merton a long time to arrive at this truth, but it came with the growing spiritual insight that surfaced in *Seeds of Contemplation*. "Many poets are not poets for the same reason that many religious men are not saints: they never succeed in being themselves."[82] One disciplines himself for his art in the same way he prepares himself for the spiritual trek, i.e., the impurities and clutter are expurgated to allow the consciousness of the mystery, which will express itself. The artist does not "use" his art any more than the spiritual man "uses" the spirit; indeed, he allows himself to be used. Each struggles to be free of the pressures, both internal and external, that interfere with and taint his work. The creative spirit strives to escape all forms of domination. The artist, like the contemplative, or vice versa, must not be bound to produce anything. He must be free to be absolutely useless by all production norms. But freedom should not be confused with unchecked license or formless anarchy. Merton was always careful when addressing either contemplatives or artists to differentiate between irresponsibility and true freedom. He offered no easy way, but one of trial and error, with occasions of disappointment and frustration.

> True artistic freedom can never be a matter of sheer willfulness, or arbitrary posturing. It is the outcome of authentic possibilities, understood and accepted in their own terms, not the refusal of the concrete in favor of the purely "interior." In the last analysis, the only valid witness to the artist's creative freedom is his work itself. The artist builds his own freedom and forms his own artistic conscience, by the work of his hands. Only when the work is finished can he tell whether or not it was done "freely."[83]

The artist emerges from his culture to stand outside social and political categories to be their unrestrained conscience, i.e., to expose the interior conditions of which external phenomena are only symptomatic. But this role is incidental to the central purpose of his existence, which is not to teach or preach or produce but only to find truth and be in harmony with it and "to point beyond all objects into the silence where nothing can be said."[84] The life and work of the artist and the mystic are consummated when they are integrated with his person and ultimate reality into an organic, spiritual whole. Thomas Merton's greatest artistic work was his own life. As Thoreau wrote: "He is the true artist whose life is his material; every stroke of the chisel must enter his own flesh and bone and not grate dully on the marble."[85]

The School of the World

It has often been said that at any given point in a man's life, he is the sum total of his experience to that moment. What does this mean for the Christian? Does metanoia mean that suddenly the mind is again a *tabula rasa* upon which the Spirit will write? Certainly, history and human experience would not support such a proposition. More likely, it is the analysis of one's life without divine meaning and the anxiety produced by the accompanying sense of futility that bring repentance and surrender to new life. Life even without a consciousness of God is a schoolmaster. But some men are better students than others; Thomas Merton was such a man.

In the twenty-three years preceding his conversion and the three years between it and his acceptance of his vocation, Merton compacted more experience than most people do in twice that span. The ordinary man would find monastic life a life of loneliness, but Merton had known intense loneliness as a child, and even in the gregarious Columbia days had never conquered his sense of loneliness. There is ample evidence in his personal journals and publications and in the work of his youthful companion Ed Rice that Merton did not deny the gratification of the senses, but momentary gratification did not satisfy his deepest needs. He knew crises both physical and mental in his personal health, in the loss of his parents and the alienation of his other relatives. His exceptional mind devoured the wisdom of the great literature of the world, but the models he found there were unsatisfactory. He tried losing himself in the crowd by immersing himself in the corporateness of modern civilization in some of the world's great cities, but this also failed to satisfy his inward longing. None of these things proved to be the thread needed to draw together his fragmented life. It was only when he plunged into the depths of his own being that he began to find the sources to pull his life together.

When Merton was baptized, he did not erase his memory of knowledge and experience, nor did he, out of hand, repudiate it. Instead, he began filtering all experience through his new perspective. He began to understand why men are lonely. The sensual drives were brought under control, but Merton would never negate them as positive human attributes. The great literature of Joyce, Richard Hughes, and E. M. Forster affirmed for Merton Augustine's assessment of the human condition. These diaries of man's anxiety, coupled with his own experience, provided analogues of Kierkegaard's discussions of dread and anxiety. Merton's own sense of lostness in the evolving massive technocracy provided the backdrop for the truth he would discover in the new loneliness of Gethsemani. Almost immediately he realized that he had only scratched the surface and that the journey inward would be a long and painful one. Nevertheless, it was one he could not resist. Thanks to his artistic disposition and his intercourse with his father's aesthetic environment and the culture of Europe, he would not only feel but also be able to share those feelings through his writing. At first it would be a mirror for personal reflection on his pilgrimage, but in due time his works would become maps to the obscure territories of the spiritual dimension of life. Merton was uniquely prepared for his vocation and was now ready for the *via purgativa*.

CHAPTER III

The Desert

The die was cast. Tom Merton had made an irrevocable decision to risk his life on the biblical proposition that one finds his life only by losing it. He wanted to bury his life with Christ. He wanted the monastery to swallow him up as a grain of wheat is swallowed by the earth, dying in order to bear much fruit (Jn. 12:24). He entered those stark white walls with joyful anticipation.

Those early days, which Merton recalled twenty years later in the Preface to A Thomas Merton Reader, were "hard" and "happy" ones.

> I was a novice in 1942–1944. Those were hard years, before the days when radiators were much in favor during the winter, when the hours of communal prayer were much longer, when the fasts were much stricter. It was a period of training, and a happy, austere one. . . .[1]

He apparently submitted himself completely to being formed by the formula tested by the centuries. All of his mental and physical resources were mustered and attuned to the "transforming and life-giving effect of the monastic tradition."[2] Merton had come to be molded into the image of God by that transformation. Water baptism had stirred in him a fervent desire to have his mind and being redeemed by the spiritual baptism of monasticism.

He came to the monastery to lay claim to the charism of the monastic life, ". . . the freedom and peace of a wilderness existence, a return to the desert that is also a recovery of (inner) paradise."[3] The desert theme was certainly no new idea in monastic or biblical thought. In biblical literature the "desert" or "wilderness" occupies a prominent place. It is the location or setting for much of the historical narrative in the Old Testament and becomes an important motif in the prophets and psalms. The Exodus and the ensuing wilderness experience are primary in the religious memory of the Jewish people. The wilderness experience was the formative one for the people of Israel.

> It is the persistent recollection of this historic experience of the Sinai desert amid the annual festival enactment of the conversion of dryness into fertility that has given the scriptural texts the extraordinary complexity and potency which was to survive in varied impulses into Christian history.[4]

The deliverance of God in these experiences is enshrined as a symbol of His salvific power and mercy. The central religious feasts and ceremonies of the Jewish people attest to this fact even today. The desert motif occurs in various forms and combinations in the later writers and in postbiblical Christian literature, but all uses include a concept of purification.[5]

The theme continues in the New Testament as John the Baptist lives and preaches in the wilderness, and it is the desert into which the Spirit drives Jesus to be tempted. Merton pointed to John the Baptist as the special "pattern and patron" of monks, both in his vocation to the desert and in his self-understanding as a prophet who must fade away as Christ comes into focus; the pscyhology of monasticism is that the monk must "decrease" in order for Christ to "increase" (Jn. 3:30).[6] It might be noted that John the Baptist provided Merton a model not only with regard to withdrawal into the desert and self-deprivation but also in the sense that the desert becomes a base for observation of a corrupt society. Both men used these observations as the source of bold denouncement of dehumanizing influences. Theirs was a prophecy rooted in their personal detachment and spiritual relationship.

It was in the desert that Jesus struggled with his identity and mission and found his way to the Father's will. In a review of a study of the desert in Mark, Merton commented on the importance of the call to the wilderness theme in biblical theology. The call is not to die in the desert but "to recover the paradise life after suffering temptation with Christ in desert solitude."[7] This motif is one that unifies much of the biblical narrative; "the *pascha Christi*, the call of the People of God out of Egypt, through the Red Sea into the Desert and to the Promised Land; the theme of the old and new man; the theme of the fallen world and the new creation" are all said to be variations of this theme.[8] The biblical testimony maps the way to the promised land through the desert, and, periodically, throughout the course of Christian history, men have gone into the desert to find God. Merton believed the Father called the monk into the desert to be nourished on Jesus himself.

The desert motif was recovered in Christian tradition in the third century as some seekers looked for alternatives to the establishment of religion. The détente between the Church and the world, instituted by the conversion of Constantine, aroused fears in some Christians that corruption would be the inevitable offspring of a wedding of Babylon and Jerusalem. Social respectability lessened the tension that sustained spiritual self-consciousness, and as a result the spiritual life became a matter of personal discipline. The most suitable environment for this pursuit was the desert. These anchorites ("withdrawers") were the Christian precursors of the various forms of monasticism that have survived into the present age. They sought escape from the distractions and temptations of society to be alone (monachus) with God and themselves. Not all disappeared permanently from view or lived impractical lives. The greatest leaders of the early Church emulated

Moses and Paul by preparing for their missions in seclusion with the Holy One. Jerome prepared himself for his scholarly contributions to the Church in a monastery and praised the uncluttered view from the desert:

> O desert enamelled with the flowers of Christ. O solitude where those stones are born of which in the Apocalypse is built the city of the Great King. . . . How long (he asks a friend) will you remain in the shadow of roofs, in the smoky dungeon of the cities? Believe me, I see here more of the light.[9]

The ecclesiastical genius of Basil was inspired by his own desert experience. He was stimulated by visions of that biblical host of witnesses who had preceded him into the desert.

> I am living . . . in the wilderness wherein the Lord dwelt. Here is the oak of Mamre; here is the ladder which leads to heaven, and the encampments of angels which Jacob saw; here is the wilderness where the people, purified, received the law, and then going into the land of promise beheld God. Here is Mount Carmel where Elijah abode and pleased God. Here is the plain whither Ezra [IV; 14:37-38] withdrew [for forty days], and at God's bidding poured forth from his mouth all his divinely inspired books. Here is the wilderness where the blessed John ate locusts and preached repentence to men. Here is the Mount of Olives, which Christ ascended and there prayed, teaching us how to pray. Here is Christ, the lover of the wilderness.[10]

Solitude was not ultimate for these men but was only a means to an end. As Merton expressed it, "Solitude therefore must translate itself into the three words: *cum Christo vivere* [to live with Christ]. . . . Solitude spiritualizes the whole man, transforms him, body and soul, from a carnal to a spiritual being,"[11] Life in the desert has never been easy, physically or spiritually. Stamina and endurance are not instantaneously acquired. A regimen to prepare men for the austere life of the desert and the vigorous inner turmoil of the life of the spirit had to be developed; to accomplish this, communities emerged to provide stimulation and support. Merton observed that there were two reasons why monks live together; first, to be "hair shirts" to one another, and, second, because "community life is safer."[12] They are drawn together and held together by the *voluntas communis*, the common will to seek the will of God. Under the leadership of such men as Basil, Augustine, and the great synthesizer Benedict, rules and patterns of life emerged to assist the beginner. The aim of the monastery is to give form to the ideal of the desert, a way of purgation where the soul may be prepared to receive God. On first glance, it would appear that the cenobitic life would be easier than the eremitic, but for many it would prove the more difficult as human eccentricities are added to the burden of an ascetical existence. Community life itself was sometimes a form of penance. "Living with other people and learning to lose ourselves in the understanding of their weakness and deficiencies," Merton wrote, "can help us to become true contemplatives."[13] The desert fathers were at least freed of the temptation to be angry at a snoring brother. One advantage to the solitary desert existence pointed out by Merton to the novices was that a man could be sure that everything in nature is working in concert to fulfill God's will. That's an assumption that cannot be made in a community of humans. Nevertheless, the impulses that lead men to their respective deserts combine with the prize they seek to overcome the cost. Community discipline was envisioned as a preparation for the true solitude of contemplative union with God. Benedict insisted in the first rule that an eremitic life should come only "after long probation in the monastery." Merton captured in verse the sense of urgency and longing that drives men into the desert, the voice of paradise that wafts over the arid sands.

And the deep ferns sing this epithalame:
"Go up, go up! this desert is the door of heaven!
And it shall prove your frail soul's miracle!
Climb the safe mountain. . . ."[14]

The fertile sands bear rich fruit when watered with the Spirit. The desert is the place least likely to be exploited by man. Merton believed the desert fathers to be correct in their assumption that the wasteland was cared for by God alone. God's plan for his chosen people, from Israel's exodus to the present, "was that they should learn to love Him in the wilderness and that they should always look back upon the time in the desert as the idyllic time of their life with Him alone."[15]

Monasticism developed for the sake of the individual. Merton subjected himself to the monastic tradition to learn the way of freedom, the way of authenticity. Monasticism "developed out of the need felt by those religiously inclined to isolate themselves, to withdraw from their worldly surroundings, in order to live more freely their own particular lives."[16] The service to the Church and the world is an indirect one, a dramatic portrayal of the gospel and its claims. The values of secular society are called into question by their renunciation. The monk's commitment to absolutes that transcend the pleasures of earthly existence is affirmed in his sacrifice of worldly pleasure and comfort. "Hence it is the function of the Christian, contemplative community on earth to imitate and reflect the perfect union of love and peace in heaven. . . ."[17] The literal desert or the simulated desert of the monastery provide only the setting in which the drama occurs. The monastic spiritual journey "is not a journey in space, but a journey in spirit."[18] The monastery serves as a laboratory where authentic spiritual encounter may take place in a controlled environment without interference or distraction. It is a battlefield where the enemies of the soul, those forces that separate deep from Deep, may be overcome. Those who come fall into the category of those

Gregory the Great alluded to when he wrote, "All who were converted to the Lord have desired the life of contemplation."[19]

Tom Merton was convinced that for him this was not just "a" way but the only way. He desired contemplation that he might be completely converted. Each seeks a place where he can ". . . live on the desire of God alone; to have one's mind divested of all earthly things and united . . . with Christ."[20] The more complex the society, the greater the need for isolation, at least separation from the fuzzy confusion of industrialized society. Almost exactly a year before his death there appeared a reiteration of Merton's concept of the *raison d'être* for modern monasticism:

> The fundamental purpose of all monastic life is . . . to deliver the individual and the charismatic community from the massive automatic functioning of a social machine that leaves nothing to peculiar talent, to chance, or to grace. The monastic vocation calls a man to desert frontiers, beyond which there are no police in order to dip into the ocean of unexploited forces which surrounds a well ordered society and draw from it a personal provision of grace and vision.[21]

Having resolved to take up his cross and follow Jesus into the desert, Merton arrived at the Abbey of Gethsemani in December 1941. He came there to die as the seed in the earth to permit the seed of life within him to grow. He was embarking on Thomas à Kempis' "royal road of the Holy Cross"; into the desert Merton went, in a way expressed centuries earlier in *The Imitation of Christ*:

> Turn to the Lord with all your heart, forsake this sorry world, and your soul shall find rest. Learn to turn from worldly things, and give yourself to spiritual things, and you will see the Kingdom of God come within you. . . . Christ will come to you, and impart

his consolations to you, if you prepare a worthy dwelling for Him in your heart. [II:1] . . . Be assured of this, that you must live a dying life. And the more completely a man dies to self, the more he lives to God. [II:11][22]

The Cistercian order, which he had chosen to nurture his faith, practiced the Strict Observance. The Cistercians claim Benedict as their spiritual father, their founders having come out of Cluny to live by a more rigorous discipline. The Cluniac reform had become establishment and the Trappists now wanted to reform the reformers. Gethsemani was the first Trappist abbey founded in America, with a heritage going back to the severe reform of La Trappe by Abbé de Rancé in the seventeenth century. From a distance, the monastic life might be enshrouded with a romantic aura; indeed, accounts of those who have entered only to leave after a brief stay suggest that some of those who enter come with a rhapsodical notion of what life there is like. "Do you . . . imagine that the monastic life is romantic?" Merton mused. "It is not. It is terribly prosaic. . . . Perhaps, we must confess, that some of us came here with a kind of secret, romantic enthusiasm in our hearts: and that we are angry because it is all shot."[23] Romantic illusions of monastic life were quickly shattered by the daily regimen in those days.

The world of a Trappist monastery in 1941 is almost inconceivable to the modern mind. It was like entering another time, if not another dimension. Tom Merton left behind him the miracles and convenience of technology; the license of self-gratification, which some men mistake for freedom; fashion and comfort, abundance of food; a myriad of luxuries that even then, a third of a century ago, affluent Americans considered necessities. He even left behind his name, symbolically burying Tom Merton to emerge as Brother Louis. Only minimal contact with the outside world was permitted. In those days there were no radios, no televisions (this is still so), no newspapers, and no newsmagazines. Visitors were allowed only once a year for three days. Letters could be sent and received only four times a year. The witty, urbane language of academia was abandoned for the silence of Gethsemani. Obedience, poverty, chastity, conversion of manners, and stability— these were the five rules accepted by the postulant, with a view to their taking them as vows at the appropriate time. The vow of stability would prove the most difficult for Merton. It was for him the "belly of the whale."[24] In *New Seeds of Contemplation* he remonstrated over this flaw:

> If you can never make up your mind what God wills for you, but are always veering from one opinion to another, from one practice to another, from one method to another, it may be an indication that you are trying to get around God's will and do your own with a quiet conscience.

> As soon as God gets you in one monastery you want to be in another. As soon as you taste one way of prayer, you want to try another. You are always making resolutions and breaking them by counter-resolutions. You ask your confessor and do not remember the answers. Before you finish one book you begin another, and with every book you read you change the whole plan of your interior life.[25]

This was a problem he never completely overcame. Periodically, throughout his life, he entertained doubts about whether he was in the right place. On more than one occasion he discussed with the abbot the possibility of changing to a stricter order or relocating in a more barren environment.[26] As prescribed by the Rule of Benedict, Louis was issued only one change of clothes. His head was shaven, and the young man of letters came under the rule of silence in order that the interior word might emerge out of silence. In the silence of concentration, the monk labors to penetrate the sound barrier of Babel to the

Word that is beyond sound and concept, that has been obfuscated by the sights and sounds that batter human senses. Bernard established the rule of silence on the basis of his experience that

> . . . the Word is apprehended not under any outward appearances but by His effect. . . . He is a Word that does not sound in the ear but penetrates the mind; He does not speak, He acts, He does not make himself heard in the senses but in the desires of the will.[27]

Commenting on Cistercian life in a photographic monograph on the community, Merton wrote, "The silence of God embraces us, consoles us, answers our question (once we have the sense to stop asking)."[28] Sleeping accommodations were dormitory cubicles where the monks were required to sleep, winter and summer, fully clothed. There was no air conditioning in spite of the stifling heat of the Kentucky summers, and the heating was inadequate for the frigid winters. Reading some of Merton's meditations on the natural environment surrounding the monastery, one might get the impression that the knobs offered a paradise rather than a wilderness, but it was not so. The weather was unpredictable and ranged from severe cold to extreme heat. Merton perspired profusely and often changed clothes several times a day, washing out by hand the soiled ones and letting them dry in the hot sun. In August 1947, he wrote, "Hot, sticky weather. Prickly heat. Red lumps all over your neck and shoulders. Everything clammy. *Paenitentiam agite!* It is better than a hairshirt."[29] Even when the weather was at its best, he was not at liberty to roam at will because the monks were restricted to the cloister except when their work assignments required them to be in the woods or fields. Work that required him to be in the fields or forests was greeted with enthusiasm by Merton, even if it was the most common task.

. . . work in the fields helps contemplation. Yesterday
we were out in the middle bottom, spreading manure
all over the gray mud of the cornfields. I was so happy
I almost laughed out loud. It was such a relief to get
away from a typewriter.[30]

The daily schedule was exacting. Everyone arose at 2
A.M., to begin a period of prayer and meditation that
lasted two hours, until time for Mass, followed by another
period of prayer and meditation, a brief "free" period for
reading, and, finally, about 7 A.M., a light repast of a cou-
ple of slices of bread and coffee. The rest of the day was
divided among labor, study, and worship. The principal
meal was served at noon. It consisted entirely of vegetables
and bread; no meat, fish, or eggs. A piece of bread and
milk or coffee was the evening menu. Self-imposed flagella-
tion was a part of the weekly routine. There is disa-
greement among his peers with regard to the severity of
Merton's personal asceticism. Some contend that he often,
at least in the early years at Gethsemani, wore a chain
under his habit as a kind of "hair shirt"; in any case, he
would have participated in the regular Friday self-adminis-
tered flogging.[31] Such a life could voluntarily be endured
only by a deranged mind or by one fortified by interior
prayer. This thought brings to mind William James' classic differentiation between the "sick soul" and the
"healthy-minded" one. The former would find gratification in severe asceticism where his "manufacture of fears"
could be nourished and his desire for every unwholesome
kind of misery satiated. The healthy-minded discovers the
interior strength to fulfill his humanity.[32] The first
months of Cistercian life are occupied with adjustment to
the routine, but the crucial test is obedience and the
submission of the singular will to the common will.
Throughout his life Merton placed great emphasis on
submission to authority, which he said "is all important
because it requires perfect humility, obedience, and interior detachment without which spiritual liberty can never

be attained."[33] In *The Waters of Siloe*, he noted
Benedict's signs of a true vocation as: "a real desire of
union with God (*si vere Deum quaerit*), a healthy interest
in the liturgical prayers of the monks (*si sollicitus sit ad
opus Dei*), willingness to learn obedience and to accept
the humiliation of hardships of the common life."[34] All
of these he would excel in all of his life. There were many
aspects of his life that he would question through the
years, but there is no real evidence he ever questioned his
call to the desert.[35] Father Matthew Kelty, a confrere
of Merton's, says that it is in the matter of obedience that
monks fail most. "To my mind all the ascetic practices
there are do not amount to much compared to the asceticism of obedience."[36] Of Father Louis, Kelty says he
was not a great ascetic characterizing Merton's asceticism
as "simple hard work"[37] and notes that he excelled in
the area of obedience. Father Kelty quotes Dom James
Fox as saying that he had no more obedient monk than
Merton. According to Father Kelty, it was "through obedience he [Merton] became a free man."[38] The only way
in which one can live by the Cistercian Rule in a monastery is "to become one flesh, one undivided organism
with all the rest of the people there."[39] Shared life is
not easy under ordinary circumstances, but the pressures
of Cistercian life surely made it a monumental task.
But it was here, under these primitive conditions, among
this strange, amorphous mass of silent humanity, that
Tom Merton found a home and a system that gave order
to his fragmented life. The discipline provided "an exterior framework, a kind of scaffolding with which he was
to help himself build the spiritual structure of his own
life with God."[40]

The Monastic Vocation

Physical labor, ascetic deprivation, self-inflicted punishment, all the curriculum of the monastery, had one purpose: to create optimum conditions for cultivating mysti-

cal awareness of God's being. The consciousness sought is mystical in the sense of piercing the darkness and resolving the mystery. That which had been present but unknown can be known under the right circumstances. Every activity, including the simplest, most natural human functions, were regimented to be means to that overarching end. "The monk," wrote Newman, "proposed to himself no great or systematic work beyond that of saving his soul."[41] This was Merton's deepest desire. He continued the course of study begun at Columbia, broadening his reading to include the principals of the Cistercian tradition: Cassian, Benedict, Ailred, and Bernard of Clairvaux. His early works reflect an assiduous study of the Scriptures, which, in the best monastic tradition, began to permeate his works. Even the Scriptures were integrated into the whole fabric of life. "The letter of Scripture must be studied and understood: but the content of revelation will not be exhausted when we have argued out all its terms and propositions to suit our own reason."[42] He perceived that while the Bible contained witness to the word of God, it was not the totality of that word. The Scriptures point beyond themselves to Christ, who is the ultimate Word and who apprehends rather than being apprehended.

"Contemplation reaches out to the knowledge and even to the experience of the transcendent and inexpressible God."[43] This was Merton's proleptic vision of the end of the journey, the paradise for which the desert must be endured. The contemplative works to direct not only his mental attention, but also the attention of his whole being to the discernment of ultimate being. "The whole meaning and purpose of Cistercian isolation from the world, of obedience, of humility and humiliations, of penance, fasting, hard manual labor, the discipline, the five vows . . . is this: to bring each monk into this close, intimate union with Christ."[44] By the force of the subdued, instructed, and formed will, the mind is disposed to recollection and attention, and the attention is fixed on God by recalling thought when it wanders, or reviving it when it fades away. The spiritual exercises of the Cistercian economy operate as calisthenics to build up the spiritual gladiators for combat. Teresa borrowed the biblical metaphor of soil to chart the course of the neophyte. Before the shoots can break through to the life-giving sun, the garden must be weeded and the soil enriched. These days were given to preparing the soil and planting the seed.

Catharsis

Merton had begun to examine the spiritual life and to practice it to some extent long before his arrival in Kentucky. He had taken for his guide the *Cautelas* or counsels of John of the Cross, and he continued to rely on them to assist him in removing the stones from his spiritual garden.[45] He referred to his entry into the monastery as the second stage of a lifetime of continuing conversion.[46] It was an act of repentance in which the communicant turned away not from acts or patterns of behavior but from self, a necessary step in the climb to God.

The ascetic life has often been misunderstood and misrepresented even by some of those engaged in it with regard to the reason for the subduing of the passions and the control of the senses. Such practices are not intended as punishment or rejection of the natural order. Rather they are means of clearing away the barriers to the experience of the goodness of creation, a means of uncovering what is now considered supernatural in the natural. The process is not unlike finding a beautiful antique piece of furniture that someone has foolishly painted over and that must be stripped to recover and refinish its original beauty. It is the work of re-creation begun in, by, and through Christ. It is the death of the old for the sake of giving birth to the new.

The death-and-resurrection theme is not the exclusive property of the Christian religion. It is common to mystical religion. William Inge's study of English mystics cited recognition of the principle of death as a prerequisite of spiritual life as "the strength of the best mystical teaching."[47] Aldous Huxley cited this self-emptying as one of the common denominators of mysticism.

> That it is possible for human beings to love, know and . . . to become actually identified with the Ground. That to achieve this unitive knowledge, to realize this supreme identity, is the final end and purpose of human existence. That there is a Law or Dharma, which must be obeyed, a Tao or Way, which must be followed, if men are to achieve their final end. That the more there is of I, me, mine, the less there is of the Ground; and that consequently the Tao is a Way of humility and compassion, the Dharma a Law of modification and self-transcending awareness.[48]

A complete metamorphosis is required, as the goal is not a difference in degree but in kind. The beginner must actively seek to remove the parasites that choke the true vine. Teresa exhorted her spiritual charges to spin a cocoon of death for the silkworm that the new creature of beauty might emerge. The annihilation of self is a familiar topic in Eckhart's discourses: "I say that if the soul is to know God, it must forget itself . . . for as long as it is self-aware and self-conscious, it will not see or be conscious of God. But when, for God's sake, it becomes unself-conscious and lets go of everything, it finds itself again in God."[49] Merton took seriously the problem of self, strove to eliminate all thoughts of self, that his mind and heart might be filled with the "wholly other." He believed that one should aspire to be at one with the Holy One. His reading of Bernard and John of the Cross led him to conclude that perfect union was beyond the reach of the cluttered soul. He once remarked that the entire meaning of Christian asceticism is summed up in Mark 8:34, when Jesus said, ". . . If any man would come after me, let him deny himself and take up his cross and follow me." The vow of poverty came to have for him a meaning more than the mere surrender of material possessions. After all, it is the poor in spirit who are promised the vision of God. While reading about the rigorous life of the Carmelites, he was struck with a more profound idea of poverty: ". . . poverty conceived as a function of solitude or 'nakedness'—detachment, isolation from everything superfluous in the interior life."[50] The riches with which we are engrossed are paste and glass. Our coffers must be emptied to make room for that pearl of great price worth our all. The obstacles must be removed, leaving a void to be filled by truth.

Merton's intellect and erudition undoubtedly presented him with special problems in stripping away the husks. The abandonment of secular comforts and conveniences was the easy part for him. The mystics have been unanimous in their assessment of the depravity of human reason. Man's intellect lacks the capacity for commerce with Wisdom Himself. Prayer, defined by Evagrius as "habitual commerce of the intelligence with God," is possible only when "intelligence goes out of the body."[51] God cannot be known via ordinary means. The tablet of the mind must be erased in order that God may write Himself across it. Such diverse philosophers as Thomas and Bonaventure instructed Louis that the way to God lay through "unknowing." Bonaventure admonished those who would experience God to

> . . . ask it of grace, not of doctrine; of desire, not of intellect; of the ardours of prayer, not of the teachings of the schools; of the Bridegroom, not of the Master; of God, not of man; of the darkness, not of the day; not of illumination, but of that Fire which enflames all and wraps us in God with great sweetness and most ardent love. The which Fire most truly is God, and the hearth thereof is in Jerusalem.[52]

The intellectual faculties have to be brought under control to deactify the field of interference that obstructs God's transmission of Himself. "As long as our faculties are absorbed in the vain work of trying to see, to grasp, to understand, they are unnecessarily standing in God's way, and prevent Him from lifting us up to Him by a knowledge that transcends our natural knowing."[53] The mind had to renounce its understanding to receive knowledge that is beyond processes of philosophical and theological speculation. He became aware of the knowledge beyond knowledge, that which Pseudo-Dionysius had in mind when he wrote

> . . . there is that most divine knowledge of God
> which takes place through ignorance, in the union
> which is above intelligence, when the intellect, quitting all things that are, and then leaving itself also, is
> united to the superlucent rays, being illuminated
> thence and there in by the unsearchable depth of
> wisdom.[54]

This was an exciting, challenging new experience, which transcended the senses, and for which Merton's appetite would grow.

Merton quickly perceived potential pitfalls and cautiously examined them. There is a danger that in disengaging the temporal, one can become encumbered with the religious. If the ritual and the routine become ends rather than means, they subvert the most devout, well-intentioned monks. One may become absorbed with one's own asceticism.

> If contemplation is arrived at by superhuman self-control and by a supreme and subtle and intense application of intellect and will, it offers, indeed, a considerable appeal to our appetite for self-glorification.
> In fact, to become a Yogi and to be able to commit moral and intellectual suicide whenever you please, without the necessity of actually dying, to be able to black out your mind by the incantation of half articulate charms and to enter into a state of annihilation, in which all the faculties are inactive and the soul is

as inert as if it were dead—all this may well appeal to certain minds as a refined and rather pleasant way of getting even with the world and with society, and with God Himself for that matter.[55]

Karl Barth, in a brief excursus on the monastic life, noted that the monk does not escape the greatest obstacle to becoming a spiritual man by fleeing to the desert, because he cannot leave himself behind. The void must be maintained until occupied by the proper tenant. There is no assurance that the expulsion of one demon will not open the way for several, more vicious and dangerous than the evicted one. Merton was unwilling to trade intellectualism for a euphoric sentimentality. Perhaps it was his brushes with Protestantism that had made him leery of a religion of emotion or chivalry. In the spring of 1941, he had insisted that religion "exists not as a 'good feeling' but as a constant purpose."[56] Eight years later he was no less wary of dependence on such stimuli. "Even religion," he grieved, "has degenerated . . . into a cult of feelings and pious emotions."[57] The fear of quietism, which never left him, was evident even in this early period. He called this kind of passive contemplation "cheap," a "feeble spiritual dilettantism";[58] he argued that ". . . quietism is as opposed to true contemplation as hell is to heaven."[59] There is a fine line between preparing oneself for what God has to "give" and trying to make oneself into an imitation of God or demanding that God do it all. The traveler begins the trip under his own steam, lured by the promise of rest at the end of the journey. Implicit in Merton's theology at this stage is a kind of synergism. Man cannot coerce God or follow a certain course to mystical experience, but man can respond in an appropriate way to God's grace.

> Mystical contemplation is absolutely beyond the reach of man's activity. There is nothing he can do to obtain it by himself. It is a pure gift of God. God gives it to whom He wills, when He wills, and in the way and degree in which He wills. By co-operating with the work of ordinary grace we can—and, if we

really mean to love God, we must—constantly grow and progress in charity and union with Him by our good works.[60]

God provides the power, but man provides the outlet. The grace that is experienced is manifested in the human embodiment of love. Theresa illustrates the progression of co-operation by extending her garden metaphor.

> Let us now consider how this garden can be watered, so that we may know what we have to do, what labor it will cost us, if the gain will outweigh the labour, and for how long this labour must be borne. It seems to me that the garden can be watered in four ways: by taking water from a well, which costs us great labour; or by a waterwheel and buckets, when the water is drawn by a windlass (I have sometimes drawn it in this way: it is less laborious than the other and gives more water); or by a stream or a brook, which waters the ground much better, for it saturates it more thoroughly, and there is less need to water it often so that the gardener's labour is much less; or by heavy rain, when the Lord waters it with no labour of ours, a way incomparably better than any of those which have been described.[61]

When the intellect and senses are freed from the illusions of Babel, the field is ready to be planted and watered. The Christian mystic is not engaged in the fabrication of a mystical experience, but, as Paul Tillich stated it, Christian mysticism is predicated on the faith expectation of "the appearance of the new reality."[62] Grace is what God does, and faith and hope are man's response, but the faith is that described by the biblical writer James, one that is visible in acts of charity.

The Search of Self

The Christian believes that God's identity and man's identity are inextricably bound together. The unmasking of the false self has as its purpose the revelation of the true self. The entire monastic ascesis is aimed at the abolition of what Bernard called the "disguise" of the illusionary self in order to expose the real self.[63] Self-scrutiny is a painful but indispensable element in all true religion. Self-awareness and self-knowledge, not to be confused with self-obsession and self-centeredness, are the beginnings of the mystical ascent. Freed from the responsibilities and claims of choosing the various roles approved by society, with no obligation to produce anything or be anything, the monk may direct all his faculties—cognitive, affective, and conative—to the discovery of the real self. The peculiar task of the monk, according to Merton, is not to "do" anything but to break through to being himself. In his notes on "the Vows" he wrote: "Our job in life is not so much to produce anything, as to be what we are supposed to be, to let the divine image come out and manifest itself in our lives by the way in which we live."[64] Unsure of who he is, man resists the image that may be imposed upon him by others. The basis for much of man's distrust of his neighbor is the fear of the other man's expectation or judgment of who he is. Walls are erected and attacks launched in self-defense. Before a man can be open to God or his fellow man, he must be open to himself. "The reason why we hate one another and fear one another," Merton observed, "is that we secretly or openly hate and fear our own selves."[65] When the illusions of self have been stripped away, the world can be seen as it is, and God can be seen as He is. The journey inward has a destination beyond personal identity. "The mystic enters into himself not in order to work but to pass through the center of his own soul and lose himself in the mystery and secrecy and infinite transcendent reality of God living and working within him."[66] What is discovered within is neither static nor complete. Implicit in the notion of growth and ascent is a kind of dipolarity of symbiotic being and becoming. Our identity lies in the discovery of the ground of being, but it must be worked out in the process of living and, for that matter, we limit God by making the creator static.

Within himself the new man does not discover a completed identity but a potential one. When the vessel has been scrubbed, the soul returns as it were to a pristine nothingness, ready to receive true being. As a polished crystal is able to reflect light, so the polished soul has the capacity to reflect the grace of God.

> The soul of man, left to its own natural level, is a potentially lucid crystal left in darkness. It is perfect in its own nature, but it lacks something that it can only receive from outside and above itself. But when the light shines in it, it becomes in a manner transformed into light and seems to lose its nature in the splendor or a higher nature, the nature of the light that is in it.[67]

The light never is fully contained by the glass; the effect is dependent on a continuing relationship. So it is with man and God. God never ceases to be creator, carving his image on the soul of man. *Ascesis* is a means of opening the self to the perpetual work of God in us. The monk is sustained by his confidence in the future consummation of his redemption, or, as Paul expressed it in the Epistle to the Philippians, confidence that God will complete the good work begun in the servants of Christ (1:6).

Merton subscribed to the recapitulation doctrine of Irenaeus, i.e., that Christ has made possible the restoration and perfection of mankind. Irenaeus described the incarnation as God becoming man so that man might become God. God keeps on creating man out of his love for him. Man's nature is determined by his relationship to God; thus the capacity of man for growth is infinite. Basil declared that man is under a mandate from God to become God. Eckhart likewise held a doctrine of mystical regeneration. According to the Rhenish mystic, man's nature is being to receive being, while it is the nature of God to be being and give being.[68] Augustinian psychology operates on the premise that human nature cannot contemplate God at all until the internal image has been "reformed by grace."[69] Augustine teaches that it is the divine image within man that impels him toward contemplative union with God. The logical conclusion of such thinking is that man's true identity is found in his identification with God, arrived at by the complete spiritual life, which actualizes the soul's potentialities and ultimately leads to transformation in God and "deification." This idea is not foreign to classical Christian thought. It is a *leitmotif* in the Nicean apologetics of Athanasius, who argues that the manifestation of the Divine Logos in Christ took the form it did "so that to the divine nature would be united human nature and so that the salvation and deification of the latter would be assured."[70] Bouyer cites the motif in the works of Clement of Alexandria, Origen, and prominently in the Dionysian Corpus.[71] Augustine proclaims that he who feeds on the Divine will have his substance transformed into His.[72] No Christian writer goes farther than the absorptionist position of Eckhart. "If I am to know God directly," he declared, "I must become completely He and He I: so that this He and this I become and are I."[73] Merton would not have felt comfortable with so extreme a position in his first decade at Gethsemani,[74] but he did long to know as intimately as possible the great "I AM." "For myself," he wrote during Advent 1946, "I have only one desire . . . to disappear into God, to be submerged in His peace, to be lost in the secret of His Face."[75] It was only in God that he believed he could find himself.

Understanding God

Critics of mysticism charge that the historical Christ is not accorded his proper role in the mystical scheme. A belief that God can be apprehended without mediation would seem to minimize the importance of Christ. Merton's early discourses seem at first glance to vindicate this judgment. There is far more focus on both man and God than there is on the man-God, Christ Jesus. When treated at all, Christology is usually discussed in relationship to sacramental practice and meaning. This does not mean, however, that there is not at work in mystical theology and practice a fundamental Christology. The mystics' intuitive sense of unity mitigates against a Jesusology that would place Jesus between God and man. The mystic considers the two, One. The Christian passes through Christ to God, and the two are undifferentiated. As Augustine expresses it, ". . . you come through Christ to Christ . . . through Christ the Man to Christ as God."[76] Christ is the living presence of God within the believer.[77] The mystic conceives of Christ as the "new reality," to return to Tillich's phrase, who has cosmic meaning that transcends events that were only evidence of the existence of such a reality.[78] Christ is the seal of assurance of the existence of the new reality. An argument could be made that the Holy Spirit is more prominent than the historical Jesus in the theology of the mystics. The mystic knows God in the form of the indwelling Spirit; he co-operates with the Holy Spirit in cultivating the life of grace within himself. It may be that mystical theology better expresses the meaning of the Trinity than does traditional dogmatic theology. The distinctions are certainly less strained as the problem of tritheism dissolves in the notion of absolute union. God in three persons, God transcendent and immanent is known only in the I-thou and not in objective logic. God is "I AM," nothing less, nothing more.

Inasmuch as no concept can satisfy the mystic's thirst, the almost ruthless safari into his inner being has as its purpose the discovery of the Word in the depths. The mystic dares to follow the instruction of Tennyson's "Ancient Sage," to experience that Word out of silence.

> If thou would'st hear the Nameless, and will dive
> Into the Temple-cave of thine own self,
> There, brooding by the central altar, thou
> May'st haply learn the Nameless hath a voice,
> By which thou wilt abide, if thou be wise.[79]

The mystic is not interested in God in the abstract but in the concrete. Contemplation has the singular purpose of initiating an ". . . experience of God revealing Himself . . . in the intimate embrace of a love so pure that it overwhelms every other affection and excludes everything from our souls but the knowledge of Love alone."[80] The knowledge of God sought by the mystic is not the kind stored in the memory bank nor what might be termed intellectual conviction; it is, rather, understanding, reality assimilated by experience into total being.

> He knows the reality of God, not in a concept, but by being in a certain manner transformed into that reality. If a pane of glass could understand the light that fills it and into which it disappears, it would be exactly like the soul of the contemplative who wakes up to the reality of God to the touch of his Gift of Understanding. For the contemplative understands God by the experience of being saturated in His Light, which is His Truth itself, poured directly into the soul and not apprehended through a sensible or rational medium.[81]

The influence of Bernard is unmistakable in both context and language—not to mention the frequent direct references. To experience God is to experience Him who is Love. God can be apprehended by man only in His purest essence, Love. The mutuality of God and man is realized as love calls to Love.

> The problem of mysticism is to endow the mind and will of God as He is in Himself and, ultimately to transform a human soul into God by a union of Love. . . . But since contemplation is an experience of God by connaturality, by union of love, St. Bernard sees that a connatural appreciation of the sufferings and sentiments of other men is an excellent preparation for the mystical knowledge of God in the obscure "sympathy" of infused love.[82]

When the soul has known God, it yearns for Him without regard to self. Indifferent to all else within and without the person, the love of God becomes its own reward. The longing for God dominates all thought, and all of life becomes a quest for Him who is "utter transcendence" and at the same time "all-pervading immanence."[83] It is the intense longing referred to again and again by Augustine, longing for divine life, a compulsion to love, hungering for experience, thirsting for truth. Here is perhaps the key differentiating factor between Christian and other forms of mysticism. Christians cling to an over-againstness of God in relationship to man. Here is one of the central paradoxes of Christianity: God is both immanent and transcendent. Contemplation is the method; God is the subject and the object. In this instance the medium and the message are inseparably conjoined. "Mystical contemplation is an intuition of God born of pure love."[84] God is known as he gives Himself to be known. True aseity precludes an adequate definition. The Christian mystic then follows Paul's admonition to grow in the grace and knowledge of the revealer who is at the same time the revealed.

Sacrament and Liturgy

Merton had abandoned the world for the spiritual college of the desert. Here in the womb of the Church he expected to lay hold of absolute and holy truth. The truth of the Church was contained in her teachings, which he studied diligently, but he was dramatically impressed with what he considered to be the embodiment of that truth in the sacraments. The life of the monk has traditionally been constructed around the *Opus Dei*, and the establishment of this priority invests the monastic life itself with at least "sign" value. The liturgical cycle is an expression of the faith of the community. "The Chief work of the Benedictine and Cistercian," Merton noted in a pious biography written in those early days, "is to praise God in

choir, in the harmonious daily round of offices that wheels
about the central hub of the Conventual Mass."[85] The liturgy provides social and religious matrices on which all the
strands of life may be woven into an organic whole. It provides the structure and form for worship, including the expression of gratitude for nature, and at the same time, it
offers rich material for meditation. Participation in the liturgy demonstrates the unity of the corporate cultus and
manifests a visible spiritual community. Moreover, in the
liturgy the participants assume a role in the *Opus Dei*;
thus it is simultaneously an act of faith and a work of
charity.

The Eucharist constitutes an object of loving attention.
It represents—indeed, to the Catholic mind it is—Jesus
Christ. Thus for Merton, Christ in the Eucharist was a
visible, tangible seal of God's love for the communicants.
The recapitulation motif appears again in Merton's eu-
charistic theology.

> We will pray for a deeper and deeper understanding
> of the great mystery which sums up the whole plan of
> God for His world, and the whole mission of Christ
> in the world: the recapitulation of all in Christ, the
> work of charity which transforms us all in Him so
> that we are one in Him as He is one with the Father
> and the Holy Spirit.[86]

Therefore, the Eucharist is not only a work effected but a
work that effects. Christ is the live seed of humanity remaking itself in history. Around the table where love is
consumed in love, all are united with one another in and
through their shared love. "The Blessed Eucharist is therefore the very heart of Christianity since it contains Christ
Himself, and since it is the chief means by which Christ
mystically unites the faithful to Himself in one Body."[87]
In the eucharistic celebration the communicant drama-
tizes his own salvation, giving concrete expression to "his
interior submission to and dependence upon a 'numinous'
power.[88] Merton, during this period, somewhat idolized the

"Blessed Sacrament,"[89] using it as an object of veneration and an aid to reflective prayer. This is not to suggest that Merton ever rejected the Eucharist as a source of grace and a special means of the presence of Christ. But like many spiritual children, he had not yet broken through the magical approach to authentic sacrament. For many the sacraments are means of manipulating God rather than a coming together of creature and creator.

Even in this early period the degree of solitude at Gethsemani was not enough for Merton. There is much in *Seeds of Contemplation* to suggest that he was becoming more and more aware of interior solitude as opposed to physical solitude. One service rendered by the order of community and ecclesiastical structure is the delineation of certain stages of advancement. Merton took simple vows in March 1944, and more and more concentrated his energies on his movement toward the third and "most tremendous step" in his conversion.[90] Each further commitment seemed to intensify his aspiration for his own incarnation into the liturgy. The priesthood appears to have represented in his mind the synthesis of his life and the sacramental expression of God's life. Anticipation of ordination filled him with "fear and trembling." Just about a year before that event, he wrote in his journals that he was sometimes plagued by the impulse to run away to avoid that awesome responsibility, but, each time, he was reassured by confidence in the direction of his superiors. "I go ahead under obedience. If my Superiors want me to be a priest, it is at least safe. God wants it and He will do me good by it although it may contain an unimaginable death."[91] The universality of the ceremonies and words of the Mass provided both a mode of adoration and an objective norm against which the subjectivism he feared might be tested. After his ordination, when he had begun to celebrate the Mass daily, he wrote of the work that he felt was being accomplished in him by this new relationship to the Word given substance. "A few months of the Mass," he wrote, "have emptied me more and filled me more than seven years of monastic asceticism."[92] Already a new sacramental relationship was being realized. The first plateau on the ascent had been reached. The sense of grace that overwhelmed him in the Mass evoked a sense of the potential oneness of God's love, solitude, and society. Physically exhausted and emotionally exhilarated, there was a taste of *quies*, rest. His solitude was shared with Christ, as they were united in the priesthood of God. A note of joy rings in his declaration that ". . . without ceasing to be who I am, I had become Somebody else—as if I had been raised to a higher and much simpler and cleaner level of being."[93] The rest he now enjoyed was only temporary, a moment of refreshment before pressing toward the prize. Even in this moment of rapture there was a ravishing of his being. He was at the same time filled with joy and terror. Such paradox was to characterize his whole life as he was swallowed up by the ark of safety.

> . . . I feel that my own life is especially sealed with this great sign which baptism and monastic profession and priestly ordination have burned into the roots of my being, because like Jonas himself I find myself traveling toward my destiny in the belly of a paradox.[94]

Following his ordination he was virtually immobilized by poor health and nervous exhaustion, unable to do any serious work for almost a year and a half. The pilgrimage toward believing and, in turn, knowing, is an arduous one, which takes its toll intellectually, emotionally, and physically.

A Third of the Journey

Eight years of study and struggle were behind him when he heard those words that seared through the flesh to be written indelibly on the heart, "a priest forever." They were years of external activity, of adjusting to a new life style, of learning, of hard labor. They were also years of inner turmoil and struggle. And they took their toll, leaving him physically ill but confirmed in the presuppositions that had brought him to Gethsemani. Ruthlessly he had exorcised the false images he had begun to question even before his conversion. He had realized, as his spiritual forerunners before him, that religious integrity requires relentless scrutiny of motivations and intentions. Self-distrust prompts a search for the potential true self. The monastery offered an environment that freed him from attachment to the world, but to be even a candidate for the life of the spirit, the self had to be purged from the everyday image of self. "It becomes overwhelmingly important for us *to become detached from our everyday conception of ourselves as potential subjects for special and unique experiences, or as candidates for realization, attainment and fulfillment.*"[95] By 1948, he was deriving some pleasure out of this cathartic leg of the journey. He apparently had little difficulty leaving the world behind, and, with anguish and perseverance, he had some sense of an inward cleansing. During this period of spiritual adolescence, he relied heavily on the teaching authority of the Church. His literary works at this time are for the most part pietistic and dogmatic. There is a danger in being too critical of these works. In the spiritual life, as in the physical life, one must walk before he can fly. Merton was enthusiastic about his new faith and the particular expression of it that he had chosen. He was determined to please God and God's instruments, his religious superiors. The latter encouraged him to write spiritual biographies and accounts of the monastic life, and he obliged with glowing panegyrics, with the usual sentimental flaws that accompany such works. Nevertheless, there are in all of these works pregnant snatches that gave promise of more original and creative thought to come later. Even among these works there are exciting glimpses of his penetrating intellect and deep spirituality. *The Seven Storey Mountain*, in spite of occasional pedantic parochialism, is an inspiring hymn of praise of thanksgiving. Dan Walsh, his teacher and life-

long friend, calls this Merton's purest mystical work. It is
the overflow of a heart filled with joy and hope. The exhaustion he experienced could be anticipated from any endeavor to which one would give himself so completely.

In giving thought to the various formulations of the
levels of the mystical ascent, it is striking how easily and
naturally they may be applied to Merton's own progression. In *What Are These Wounds*, he discusses the three
"sabbaths" or "rests" of the Cistercian teacher Ailred of
Rievaulx. By the time of his ordination, Merton had
passed through the first, the period of struggle and external activity, and entered the second, that of fraternal
union or peace with his brothers. A measure of freedom
had been achieved, and he knew that he was on the bor-
der of a new experience. An excerpt from his poem *The
Quickening of St. John the Baptist*, originally included in
his collection *The Tears of the Blind Lions* (1949), may
well be indicative of his own state at that juncture of his
life:

Night is our diocese and silence is our ministry
Poverty our charity and helplessness our tongue-tied
    sermon.
Beyond the scope of sight or sound we dwell upon the air
Seeking the world's gain in an unthinkable experience.
We are exiles in the far end of solitude, living as listeners
With hearts attending to the skies we cannot understand:
Waiting upon the first far drums of Christ the Conqueror,
Planting like sentinels upon the world's frontier.[96]

With his mind and his heart, Merton had listened to
the wisdom of the desert "cloud of witnesses" as well as
the silence. He had, he told his colleagues twenty-five
years later, been "turned on" by the liturgy and the life in
his first days in Gethsemani. Trappist life had given him
". . . the key to profound, deep things" that were not
accessible to him outside.[97] But if he had unlocked and
opened the door in 1949, he had discovered a new series
of obstacles to be overcome. He had abandoned the

world and was willing to abandon himself to obtain that "pearl of great price" that seemed to lay just beyond his grasp. He had filled himself on the manna of the Church, its prophets, its law, its liturgy. Yet his hunger and thirst were not yet satiated, and he pushed on, desiring that purity of heart that would let him see God. With honest trepidation, he was resolutely determined to press on into the presence of the Holy.

CHAPTER IV

World into Silence

Father Louis' "rest" was the rest of physical and emotional exhaustion. He had been ill at the end of his novitiate and, in 1949, was again somewhat incapacitated by a period of "poor health and nervous exhaustion," which left him "incapable of writing for at least a year and a half after I became a priest."[1] Before he could emerge from his cocoon, the world intruded into his life and shattered the silence he prized so highly. The unexpected success of *The Seven Storey Mountain* thrust the monk into the public spotlight and severely complicated his life. Mail by the sackful began to arrive, addressed to the author of the best seller. The sudden interest of the world disrupted the routine of the entire monastery, and Father Louis' problems were increased by the chagrin of some of his brother monks, who were scandalized by the fame of their colleague.

By design he had sought anonymity that he might be known by God alone. Even as the book was being prepared for market, he wrote, "Now my whole life is this —to keep unencumbered. . . . I own nothing and am owned by nothing and I shall never even be forgotten because no one will ever discover me."[2] Now this hope could never be realized. His suffering was all the greater because it was what he considered to be a flaw in his own character that was creating the problem—his inability to suppress the compulsion to write. His conscience was troubled continually by this inner conflict. He had hoped that his superiors would command him to stop writing, but each time he sought counsel, he was encouraged to develop his talent. Unsatisfied by the advice of his abbot, he discussed the problem with the general of the Cistercian order during the annual visitation to Gethsemani, only to have the decision of the abbot confirmed.[3] It was to be some time before he would cease to struggle and accept Tom Merton the writer. He attempted to work out the problem in an article entitled "Poetry and the Contemplative Life," but doubt was still evident in what never quite came off as a dénouement.

> The sacrifice of an art would seem small enough price to pay for this "pearl of great price." But there is a further complication, which we can only adumbrate, before closing this article. What if one is morally certain that God wills him to continue writing anyway? That is, what if one's religious superiors make it a matter of formal obedience to pursue one's art, for some special purpose like the good of souls? That will not take away distractions, or make God abrogate the laws of the spiritual life.[4]

The purpose for which he had come to the abbey, the primary goal of life, the contemplation of God, was threatened by the publication of his fervent testimony.

> Contemplation will be denied to a man in proportion as he belongs to the world. The expression "the world" signifies those who love the things of this world. They cannot receive the Holy Spirit Who is the Love of God. As St. John of the Cross says: "Two contraries cannot coexist at the same time in the same subject."[5]

The success of the book, which shocked him, is really not difficult to understand. Manifestly modeled after Augustine's *Confessions*, the power of the honest unveiling of one man's struggle with the most fundamental questions of life was sufficient to overcome the patent parochialism and piety of a zealous new convert. The burden of his success was with him to the end of his life. Everywhere he turned he was confronted with the expectations of readers who insisted that he remain the callow zealot of *The Seven Storey Mountain*.[6] The situation was complicated by Merton's determination to be a living expression of the love of Christ. He tried to imitate Paul in being all things to all men for the sake of Christ (1 Cor. 9:22). Love was his theme and the chief motivating force of his life. "Love is above all things," he wrote, "the *Super omnia*, the sum total of mystical theology."[7] Even in his dealings with the hero worshipers and bores who were forever violating his privacy and interfering with his life of prayer, his motto was *caritas Christi urget nos* [the love of Christ compels us].[8] Although later years would cause him to reflect with some anguish on his shallow theology and experience at the time of the writing of *The Seven Storey Mountain*, he never repudiated it, recognizing that it was as true as an old photograph, which captures a man in a given moment in his personal history. In 1966, in the Preface to the Japanese edition of the work, he wrote, "The story no longer belongs to me, and I have no right to tell it in a different way, or to imagine that it should have been seen through wiser eyes."[9] Nevertheless, he was able to perceive that it was not the story that had changed, but the author.

Now the world had a claim on him; his own pen had drawn an image that would mock and play havoc with him throughout his life. He considered a number of possible means of escape, which included transferring to one of the more severe orders. He carried on correspondence with several orders, but some were not reluctant to express their hesitation to accept the Trappists' problem. He explored a number of avenues, all in the context of his vows, but none worked out.[10]

Another factor that affected his development during the fifties was his appointment to the post of master of scholastics. This added responsibility required a more conscious correlation of the vast and varied reading that was his habit. Perhaps it was this teaching task that motivated him to systematize his own thought and to make his only serious and conscious attempt to publish in the field of theology. The combination of the readers of his book and the students under his tutelage locked him into a new role of teacher and role-model. Nothing so intensifies a man's scholarship as the burden of directing the mental and spiritual growth of others. This responsibility surely intensified his own inner exploration and study.

In 1956, an event occurred that left a permanent scar on his pysche. Some of Merton's friends outside the monastery became concerned about his increasing divergence from their stereotype of a Cistercian monk. Father Louis did not act and talk enough like a monk, and they wanted to assist him in destroying the playboy image and in molding himself into the proper image. An internationally prominent psychiatrist was contacted and, incredibly, agreed to read Merton's works to make some kind of a diagnosis on that basis. The abbot was drawn into the conspiracy, convinced, as all those involved, that it was in the spiritual best interests of Father Louis. The psychiatrist was to participate in a symposium at St. John's University in Collegeville, Minnesota, on the subject, "Religion and Psychiatry." Merton was invited to go along with the abbot and another monk, supposedly because of Merton's interest in the psychological aspects of the spiritual life.

Merton had read Freud and Jung in his European student days, and, in the summer of 1948, he had reflected on the reading of some articles on conversion that had included reactions of Freud. Merton expressed disappointment that his confreres had not taken the material more seriously.

> On the whole I think it will do Trappists no harm to have heard about Freud, although the little there was probably won't have much effect on them one way or the other except to give them the complacent notion that psychoanalysis is much more crazy than it actually is. Personally I have always felt that a clearer understanding of the subconscious mind would help priests to be better spiritual directors.[11]

The prospects of participation in such a conference excited Merton, and he was quick to accept the invitation. He had written a paper on the subject, and, as soon as he was introduced to the doctor, he asked him to read it and respond. Later, when the two men conferred, the therapist unleashed a merciless attack on Merton. An exhibitionist who wanted to have a hermitage on Times Square was the way he mirrored the unprepared priest. He hit Merton where he was most vulnerable, accusing him of being enamored with his own words. According to witnesses present, Merton was reduced to tears, emotionally disemboweled. It is doubtful that later reassurances by other professionals, including a Louisville psychiatrist who is reported to have said that Merton was the healthiest, most normal man he had ever met, ever completely erased the memory of that trauma. It must have confirmed some of his own self-doubts relating to the real and the illusionary self. In the ensuing years, he became more and more obsessed by the idea of withdrawing to a hermitage and talking and writing less.[12] As far as an interest in spiritual psychology was concerned, Merton's interest was only fueled, and some of his last essays have a strong psychological orientation.

The Ascent to Truth

The Ascent to Truth is the only one of Merton's publications that approaches formal theological writing. Perhaps it was inspired by the requirements of his teaching assignment or by a personal need to organize his own mystical philosophy in order to be an effective spiritual director. In any case, the book is worthy of special attention because it is primarily an exposition of and commentary on the mystical theology of John of the Cross, whose works seemed to have constituted a kind of manual for Merton's own spiritual evolution. Merton's first title for *The Ascent to Truth* was *The School of the Spirit*, which is indicative of his appreciation for the theology of John of the Cross. By his own admission, Merton found John of the Cross not only "one of the greatest" mystical theologians, but also the "safest." John, at least in his choice of language, was not as radical as others, such as Eckhart and Ruysbroeck, and was more acceptable to the teachers (and censors) of the Church. The book evidences Merton's continuing efforts to correlate the logical theology of Thomism with the intuitive religion of the mystics. The work is strained by Merton's endeavor to erect a theological system with incompatible components. In *Ascent*, he frequently draws on the Scholastics to support the theories of mysticism. It is implied that the problem is only a matter of clarifying the relationship of the two. According to Merton, Thomas, the "angelic doctor" and patron of the lesser Scholastics, did not view his analogical theology and mysticism as opposites. The two ways are only different approaches to truth. What Merton had not yet realized, or would not yet admit, was that men often disagree on the nature of truth. Mystical practice and theology are not in competition or conflict, Merton insisted, but really complement each other. According to Merton, "Theology is not made by mystics: mystics are formed by theology."[13] The purpose of moral theology and dogmatics is to form a frame within which the new man can be molded. The end of the Christian life is not conformity to a set of rules or propositions but transformation by union with God. *Ascent* was not well received by the critics, and the negative criticism may have been the reason Merton never published another book that could be placed in the same category.[14] Adverse criticism notwithstanding, *Ascent* furnishes a valid stackpole for the examination of his other works during this period. This book attests to the importance of the thought of the sixteenth-century Spanish mystics, especially that of John of the Cross, in the formation of Merton's spiritual thought.

The Via Negationis

Merton begins with a juxtaposition of the two traditions in Christian history, the affirmative way, or theology of light, and the *via negationis*, or theology of darkness. Among the "theologians of light" Merton lists Origen, Augustine, Bernard, and Thomas; the representatives of the *apophatic* thinkers included in his panel are Gregory of Nyssa, Pseudo-Dionysius, and John of the Cross. The theologians of light stress illumination, which has intellectual form and is more palatable to the man of reason than the more passive, affective experience described by the theologians of darkness. The former advocate pressing on to the boundary line of ordinary human knowledge and breaking through to the transcendent suprarational knowledge of truth. "Truth" is a favorite topic of this school. The "way of negation" is exactly that, a way of wiping clean the soiled slate of denigrating human philosophical and religious knowledge in order to be free to be immersed in the pure presence of God, to experience authentic Love. The two traditions could easily be reconciled by modern theologians, Merton argued, implying that the two ways are really only opposite sides of the same coin. If the imagery is not pressed too hard, there is great similarity between the accounts of the spiritual journey in the two traditions. There seems to be a consensus that the seeker finds himself in alternating rhythms of anxiety and felicity. Origen's commentary on Israel's journey through the desert notes the irregular process through phases of aridity and fertility. Augustine wrote of "light, ineffable and uncreated . . . above the intellect."[15] It is perhaps this same light, greater in its intensity than direct sunlight, that blinds the eyes of man and leaves him in the "deep yet dazzling darkness" revered by the disciples of Pseudo-Dionysius. It is the "darkness of surpassing brightness . . . as the shining of the sun on his course is as darkness to weak eyes."[16] All the descriptive propositions formulated by man are fallible according to the limited knowledge of finite being. At best, man is only capable of "seeing through a glass darkly." He is not free to elect the way of affirmation without the corrective of negation. "If we go on affirming, without denying, we end up by affirming that we have delimited the Being of God in our concepts. If we go on denying without affirming, we end up by denying that our concepts can tell the truth about Him in any sense whatever."[17] In Dionysian literature, "darkness," "unknowing," and "ignorance" are the significant terms. One's potential for ascending the "Ladder of Perfection" is, according to the masters of this school, directly proportionate to his willingness to pass through the darkness. Walter Hilton believed it impossible for an individual to "attain the love of God and the light of understanding" if he is unwilling "to pass through the darkness."[18] This darkness is the vault of the

> . . . immutable mysteries of theology [that] are veiled in the dazzling obscurity of the secret Silence, outshining all brilliance with the intensity of their Darkness, and surcharging our blinded intellects with the utterly impalpable and invisible fairness of glories surpassing all beauty.[19]

The paradox of the darkness born of light is one of the religious experiences attested to by almost all of those who have earned a place of honor in the mystical tradition. It is one of those elements that can only be categorized as "mysterious." Such an experience eludes logical expression or programmed accomplishment. "Christianity," Merton observed, "is not so much a body of doctrine as a revelation of a mystery."[20] A new anxiety sets in when the rest (quies) at the end of the *via purgativa* may be momentarily jejune, but the state soon becomes one of barrenness. Added to the anxiety of the awakened soul's sense of estrangement is the agony of expectation.

In Merton's own spiritual campaign he was experiencing only one installment of the crisis and anguish that mark the mystic's life. He had learned already that contemplation is at the same time the source and result of crisis. The exercises of the ascetic gymnasium serve only to free the monk from something, for the purpose of attaining something else. Even the *Opus Dei* is but a means to the end of union with God. The primary concern of the mystic is for interior spiritual experience. John related his dark night to the three stages of ascent.

> These three parts of the night are all one night; but like night itself, it has three parts. For the first part, which is that of sense, is comparable to the beginning of night, the point at which things begin to fade from sight. And the second part, which is faith, is comparable to midnight, which is total darkness. And the third part is like the close of night: which is God, the part which is near to the light of day.[21]

To be disposed for divine union, the subject must be grounded in faith, as tenuous as it may be. According to John of the Cross, "Such a one must walk by faith, with his understanding in darkness and in the obscurity of faith only: for in this darkness God unites Himself to the intellect."[22]

Faith, its nature and importance, was a subject that found its way into Merton's work with increasing frequency. In *Ascent* he contended for the perspicuous nature of faith, in keeping with the fundamental thesis of the book that mystical theology is not counter to the Aristotelian logic of Thomism. He maintained that even the spiritual crises that lead to faith "must first of all have an intellectual element."[23] The evolution of his understanding of faith moved more and more in the direction of the irrational obscurity of faith.

> The very obscurity of faith is an argument of its perfection. It is darkness to our minds because it so far transcends their weakness. The more perfect faith is, the darker it becomes. The closer we get to God, the less is our faith diluted with the half-light of created images and concepts. Our certainty increases with this obscurity, yet not without anguish and even material doubt, because we do not find it easy to subsist in a void in which our natural powers have nothing of

their own to rely on. And it is in the deepest darkness that we most fully possess God on earth, because it is then that our minds are most truly liberated from the weak, created lights that are filled with His infinite Light which seems pure darkness to our reason.[24]

Faith is that moment of insight, that plot of high ground, from which one can see spiritual alternatives. It is often evoked more by the dread that results from the unmasking of the false in the world than by the joyful anticipation that all "will be well with one's soul" or that "all's right with the world." To the edge of the darkness the process is primarily one of unlearning—unlearning in order to uncover the truth intrinsic in human nature. In a paraphrase of a familiar Augustinian statement, Merton noted that ". . . all men are born with an instinctive desire to know the Truth and an instinctive (though unrecognized) desire for . . . the wisdom of God in heaven."[25] At the second stage of emergence this desire for truth drives the bold into the dark desert of his own inner being. The taming of the exterior man is a lark compared to the second excursion, which John depicted:

> . . . darker than the first part . . . this second part, which is of faith, belongs to the higher part of man, which is the rational part, and, in consequence, more interior and more obscure, since it deprives it of the light of reason, or, to speak more clearly, blinds it; and thus it is aptly compared to midnight, which is the depth of night and the darkest part thereof.[26]

Faith, then, is the door through which one passes into the "dazzling darkness."

Faith and Reason

The relationship of faith and reason is one of the perennial problems encountered by the philosopher and theologian. It presupposes the question of the nature of reality and how it may be perceived. How far may a man trust his senses, and to what extent can he trust his intellect to discern Reality? Does the intellect inform faith, or faith the intellect? These were the questions that continued to plague Merton, whose "Augustinian bent" conflicted with the Thomistic color of his own instruction as a novice and professed student. The sectarian tone of his literary output in his first decade in the order is indicative of his determination to be a "good Catholic." Excerpts from his journals of the forties included in *Sign of Jonas* divulge his dissatisfaction with the quality of these works, even at the time of their writing. Readers of *Seeds of Contemplation* were assured in the Introduction that they would not be exposed to "a line that is new to Catholic tradition or a single word that would perplex an orthodox theologian."[27] Through the early fifties, his writings are replete with references to Thomas as the guarantor of the orthodoxy of the mystics. The natural disparity between Merton's mode of thinking and that of the Schoolmen became more and more difficult to ignore.[28] His journals reveal a continuing interior dialectic with regard to the authority and importance of Thomas Aquinas. Gleefully, Merton pointed out that when Thomas had begun his study of Aristotle, the Church had a prohibition against either the study or teaching of the Greek philosopher's ideas. Merton argued that Thomas never intended his work to be authoritative. Thomas had been the victim of the Thomists, who had installed him as a "scholastic machine."[29] But it was some time before Merton was free enough of his personal image of an ideal Catholic's theology to admit to himself that these were rationalizations to absolve his conscience from adherence to the Scholastic tradition. For the time being, he toiled to think the way he thought a Catholic priest was expected to think. "I wish I had gone into my study of theology," he lamented, "with something more of the mind of St. Dominic."[30] He chided his lack of the Dominican characteristics of "sharpness, definiteness, precision . . ."[31] It was disturbing for him to discover that the intellect was not always the willing ally of the spirit.

Merton's was not the first powerful Catholic mind to grapple with this problem and arrive at an opinion incongruent with the Scholastic position. Augustine wrote in the fifth century: "Understanding is the reward of faith. Therefore do not seek to understand in order that you may believe, but make the act of faith in order that you may understand; for unless you make an act of faith you will not understand."[32] A thousand years later, with the Reformation in the making, Nicholas of Cusa argued that this principle applied to scientific inquiry as well as to the domain of the spirit.

> For in every discipline certain things are presupposed as first principles, which are apprehended by faith alone and from which springs the comprehension of the matters treated. Every man who wishes to raise himself to knowledge must necessarily believe in the things without which he cannot raise himself. As Isaiah says, "Unless you believe, you will not understand." Faith, therefore, comprises in herself all that is intelligible. Understanding is the explication of faith. Understanding is, therefore, directed by faith, and faith is developed by understanding. Where there is no sound faith, there is no true understanding.[33]

Man's knowledge is itself subjective and shares in his finitude; therefore, it does not just lack the ability to comprehend or apprehend God; it is capable of being an obstacle to that attainment. John articulated it this way:

> . . . there is no ladder whereby the understanding can attain to this High Lord. Rather it is necessary to know that if the understanding should seek to profit by all of these things or by any of them as a proximate means to such union, they would be not only a hindrance but even an occasion of numerous errors and delusions in the ascent of this mount.[34]

Man cannot trust his own rationality to lead him to truth. Meister Eckhart warns that man's knowledge, which is in reality ignorance, is a siren luring the individual to the rocky shoals; ". . . this outward ignorance lures and attracts thee from all understood things and from thyself."[35] More recently, David Steindl-Rast has written that faith is conceived in doubt. "You can't have faith without doubt. Give up the business of suppressing doubt. Doubt and faith are two sides of the same thing. Faith will grow out of doubt, the real doubt."[36] Not in security, but in uncertainty that breeds a sense of personal contingency is man driven out of the exterior sureties to authentic dependency.

Merton had arrived at an early appreciation of faith as a requisite of religious life and as an entity apart from mental assent. "Faith is higher and more perfect than all knowledge that is accessible to us on earth."[37] Faith is the destination at the end of the journey that originates in the crisis that results from the Sisyphean efforts of man to reach God by means of his own abilities. With simple directness, Merton states in Thoughts in Solitude, "By faith I find my own true being in God,"[38] but such statements are qualified throughout his early writings by connecting them in some dependent way to reason. Merton concurs with John that the power of the intellect to arrive at union with God is even less than that of ascetic techniques. Then he hurries on to assert that the work of the intelligence is as important to John as to Thomas Aquinas. Conceptualization, while not a means of union, is essential to the apprehension and interpretation of mystical experience. Only the cosmology of Aquinas is adequate to support John's apophatism. ". . . even the dark mystical knowledge of God which is beyond concepts . . . depends upon the existence of concepts,"[39] Merton argues. These concepts constitute the launching pad that propels the mystic into the darkness of God. Merton points out that even Aquinas recognized that the end of man's intellectual ascent is the realization of his ignorance. "The final attainment of man's knowledge of God consists in knowing that we do not know Him, insofar as we realize that He transcends everything that we understand concerning Him. . . . Having arrived at the term of our knowledge we *know God as unknown*."[40] The nature of the truth dictates the means of acquisition. Nicholas of Cusa had stressed the fact that the object of faith is Truth, which is not a substance or a thing, but a person. Merton reiterated this belief in *Thoughts in Solitude*.

> Ideas and words are not the food of the intelligence, but truth. And not an abstract truth that feeds the mind alone. The Truth that a spiritual man seeks is the whole Truth, reality, existence and essence together, something that can be embraced and loved, something that can sustain the homage and service of our actions: more than a thing: persons, or a Person. Him above all Whose essence is to exist. God.

Christ, the Incarnate Word, is the Book of Life in Whom we read God.[41] It is a truth that is not assimilated but that assimilates. It is not so much a matter of one object becoming related to another as it is the integration of disjointed elements into the natural whole. "Wisdom knows God in ourselves and ourselves in God."[42] Faith frees one from efforts of the senses, mind, and will so that the total being may be illuminated by the grace of God. The experience that occurs in the context of faith defies human categories. It affects all the faculties, but at the same time transcends all of them. In *Thoughts in Solitude*, Merton could only say what it is not: "Spiritual life is not mental life. It is not thought alone. Nor is it, of course, a life of sensation, a life of feeling. . . . Nor does the spiritual life exclude thought and feeling. It needs both."[43] Every man has the ontological ability to grasp God intuitively in faith without regard to his ability to absorb conceptual knowledge about Him. In the tradition of Augustine and Nicholas, Merton concluded that it is faith that informs and energizes human intelligence. There is no scientific evidence that can evoke commitment; only the experience of God can accomplish that. And Merton is almost Barthian in his conviction that perception of the divine reality is beyond man's ability. All man can do is open himself to the illumination of God, who is known only as He chooses to be known. The soul may have intercourse with God only "in the darkness and obscurity of a blind and naked faith."[44] Moreover, even faith is bestowed according to the will of God.

> It [faith] is a gift of God. It is produced under the inspiration of grace. This inspiration acts directly upon the faculties of the soul which are moved, so to speak, by the "finger of God." In every act of faith, the Holy Spirit takes our will, which has been deflected away from God by sin, and "corrects" its aim and at the same time illuminates the understanding, so that we believe.[45]

The healing restoration of harmony between man and God is possible only "through faith; and this not of your own doing, it is the gift of God" (Ep. 2:8). Such a position was not a comfortable one for Father Louis on two counts: one personal, and the other theological.

Infused Contemplation

The problem of how man participates in the work of God is one that occupies theologians in every age. It is a problem that has particular significance for the mystic. Can one diligently pursue a particular course in assurance that it will lead to God? Is there a technique that, assiduously practiced, will bring man into union with God? Positive responses to these questions would affirm the gnostic heresy with its initiation and graduation to higher spiritual levels by the successful assimilation of certain knowledge. Implicit in such an idea is the possibility that a man can save himself. Can man bargain with God or manipulate Him? This position is vigorously repudiated in the doctrine of revelation as the unique prerogative of God.

At the opposite end of the spectrum is the position of the Quietists, who advocate "complete passivity in spiritual life from the word go."[46] Merton was almost violent in his refutation of Quietism. His sensitivity to any appearance of this unorthodox practice was most likely due to his Quaker background, and a fear that he might regress into this "heresy." As a young child he had attended Quaker meetings with his mother, and his first religious stirrings had inclined him in that direction.[47] In his early writings, he indicted oriental religions for their Quietism. His aggressive repudiation of any position that suggests inertia on the part of the postulant seems to be rooted in the fear that it relieves the subject of any responsibility and tends to be anti-intellectual. A bill of particulars against Quietism was included in *Ascent to Truth*.

> The errors of Quietism with respect to the knowledge of God consist in a formal rejection of theology, a depreciation of God's revelation to Himself to man in Christ the Incarnate Word, in the complete rejection of formal prayer and meditation, and in the theory that supernatural contemplation can be "acquired" by the mere cessation of mental activity. These errors . . . actually make true contemplation impossible.[48]

In spite of his frequent disclaimers, the "infused" contemplation advocated by both his teachers and himself bears strong resemblance to Quietist passivity. Merton's discourse on the "Prayer of Quiet" points out that Teresa of Avila and John of the Cross are in agreement that the human faculties are passive in that experience. Reason, imagination, and will are only capable of registering the experience and remaining alert to distractions and detours that might render the careless or inert soul unreceptive to God's gift. Human effort cannot invoke the Prayer of Quiet. The experience itself is one of enlightenment and liberation, not an enlightenment of mind but of being.

God is not brought into the focus of thought, but He brings the soul into Himself. The blessing of the divine presence is "a pure gift of God."[49] The Quietist would undoubtedly have little problem with John's description of the proper state for the occurrence desired. "In order to receive (these graces) the soul must be quite disencumbered and at ease, peaceful and serene, according to the manner of God; like the air which receives greater illumination and heat from the sun when it is pure and cleansed and at rest."[50]

Merton's efforts to differentiate between his mentor and the Quietists are equivocal at best. He compares John of the Cross with Michael Molinos, differentiating between the two according to the degree they advocated the abandonment of intellectual and affective activity. John of the Cross is said to advocate suspension of the affective and intellectual faculties only at certain advanced stages of the spiritual life, while Molinos demands the total surrender of them from the beginning. The truth of the matter is that Merton seems to beg the question. John is very clear as to what occurs and who is the central actor in the darkness.

> This Dark Night is the inflowing of God into the soul which purges it of its ignorances and imperfections, natural and spiritual, and which is called by contemplatives infused contemplation. . . . Herein God secretly teaches the soul and instructs it in perfection of love without its doing anything or understanding of what manner is this infused contemplation.[51]

Human effort is sufficient only in the sensitizing of his natural longing for God. God fills the void left by the exorcism of the false self. Implicit in such a position is the argument of the early Protestant reformers that man apart from God is incapable of any act that can be termed "good" and that man does nothing to ascend to God but dispose himself to the work of the Spirit. Man only removes the obstacles, unlocks the door, and awaits the entry or at least the unleashing of the Spirit. Merton admitted the necessity of God's power and action but could not negate man's freedom and responsibility. The ability of man to respond was a divine gift, but nevertheless it was a part of human existence.

Merton believed he was following the instruction of John of the Cross in opting for a period of intellectual endeavor for the purpose of grasping philosophical and theological principles in order to construct a substratum for the spiritual life. In this preliminary stage the neophyte undertakes a program of training in self-denial and the practice of virtue. God rewards the initiative of the seeker with guidance and strength, but the control remains with man. Man's capacity for the experience of God is directly proportionate to man's willingness to undergo the experience of nothingness in which the mind and the will can be possessed and transformed by the action of the Holy Spirit. With a brush stroke of Augustinian "desire," Merton dismissed any possible efficacy of human activity. Man's will is so corrupt that he desires knowledge and even religious experience for its own sake; thus it is not knowledge that is the obstacle but the wrong motivation for its appropriation and use. Even God must not be desired for unworthy, selfish reasons, and false motivation debilitates even attributes ordinarily to be prized. One can in the words of T. S. Eliot do the "right thing for the wrong reason." Some people escape true spirituality by hiding in "religious" institutions and ceremonies. John of the Cross's caution is cited on this point:

> However little a man may drink of this wine (of rejoicing in created things for their own sake) it at once takes hold upon his heart and stupefies it and works the evil of darkening the reason . . . so that if some antidote be not at once taken against this poison whereby it may be quickly expelled, the life of the soul is endangered.[52]

Man can trust nothing of his own in the apprehension of God; all faculties must be subjected to the Holy Spirit.

In a pamphlet published in 1950, entitled *What Is Contemplation?*, Merton outlined in some detail his understanding of contemplation. The propensity for contemplation, he said, is a gift of the Holy Spirit to all Christians. The potentiality for mystical prayer is one of the components of the baptismal experience. However, the realization of this potential is the exclusive prerogative of God, who dispenses His gifts according to His wisdom. Moreover, Merton said, such gifts are not granted capriciously; ". . . the Holy Spirit will not waste any of His gifts on people who have little or no interest in them."[53]

Merton is not evasive in defining the problem. According to him, contemplation describes only one phenomenon, which is "infused or mystical," sometimes called "passive."[54] The phenomenon, condition, or state designated by this term is induced by God, who ". . . is the principle agent Who infuses it into the soul and Who, by this means, *takes possession* of the soul's faculties and moves them directly according to His will."[55] What is generally referred to as "active" contemplation, Merton asserts, is merely the ordering of resources, personal, aesthetic, and theological, in such a way as to direct the aspirations of the individual toward God. Merton does not neglect his favorite quixotic windmill in this short treatise, but moves in to differentiate between orthodox passivity and the heinous specter of "Quietism."

> The Quietist on the other hand, pursuing a false ideal of absolute "annihilation" of his own soul, seeks to empty himself of all love and all knowledge and remain inert in a kind of spiritual vacuum in which there is no motion, no thought, no apprehension, no act of love, no passive receptivity but a mere blank without light or warmth of breath of interior life.[56]

But the question that is not satisfactorily dealt with is how the purified obscurity of the properly disposed Christian mystic can be distinguished from the heretical selfish blank of the Quietist. Merton is about as definite as one can be in his deprecation of man's feeble efforts to effect union with God:

> No system of meditations, of interior discipline, of self-emptying, of recollection and absorption can bring a man to union with God, without a free gift on the part of God Himself. Still less can a man arrive at mystical union with God by an effort of the intellect on his own natural level.[57]

The paradox is inescapable; man must not abrogate his faculties, but neither can he effectively employ them for attaining contact with the Absolute.

Merton did attempt to establish criteria for discriminating between the two. True contemplation is said to contain positive elements that give purpose to the agony of loneliness and the sense of having been forsaken by God, which is a stage of the pilgrimage. According to Merton, the "dazzling darkness" of God has a magnetism that holds the soul without fear or desire to escape the desert. The soul is buoyed by "a growing conviction that joy and peace and fulfillment . . . [are] to be found somewhere in this lonely night of aridity and faith."[58] Similar assessments are interspersed throughout *Ascent to Truth*. At one point Merton calls on Ruysbroeck to indict Quietist stultification. The Quietist is accused of selfish introspection, as opposed to concentration on the Absolute. ". . . this man . . . turns away from God in order to concentrate on himself with natural love. All he is looking for is consolation, sweetness and satisfaction. . . . Everything he does is done for his own personal interests, not for the honor of God. . . ."[59] All these dangers are unquestionably real and threaten authentic union. But they may be applied to all modes of ascetic practice, which has as its end the contemplation of God. Time and again one is impressed with the fact that even salvation must not be a selfish aspiration. One who seeks God only to escape hell, who takes the sacrament as insurance investments, who uses worship as a retainer for an intercessor, is engaged in a religious fantasy. The true seeker is willing to really risk all, to enter the furnace like the Hebrew children with no assurance of insulation from the heat. Indeed, there are insidious elements with the capacity to infect and nullify all religious activity. However, this fact does not obliterate the tranquil components inherent in the contemplative modes advocated by Merton and the apophatic legacy he claimed.

Certainly Merton is not inaccurate in his judgment of religious experience, which begins and ends with self. He stands in the best mystical tradition of Gregory of Nyssa, Bernard of Clairvaux, John of the Cross, Ruysbroeck, et al., in defining the presence of God within as the manifestation of love. *"The most important element in the contemplative life,"* Merton wrote, "is not knowledge but love."[60] The real test of the contemplative life is its fruit, love.[61] Love has its existence in loving. Love is the sign of man's regeneration. As the individual's life is characterized by love, it takes on the new image, the form of God. The more one loves, the more he is absorbed into Him who is Love.

In Bernard's language this form, this divine likeness, is the identity we were made for. Thus we can say *"caritas haec visio, haec similitudo est."* By love we are at once made like to God and (in mystical love, pure love) we already "see" Him (darkly), i.e., we have experience of Him as He is in Himself. Thus by loving we know God in God and through God, for in love the three Divine Persons are made known to us, sealing our souls not with a static likeness but with the impressions of their infinite life.[62]

One who has been to the well of God's love becomes a fountain at which others can drink. This leads Merton to the conclusion that action, in the sense of Christian acts of charity, is not the antithesis of contemplation but rather the stream that flows from the contemplative spring. Indeed, Christian incarnation of love may ignite the fuse that lets love burst forth in others. Love calls to love, and we may be the means by which the dormant inner man may be activated. Merton points out that one needs to be loved in order to know what it is.

> If men do not love, it is because they have learned in their earliest childhood that they themselves are not loved, and the duplicity and cynicism of our time belongs to a generation that has been conscious, since its cradle, that it was not wanted by its parents.[63]

In an essay on the contemplative life, Merton states that social action is an indirect product of contemplation. "Contemplation, at its highest intensity, becomes a reservoir of spiritual vitality that pours itself out in the most telling social action."[64] This discovery provoked a reassessment and, ultimately, a readjustment of Merton's own attitude toward the world.

The City of God and the City of Man

Arnold Toynbee identifies retreat by a group or an individual as a recurring agent of change in history. He plots the sequence as a period of isolation followed by a period of aloofness, during which periods a process of incubation occurs. The third stage marks a re-entry into society where the subject assumes a new role. Toynbee observes that in this new role the former recluse "makes a greater impression than it had ever made in its original role, and this gives it a chance of converting the other members of the society to its own new ideas and ideals."[65] With only slight modification, Toynbee's analysis constitutes a blueprint of Thomas Merton's emergence from Teresa's cocoon. One of the conclusions drawn by Workman in his study of the monastic ideal is quite similar; he states, ". . . the whole history of monasticism is the emphasis on the importance of the conquest of self . . . as the one condition of work in the world."[66] Although he did not physically return to secular society, Merton did recognize that he was a part of the world, and it was a part of him, that in belonging to God, he belonged to the world. Spiritual illumination includes the correction of man's distorted vision. As the scales fell away from his eyes, he acquired "the ability to respond to reality, to see the value and beauty in ordinary things, and to come alive to the splendor that is all around us in the creatures of God."[67]

Encounter with Truth brings a person into contact with reality, the reality of the world and the persons who people it. Merton discovered that when he was freed from dependence on the world, when it ceased to define him, he found he was free to filter the chaff from the wheat and to relate to it in a positive way. As early as 1948, the possibility of rapprochement was apparent to him.

> We drove into town with Senator Dawson, a neighbor of the monastery, and all the while I wondered how I would react at meeting once again, face to face, the wicked world. I met the world and I found it no longer so wicked after all. Perhaps the things I had resented about the world when I left it were defects of my own that I had projected upon it. Now, on the contrary, I found that everything stirred me with a deep and mute sense of compassion. Perhaps some of the people we saw going about the streets were hard and tough—with the native, animalistic toughness of the Middle West—but I did not stop to observe it because I seemed to have lost an eye for merely exterior detail and to have discovered, instead, a deep sense of respect and love and pity for the souls that such details never fully reveal. I went through the city, realizing for the first time in my life how good are all the people in the world and how much value they have in the sight of God.[68]

He felt remorse at his aloofness, realizing that his identity was tied to the identity of mankind. Recapitulation for the individual was possible only as he participated in the phylogenetic spiritual development of the human race.

In some way the individual's freedom was linked to universal freedom. To be a spiritual man, Merton discovered, was to be a man. He decided that God had called him to Gethsemani to discover his place in the world, and, if he did not achieve that goal, it would all be for naught. One of the lessons he learned from the contemplative life was that growth in Christ meant finding Him in new and unexpected places. Christ represented the humanity of God and symbolized the unity of being. Merton had committed his life to the quest for God and himself in God, but now his intuition impelled him to look for God and himself in the world that he had rejected. In *New Seeds of Contemplation*, he recorded the decision that would in only a few years cast him in the role of a spokesman for the national conscience. "I must look for my identity, somehow, not only in God but in other men. I will never be able to find myself if I isolate myself from the rest of mankind as if I were a different kind of being."[69] His love of God generated in him a love for others, though he had not yet learned to love himself. He wrote in *The Sign of Jonas* that the self-image projected in his works was not pleasing to him. He would now begin to bear in himself the frustration and despair of technocratic man, threatened with annihilation by the work of his own hands.

Sanctification of the Ordinary

Beginning in the late fifties, Merton's correspondence and teaching notes reveal an increasing interest in the English mystics, particularly Julian of Norwich. While his enthusiasm for the theology of the Spanish mystics does not diminish, his work has less of the melancholy tone of the somber Spanish and more of the serene joyousness and sunny hopefulness of Julian.[70] *Seeds of Contemplation* is the first of his major works to sound a strong chord of hope and resolute affirmation of the goodness of creation. "There is no evil in anything created by God. . . ."[71] he declared; ". . . everything made by God is good."[72] Man's anxiety is the result of living in delusion, inauthenticity. Merton elaborates a Neoplatonic doctrine of sin as incompletion or nonbeing. Sin is not an evil presence but an absence of authentic presence. "Evil is not a positive entity but the absence of a perfection that ought to be there. Sin as such is essentially boring because it is the lack of something that could appeal to our wills and our minds."[73] Perhaps what Paul was teaching when he admonished the Philippians to "work out your own salvation with fear and trembling" was to nurture the seeds of life and grow into the identity God intended. Merton defined salvation as the individual's "full discovery of who he himself really is."[74] The false world is the world of illusion created by the false self to disguise its despair. Sinners, according to Merton, are bored people who spend their lives glossing over "the tedium of life by noise, excitement, and violence—the inevitable fruit of a life devoted to the love of values that do not exist."[75]

Merton broadcast his message of the affirmation of life to the world through his relatively short and, on the surface, simple books of meditation. Every event that transpires in human history or in the life of the individual is an expression of the divine judgment. "Everything that exists and everything that happens bears witness to the will of God."[76] The Christian is not a pawn of divine caprice but a son of God called by Him to participate in His life. God's own humanity expressed in Jesus bears witness to the fact that life has meaning. The special vocation of the Christian is to give form to that meaning and share in the world's transformation. The common task that binds all Christians together "is to deliver the whole world from evil and to transform it in God. . . ."[77] Life is neither a riddle to be solved by the clever operation of the mind nor an organism to be analyzed; it is an experience to be lived. This was the lesson of the Christological drama that God chose to reconcile and unite men to Himself through the sacred humanity of Christ. "Jesus lived the ordinary life of the men of His time, in order to sanctify the ordinary lives of men of all time. If we want to be spiritual, then, let us first of all live our lives."[78] How could this be? Where should one begin? Merton believed that each individual must begin with himself.

A Christian Personalism

The love of others is rooted in the acceptance of self. Merton proposed the giving of oneself to others in order to find oneself. Here emerges in his thought the unity metaphysic of mysticism. It is humanity that contains man. "Every other man is a piece of myself," he wrote, "for I am a part and a member of mankind."[79] It is the nature of man to love, but society restricts his nature by turning his attention upon himself. The man who is consumed with himself wastes himself in trying to define himself. Man against himself generates conflict and evokes violence in the society of which he is a part. Any effort to live at peace with others is contingent upon the individual's ability to accept himself as he is. Merton begins to speak of the person as a sacrament of God in the fullest sense of sacrament, i.e., participation in that which it symbolizes and in communicating its referent.

> Christian personalism is, then, the sacramental sharing of the inner secret of personality in the mystery of love. This sharing demands full respect for the mystery of the person, whether it be our own person, or the person of our neighbor, or the infinite secret of God. In fact, Christian personalism is the discovery of one's own inmost self, and of the inmost self of one's neighbor, in the mystery of Christ; a discovery that respects the hiddenness and incommunicability of each one's personal secret, while paying tribute to his presence in the common celebration.[80]

Inferred here in the most lucid terms is a fundamental attitude about one's self. The vocation to serve God through service to others presupposes another vocation. Man cannot make himself other than what he is. As Merton put it, "Every man has a vocation to be someone: but he must understand clearly that in order to fulfill this vocation he can only be one person: himself."[81] The experience of self is prerequisite to the experience of God, or at least concurrent with the discovery of Absolute Being. According to Merton, "His presence is present in my presence. If I am, then He is."[82] Self-awareness of ontological existence lures the "I" into the deep center and through to the eternal "I AM." The depth of human existence is the hiding place of God, and it is there He is encountered. This encounter frees the man to be a person who can relate to other persons. The man who had experienced "salvation" knows who he is and who is within him. Salvation is the discovery of who you are. Man is one with God in Christ and is revealed as a bearer of the incarnate Word with all the worth, dignity, freedom, and responsibility that that implies. It is this reality that frees the person to give himself to society. Such a doctrine of man imputes dignity to almost all work. A man is not expected to be any more than what he is. The ordinary is elevated to the extraordinary as it is in harmony with the divine. The path to union is not necessarily through the monastery or through a religious route. "It is supreme humility to see that ordinary life, embraced with perfect faith, can be more saintly and more supernatural than a spectacular ascetical career."[83] Such statements should not be interpreted as any kind of repudiation of monastic or religious life. The priest and the monk each have their own function in the world, of neither more nor less value than the function of any other person in the center of God's will. As Karl Rahner has observed, each man or woman is a unique and unrepeatable term of God's creative love and must find the way to God appropriate for him.[84]

Interior Solitude

Merton's new openness to and sense of responsibility for the world were in no way indicative of abandonment of

his monastic vocation. There was only a new understanding of what that vocation entailed. The rest that had
climaxed those first eight years at Gethsemani was the qui-
escence of exhaustion rather than the sweet repose associated with religious consolation. As generations of
monks before him, he had fasted, prayed, meditated,
studied, and kept the silence in order to know the inner
peace of God's presence, but the experience had not come
as an automatic consequence of the strict observance of
these practices. In fact, he discovered that the "quiet"
could be deceptively noisy, and the "order" could be as
busy as the secular society he had fled. In the language of
MacLuhan, he analyzed the encumbrance of the methods
devised to disencumber.

> The monastic life as a whole is a hot medium. Hot
> with words like "must," "ought" and "should." Com-
> munities are devoted to high definition projects:
> "making it all clear!" The clearer it gets the clearer it
> has to be made. It branches out. You have to keep
> clearing the branches. The more branches you cut
> back the more branches grow. For one you cut you
> get three more. On the end of each branch there is a
> big bushy question mark. People are running all
> around with packages of meaning. Each is very anx-
> ious to know whether all the others have received the
> latest messages.[85]

The peaceful routine of community life was at times itself
violent and disruptive to contemplation. He recorded
these painful elements in *No Man Is an Island*: "Usages
and observances are sometimes twisted into ridiculous
formalities," which seemed to him ". . . to conspire to
make peace and prayer impossible."[86] He had written in
The Waters of Siloe that men come to the monastery not
to escape reality but to find it. However, he could not ignore the fact that the monastery was a place where a man
might hide from himself, the world, and God. The austere
religious life offers unique opportunities for pride, always a
scandal to the mystic. Merton was on occasion gripped by

the fear that he might succumb to the temptation to glory in his ascesis; "I have a peculiar horror of one sin: the exaggeration of our trials and of our crosses."[87] The way of purgation had brought him into the "dark night of the soul," where every aspect of his being would be in the intense light of desire for God. Even those structures and vehicles that had brought him to this point were subject to the closest scrutiny.

This agonizing, further examination of himself and his mode of life resulted in changed attitudes not only about the world, but also about the nature of contemplation. The flight to the desert, into the arms of Christ, must not be a flight from self. A genuine discovery of Christ within one's own being is not possible until one has courageously faced the truth about who he is, accepting all his limitations and being freed to accept others as they are with all their limitations. Merton discovered about himself that he was as incapable of being a modern Simon Stylites as he was of being an itinerant religious soldier of fortune. He had, by 1958, become more obsessed with the eremitical life as a viable alternative for himself. All things considered, it was the life of the hermit that he believed offered to *him* the conditions most conducive to living "in God *always*, speaking to Him with simplicity. . . ."[88] This was the pattern he would opt for as opposed to "a life of disjointed activity sublimated by a few moments of fire and exaltation."[89] It was still constancy in the pursuit and presence of God that he sought.

The existence of anxiety in the contemplative indicates a misplaced confidence, Merton concluded through recollection during this period. Anxiety that eats away at faith is the product of too much "dependence on ourselves, on our own devices, our own plans, our own idea of what we are able to do."[90] Monastic discipline has only one purpose: to emancipate the monk. It is "utterly useless," Merton wrote, "if it turns us into freaks."[91] The change that is the goal of monastic retreat is interior. The conversion of manners is simultaneously to contribute to and to

reflect a *metanoia* of the inner man. The physical clothing, the more rigorous mode of life are all incidental to
the transformation of "man" into "spiritual man."[92]

Merton believed that spiritual solace was directly related
to man's development of his natural capacity for solitude.
Such solitude is not the singular province of the monk,
nor is it always determined by external conditions.

> Solitude is not merely a negative relationship. It is
> not merely the absence of people. True solitude is a
> participation in the solitariness of God—Who is in
> all things. His solitude is not a local absence but a
> metaphysical transcendence. His solitude is His Being.
> For us, solitude is not a matter of being something
> more than other men, except by accident; for those
> who cannot be alone cannot find their true being and
> they are always something less than themselves. For
> us solitude means withdrawal from an artificial and
> fictional level of being which men, divided by original
> sin, have fabricated in order to keep peace with con-
> cupiscence and death.[93]

He differentiated very clearly between isolation and solitude. In his books of meditations published during this
period—*Seeds of Contemplation, No Man Is an Island,*
and *Thoughts in Solitude*—he advocated solitary experience for all. Every man who is to discover his personhood
needs true solitude. Merton contended that man's attempt
to lose himself in the crowd was an attempt to escape this
need in a "formless sea of irresponsibility."[94] Even authentic society is rooted in interior solitude, which makes it
possible for a man to accept his proper relationship to
other men. In *No Man Is an Island*, solitude is posited as
an inalienable right of human personality:

> Secrecy and solitude are values that belong to the very
> essence of personality.
>
> A person is a person insofar as he has a secret and is a
> solitude of his own that cannot be communicated to
> anyone else.[95]

In his inner being a man discovers what it is to be a man, and, in so doing, becomes aware of all that the total secularization of life has done to deprive him of his humanity. "In an age when totalitarianism has striven, in every way, to devaluate and degrade the human person, we hope it is right to demand a hearing for any and every sane reaction in the favor of man's inalienable solitude and his interior freedom."[96] The soul that has drunk at the fountain of hope in true solitude will find itself gravitating toward the desert, but it will not die in the city, for it has been endowed with the strength to live there. The soul that has truly been alone with God will be everywhere alone with God. Man's discovery of his self-transcendence in solitude contributes to his union with God, but also it makes possible his "supernatural love for his friends and his relatives and those with whom he lives and works."[97]

Illumination

Merton's first eight years in the monastery had been devoted to peeling away the encrustation that imprisoned him. It was in the most technical and classical sense a period of purgation. Relentlessly Merton had subjected himself to the most rigorous spiritual tradition, holding nothing back. This had brought him with naked soul shrouded in loneliness, into the darkness. In the collection of his poetry, *The Strange Islands*, are words that reflect both the disappointed anguish and the expectation of his state.

I studied it and it taught me nothing.
I learned it and soon forgot everything else:
Having forgotten, I was burdened with knowledge—
The insupportable knowledge of nothing.
How sweet my life would be, if I were wise!
Wisdom is well known
When it is no longer seen or thought of.
Only then is understanding bearable.[98]

The experience of nothingness filled him with both despair and hope. The fifties were the context in which he discovered the unity of society, history, God, and himself. The darkness was the darkness of light, and the cloud of unknowing intimated truth beyond the expression of human knowledge. Words were inadequate to express the reality that was intuitively perceived.

Words create history, But they, in turn,
Must be destroyed by the history they have created.
The word supersedes the event, as light emerges from
    darkness,
Transforming the event into something it was not.
But the event, in turn, supersedes its interpretation as
    darkness
Replaces light, and in the end it is darkness that wins.
And the Words of the historian are forgotten.[99]

Merton was discovering what had been the "hidden wholeness" of himself and all creation. He had climbed partway and demonstrated a willingness, even an aspiration, to love God for the sake of Merton and to love others for the sake of himself. Now he would direct his energies toward loving God for God's sake and loving Tom Merton for God's sake.

CHAPTER V

The Desert of the Heart

Tom Merton began the sixties on the edge of a new desert. He had been through the geographical wilderness of isolation, through the physical wasteland of asceticism; now he was moving into the desert of the heart, where "created joys are consumed and reborn in God."[1] In an article published only a short time before he embarked on the fatal Asian journey, he wrote, "The real wilderness of the hermit is the wilderness of the human spirit which is at once his and everyone else's."[2] Even the monastic community must not impede the contemplative's exploration of the inner waste of his own being. The desert he longed for was one without social, political, or religious props, where the only oasis would be the fountain of eternal waters, which would truly quench the most intense thirst. Only in this desert could he learn the meaning of complete and continual dependence on God alone.

The sixties were years of consolidation and reintegration for Merton. The various colors and textures of his thought began to come together into a discernible pattern. The strength of the evolving unity within him enabled him to embrace the exterior diversities behind which he perceived the unity of Christ. He rediscovered Meister Eckhart, whose thought was in harmony with his own perception of mystical union as the experience of the unmediated apprehension of God in His essence, which He chooses to bestow on man, i.e., that God's essence provides the core of human being. Although there was much in the thought and language of Eckhart's "God-mysticism" that Merton adopted, there emerged at the same time Merton's most lucid expression of a high Christology. Merton held to

Christ as the fountainhead of the new creation, as the chief agent of reconciliation and recapitulation. Merton's keen interest in Eastern religions, which was indicated by the domination of their discussion in his published works of the sixties, was not the curiosity of a dilettante, but rather the acknowledgement of the natural affinity of Christian mysticism and Eastern mysticism on a number of important points. His own increased sense of intellectual and spiritual freedom relieved him of the burden of delimiting his study and analysis to the "safer," more orthodox thinkers; thus, with relish, he attacked these affinities, opening himself to what he thought the East could teach Western Christianity. In Eastern thought he found a perception of reality that penetrated the illusionary world of Western (and Marxist) materialism. The unmasking of reality would preoccupy him for the rest of his life. He would find in Eastern thought, and particularly in Zen, an idea that he had already intuited, that the key to reality is the self.

> The world as pure object is something that is not there. It is not a reality outside us for which we exist. . . . It is a living and self-creating mystery of which I am myself a part, to which I am myself, my own unique door. When I find the world in my own ground, it is impossible for me to be alienated by it.[3]

His sorties against the establishment and the social injustices tolerated and supported by it were attacks upon the false values it represented.

He continued to struggle with his own identity and with the burden of his public image created by *The Seven Storey Mountain* constantly confronting him in the endless flow of correspondence from old and new disciples, and in the even more irksome parade of visitors and retreatants at Gethsemani, who stalked him in the cloister like a movie or athletic hero. In 1966, he wrote:

> I notice that for nearly twenty years my society—or those in it who read my books—have decided upon

an identity for me and insist that I continue to corre-
spond perfectly to the idea of me which they found
upon reading my first successful book. . . . They
demand that I remain forever the superficially pious,
rather rigid and somewhat narrow-minded young
monk I was twenty years ago. . . .[4]

Two years later this thorn still pricked him.

. . . I am personally involved in the absurdity of
the question; due to a book I wrote thirty years ago, I
have myself become a sort of stereotype of the world-
denying contemplative—the man who spurned New
York, spat on Chicago, and tromped on Louisville,
heading for the woods with Thoreau in one pocket,
John of the Cross in another, and holding the Bible
open at the Apocalypse. This personal stereotype is
probably my own fault, and it is something I have to
try to demolish on occasion.[5]

This problem of a public image became even more complex in the sixties, as the "image" became "images." Merton's cogent, vigorous attacks on social injustice and mili-
tarism attracted a new audience for him so that he joined
such radicals as the Berrigan brothers as a leader of the
crusade for peace and justice, while remaining the patron
of untold numbers of spiritual seekers. However, he had
developed some coping devices by this time. He had
learned how to live with physical pain and mental depression. Indeed, he learned how to rise out of his own
ashes, how to turn liabilities into assets. "Paradoxically, I
have found peace because I have always been dissatisfied.
My moments of depression and despair turn out to be
renewals, new beginnings. . . ."[6] By 1961, he was able to
live with Tom Merton, writer. "It is possible to doubt
whether I have become a monk (a doubt I have to live
with), but it is not possible to doubt that I am a writer,
that I was born one and will most probably die as one."[7]
This was all part of his evolving discovery of the unity of
life. He had adopted a philosophy of life, a philosophy

that presupposed God as creator and the intrinsic goodness of all His creation. Life is not to be analyzed,
endured, or even to be enjoyed; it is to be accepted and
shared. It is as God is and as man is.

> In religious terms, this is simply a matter of accepting
> life, and everything in life as a gift, and clinging to
> none of it. . . . You give some of it to others. . . .
> Yet one should be able to share things with others
> without bothering too much about how they like
> it. . . . All life tends to grow like this, in mystery in-
> scaped with paradox and contradiction, yet centered,
> in its very heart, on the divine mercy.[8]

Each man, each moment, each created thing was invested
with its own worth and meaning.

In those months of turmoil following his conversion
when he was pondering what course he should take, Merton had been attracted to those religious orders offering
the most severe rules and the greatest solitude. In his early
monastic career, he had struggled with the temptation to
seek another order where he could lose himself. His admiration for the eremitical life is evident in his early writings
and his reverence for the desert fathers. He acceded to
community life as a means of formation for the life of solitude, the environment most conducive for union with
God. In *Thoughts in Solitude*, he had written: "Do not
flee to solitude from the community. Find God first in the
community, then he will lead you to solitude."[9] As the
years passed, eremitical solitude emerged in his mind as
the monastic ideal and the goal of his life. Allusions to his
desire for solitude and statements to the effect that he felt
this was what God wanted of him pervade his personal
correspondence and notes during this period. As early as
January 1953 (two years after the publication of *The Ascent to Truth*), Merton had written Father Barnabas
Ahern, a member of the Passionist order and a frequent
correspondent in the fifties, of his thoughts about greater
solitude and the consideration of the Camaldolese hermit

order. In a letter dated January 22, 1953, Merton complained of the "perpetual motion of exterior exercises," the gregarious conditions and the noisy machines of Gethsemani that posed a problem for his spiritual growth. He spoke of a concern that even a move to more solitary conditions within the community would bring critical comments on his "defection" from "duty." He spoke kindly of the abbot's sympathy for his duress and reported that he had been permitted to exist as a "part-time hermit." It was pointed out that theologians such as Dom Anselme Stolz and Dom Jean Leclercq were writing with favor of more solitude in contemporary monasticism. With *Ascent* quite possibly still in his mind, Merton wrote, ". . . I do not feel that I will ever write anything worthwhile if I cannot have access to the depths which solitude alone seems able to lay open to men. In other words there is simply no point in my rehashing other people's books as I am not a true theologian. . . ."[10] *Life and Holiness* and *Thoughts in Solitude* soon followed in the wake of his "part-time" solitude. The greatest obstacle was the fear of the leaders of his order that solitaries would violate the Cistercian fraternity and interrupt the common life. Events were taking place that would so alter attitudes and circumstances as to permit the realization of Merton's passionate desire. One of the first breakthroughs was the building of a place suitable for solitude, but in such proximity to the monastery as to permit community communication. The rudimentary structure that would eventually become his last place of residence was contructed in the late fifties, ostensibly to house conferences for the growing number of Protestant groups visiting the monastery and anxious to meet and talk with Merton. The cottage was completed in 1960.

Merton began immediately to spend as much time there as possible and was absolutely elated when he was allowed to spend six full days there in the summer of 1963. Beginning early in 1965, he was given permission to sleep at the hermitage, returning daily to the cloister for regular offices. During that same year, his ambition was finally realized, and his full-time occupation of the hermitage and his resignation as novice master were approved. Merton wrote his friend Dom Jean Leclercq that for the first time he felt that he was living a really monastic life. The day before his fifty-first birthday, Merton responded favorably to the news that newspapers throughout the country were carrying the story of his self-imposed exile from the world of commerce. John Howard Griffin records Merton's joyous reaction to this particular publicity.

> He hoped it would be considered his way of saying goodbye "and getting out (of public life) for keeps." His profound involvement with the works of Chuang Tzu and other Tao and Zen masters over the past years made any public notice appear to be almost a betrayal of his true vocation. His renderings of Chuang Tzu, "The man of spirit . . . hates to see people gather around him." And "Achievement is the beginning of failure. Fame is the beginning of disgrace," and similar aphorisms were now Merton's own convictions, convictions derived from his own solitude and contemplation. Merton resolved that the one central option for him lay in letting go of all that might suggest getting somewhere, being someone, having a name and a voice, following a policy and directing people in "his" ways. What mattered was to love and to be in one piece in silence and not to try to be anybody outwardly.[11]

This kind of solitude was never to be Merton's lot. In 1968, his journal entries record frustration at the intrusions of friends and famous personages who came to dialogue with him, but in the process interrupted his contemplation. In February 1968, he indicated his concern about such well-intentioned interference.

> I am interested in being more honest and more serious—and a better hermit. It will be a struggle be-

cause I have let things get potentially out of hand by
thoughtlessness and carelessness with people, visitors,
etc. Just to aim at moderation does not really work
. . . something more absolute is required and a more
real solitude. I really think that the idea of "helping
others" and "being open" has led me into a real illusion.[12]

However, there was never any question that any less solitude would be desirable. After his first year as a recluse he
signed this vow, dated September 8, 1966: "I Brother M.
Louis Merton solemnly professed monk of the Abbey of
Our Lady of Gethsemani, having completed a year of trial
in the solitary life, hereby make my commitment to spend
the rest of my life in solitude, in so far as my health may
permit."[13] Never did he give any hint of having a desire
to renege on that vow. He did write Dom Leclercq in the
spring of 1968 that he was concerned about being
identified with the United States and its domestic injustice and involvement in Vietnam. He expressed a belief
that the nation was under the judgment of God but came
to say in the same letter that most likely he should stay
and share in the suffering. Much of the speculation about
Merton's intention to relocate permanently, or at least to
divide his time between Gethsemani and some other,
more remote spot, was spawned by his oft-expressed fear
that he would always be too accessible in the knobs. Just
before he left for Asia, he wrote in his diary, "I am not
starting out with a firm plan never to return or with an absolute determination to return at all costs."[14] In a letter to
Brother Patrick Hart, dated two days before Merton's
death, he wrote, "I think of you all on this Feast Day—
and then with Christmas approaching I feel homesick for
Gethsemani. . . ." Almost exactly a month before the accident that claimed his life, he noted in his journal that
there were few places where one would not encounter
noise and crowds and that he was beginning "to appreci-
ate the hermitage at Gethsemani more" than he had.[15]

Merton's View of the World from the Desert

One of the paradoxes of Merton's life was his desire to live in genuine solitude and at the same time to assume responsibility for the world. His longtime friend Naomi Burton Stone admitted her difficulty in reconciling "his real need for seclusion and his real need to give himself to people."[16] His Cistercian brother Father John Eudes Bamberger recognized in Father Louis a tension between his commitment to solitary contemplation and his concern for humanity, but notes that open warfare never erupted because of Merton's awareness of the two drives within him, which he kept in balance.[17] Merton realized that he was a part of the world and must participate in its existence and share the responsibility for its becoming. By 1968, he had learned that it is not easy to dichotomize "good" and "evil" and that he could not accept everything within his "city" in the heart of America, nor could he renounce everything and everyone outside its walls. It is neither creation nor creature that the Christian is called to reject, but rather "the perverted standards which made men misuse and spoil a good creation, ruining their own lives into the bargain."[18] The monastery could be a place of refuge, but not of escape from the rightful responsibilities of children of God.

> Even the cloistered "contemplative" is inevitably implicated in the crises and problems of the society in which he is still a member (since he participates in its benefits and shares its responsibilities). Even he must to some extent participate "actively" in the Church's work, not only by prayer and holiness, but by understanding and concern.[19]

Merton was, he realized, a part of the nuclear age, of the century of Hitler, of Vietnam, poverty, disease, and the most insidious kind of materialism. "In such a situation," he said, "it is no longer permissible for Christians

seriously and honestly to devote themselves to a spirituality of evasion, a cult of otherworldliness. . . ."[20] Merton's interest in social issues, even his unorthodox positions, were not completely new. As indicated in Chapter
II, in 1941 he had been torn between the possibilities of
laying his life down in Harlem or in a monastery. In his
chronicle of 1940, he had written that the racial prejudice
of Christians was akin to the "prudence of Judas."[21] His
penetrating analysis of the war-peace syndrome of the sixties was rooted in his insights of the forties. Merton's
Quaker mother had been a strong enough pacifist to
prevail on Owen Merton to avoid service in the First
World War, and Tom had elected to refuse combat
service in the Second World War, which was going to
guarantee eternal peace. ". . . I made out my papers with
an application to be a noncombatant objector . . . so long
as I did not have to drop bombs on open cities, or shoot
at other men."[22] But these were the cries of a sensitive,
perplexed young man, struggling with a world of suffering
and imperfection. Merton's pronouncements of the sixties
had the ring of the prophet whose vision has been
sharpened by the purification of the desert and whose
tongue stung like a desert wind. He had discovered that he
was a part of it all and must bear responsibility not only
for acts of commission but also for failures of omission—
he could not remain silent. *Conjectures of a Guilty Bystander*, the title of his most popular work of this period
of his life, reflects his feelings and the renewed struggle to
accept his role in the historical context of his life. This
theme was sounded in other works as well:

> My very existence is an admission of guilt. . . . All I
> have to do is think, and immediately I become
> guilty. . . . Everything that is written is a potential
> confession of crime. . . . My indifference will make
> me the partisan of all opposition. . . . The worst
> traitor is the one who simply takes no interest. . . .
> That's me. Here I sit in the grass. I watch the clouds
> go by, and like it.[23]

Merton was to become the voice of conscience in the prophetic plea, not just for reform but also for transformation of a whole culture and its warped values. He recognized and often pointed out the "seeds of destruction" in the reformers as well as the "establishment." Dom Jean Leclercq is essentially correct when he asserts about Merton that his monastic vocation and experience were "at the heart of everything he said."[24] "This was," his Benedictine friend goes on, "both his limitation and his strength: a limitation, because, after all, monastic life is not the totality of the Church or of society; a strength, because he was a man of single purpose, a lone warrior."[25] Merton argued that the Church as a body of Christ had no alternative to sacrificial involvement in the fight for human rights. Christians would be judged, he contended, not by their dogmatic orthodoxy or ritual piety, but by their identity with and immersion in the transformation process, the remaking of the world from the live seed of Christ. He noted hopefully that

> . . . the developing Christian consciousness is one which is activistic, antimystical, antimetaphysical, which eschews well-defined and concrete forms, and which tends to identify itself with active, progressive, even revolutionary, movements that are on the way but that have not yet reached any kind of clear definition.[26]

Merton advocated an acceptance of the burden of the struggle and of the suffering of the word of judgment that was being acted out in the shaking of the foundations in the riots and revolution in America, as well as on the world's slaughterblocks that romanticists call "battlefields," but he also cautioned those who came in the "name of the Lord" to remember who they were. ". . . In our eagerness to go out to modern man and meet him on his own ground, accepting him as he is," he said, "we must also be truly what *we* are."[27] Merton's role then was truly that of a prophet as he himself defined a prophet. "A prophet is a man who has been struck by the word of God. The word of God has entered his life and disrupted it and through his life disrupts the lives of others."[28]

The messages of the biblical prophets were often declarations of judgment, and Merton's pronouncements had a strong eschatological orientation, announcing judgment and calling for a new day of the Lord. Contemporary society is witnessing the failure of its schemes and structures. Modern man has succumbed to his own propaganda.

> When one has too many answers, and when one joins a chorus of others chanting the same slogans, there is, it seems to me, a danger that one is trying to evade the loneliness of a conscience that realizes itself to be in an inescapably evil situation. We are all under judgment. None of us is free from contamination. Our choice is not that of being pure and whole at the mere cost of formulating a just and honest opinion.[29]

In particular, the American individualist has been hypnotized by the siren songs of independence and "private heavens."[30] Man has wasted his inheritance trying to construct his own "kingdom" and in the process has decided against the Parousia. Merton chastises the inclination of modern Christians to pray for an indefinite postponement of God's judgment in order that they may repeat their mistakes and rebuild their towers of Babel. Caustically he suggests that the phrase in the Lord's Prayer, "thy Kingdom come," be changed to, "give us time!"[31] The crisis of contemporary Christianity is most acute where Christians are striving to perpetuate "fundamentalist and conservative superstitions" and to vindicate their past mistakes on the grounds of "good intentions." It is by its fruit that the Church must be judged.[32] Liberal utopianism has failed no less in its confidence in inevitable progress. False optimism is as useless as misguided patriotism is dangerous. What the Christian must do is to commit himself to an eschatology of hope, which is judgment on the false kingdoms that wither in the sun.

For eschatology is not *finis* and punishment, the winding up of accounts and the closing of books: it is the final beginning, the definitive birth into a new creation. It is not the last gasp of exhausted possibilities but the first taste of all that is beyond conceiving as actual.[33]

Christians were called to be citizens of the heavenly city, to transcend earthly political boundaries, to become agents of transformation in history. Each individual must be a martyr, i.e., a living witness of the present eschatological reality.

For a Christian, a transcultural integration is eschatological. The rebirth of man and of society on a transcultural level is a rebirth into the transformed and redeemed time, the time of the Kingdom, the time of the Spirit, the time of "the end." It means a disintegration of the social and cultural self, the product of merely human history, and the reintegration of that self in Christ, in salvation history, in the mystery of redemption, in the pentecostal "new creation." But this means entering into the full mystery of the eschatological Church.[34]

It was this understanding of the meaning of being a Christian in the world that made Merton a "contemplative at the heart of the world, a world in revolution."[35] A brief sampling of Merton's social thought will be helpful in assessing the practical ethical implications of his spirituality. However, before going on to that, it should be noted that Merton never seems to have had much confidence in the mass of humanity's ability or willingness to alter the course of history. The contribution of each man must be to assert his own integrity, depending on God to ultimately restore the integrity of the universe. Merton came to believe by the midsixties that one might have to accept just being a part of the whole and acting as a leavening agent and not always a vocal or exercised one. In "Rain and the Rhinoceros," he wrote, "Thoreau sat in *his* cabin and criticized the railways. I sit in mine and wonder about a world that has, well, progressed. I must read *Walden* again, and see if Thoreau already guessed that he was part of what he thought he could escape. But it is not a matter of 'escaping.' It is not even a matter of protesting very audibly."[36]

THE CITY OF MAN

Merton viewed contemporary decadence as a complex problem of spiritual ecology. The civilization that man had constructed was a world of illusion that oppressed man's spiritual nature and stifled his innate longing for ultimate reality. Merton's conversion to a philosophy of affirmation of man and the natural world did not alter his evaluation of the antispiritual nature of the mass urban mentality of contemporary society, particularly Western society. Time did not temper Merton's critique of the sterility of the modern city. He shared Augustine's hope for the spiritual city "not made with hands," as promised by the writer of Hebrews. It is in this vein that he spoke of Gethsemani as the "only real city in America." Even Louisville, a middle-sized city by American standards, was seen as a part of the contemporary heteronomy that precluded autonomy, let alone the freedom of theonomy.

> Cities, even Louisville (which, being the city nearest to home is in some sense my city), leave me with a sense of placelessness and exile. There is an immense movement spread all over everything; the ceaseless motion of hot traffic, tired and angry people, in a complex swirl of frustration. While one could easily have all that one needs within easy reach, the purpose of a city seems to be to guarantee that everybody has to travel eighteen to fifty miles a day just in the performance of the routine duties of everyday life. One must move through noise, stink, and general anger,

through blocks of dilapidation, in order to get somewhere where anger and bewilderment are concentrated in a neon-lit air-conditioned enclave, glittering with "products," humming with piped-in music, and reeking of the nondescript, sterile, and sweet smell of the technologically functioning world.[37]

Merton picked up the Old Testament conflict between agrarian society and urban society. The city represents the mass that denies man his true identity and enslaves him in the pseudocorporateness of modern civilization.

They are not even replicas of the great tower of Babel that once rose up in the desert of Senaar, that man "might make his name famous and reach even unto heaven." (Gn. 11:4). They are brilliant and sordid smiles of the devil upon the face of the wilderness, cities of secrecy where each man spies on his brother, cities through whose veins money runs like artificial blood, and from whose womb will come the last and greatest instrument of destruction.[38]

There emerges in Merton's discussion of the city and technology one of his central themes, that of freedom. Although he acknowledged the potential of technology for improving the human lot, he feared the establishment of a cybernetic technocracy. Mechanical perfectionism threatens the natural impulses and reduces man to a computer. The Puritan ethic has reached its apogee when art and leisure are a part of a utilitarian blueprint. Merton cried out for a renaissance of humanism and a recovery of priorities established by man rather than imposed upon him by society.

Technology was made for man, not man for technology. In losing touch with being and thus with God, we have fallen into a senseless idolatry of production and consumption for their own sakes. We have renounced the act of being and plunged ourself into

process for its own sake. We no longer know how to
live, and because we cannot accept life in its reality
life ceases to be a joy and becomes an affliction.[39]

Merton's humorous illustrations of neopaganism were bit-
tersweet to those who understood the ramifications of
their veracity.

Compare our monastery and the General Electric
plant in Louisville. Which one is the more serious
and more "religious" institution? One might be
tempted to say "the monastery," out of sheer habit.
But, in fact, the religious seriousness of the monastery
is like sandlot baseball compared with the big-league
seriousness of General Electric. It may in fact occur
to many, including the monks, to *doubt* the monastery and what it represents. Who doubts G.E.?[40]

The order of our lives reflects the priority of our commit-
ments and those things that are the objects of our faith.

Technological progress had resulted in the enslavement
of man to work and of society to industry. The United
States government's budget provides ample evidence of
the priorities of a technocracy. Our success in the laboratory and shop has launched an exploding GNP and a
moral code calibrated to greater wealth, greater military
capacity and sophistication, and a controlled society. Process and power become supreme ends. Father Frederic
Kelly articulated Merton's concern when he wrote, "The
problem for religious man is how to maintain that inner
peace, personal identity and personal freedom that are
necessary to be truly religious in the modern world that is
dominated by activism, science, machinery and the drive
to acquire power and proficiency."[41]

Merton did not advocate the abandonment of the city
nor the renunciation of scientific achievement. He did encourage a recovery of the personal, a sense of the authentic. Man can experience an inner solitude that will enable
him to be an instrument of renewal and transformation.

Indeed, one should accept his station in the city as a Christian vocation, a means of expressing Christ's love.

> But if you have to live in a city and work among machines and ride in the subways and eat in a place where the radio makes you deaf with spurious news and where the food destroys your life and the sentiments of those around you poison your heart with boredom, do not be impatient but accept it as the love of God and as a seed of solitude planted in your soul.[42]

The central issue with Merton was whether or not man was still in charge of his destiny. Merton observed that the most affluent nation in history was enslaved to its wealth. Our possessions possess us. Merton was not blind to the potential of our knowledge and resources to deliver men from the traditional enemies of disease and poverty, but he also saw the gap between the haves and have-nots grow wider and wider. He feared that his contemporaries had become like those people Paul described when he wrote, "They exchanged the truth about God for a lie and worshiped and served the creature rather than the creator." His concern was that we seek the Kingdom of God first.

RACISM AND A CHRISTIAN CONSCIENCE

Merton followed closely the development of the civil rights movement in the fifties and its changing complexion in the sixties. Martin Luther King, Jr., occupied a special place in Merton's mind alongside Gandhi.[43] King provided a model for Christian opposition to injustice.

> Dr. Martin Luther King has appealed to strictly Christian motives. He has based his non-violence on his belief that love can unite men, even enemies, in truth. That is to say that he has clearly spelled out the struggle for freedom not as a struggle for the Negro alone, but also for the white man.[44]

In a discussion with the novices the day after Dr. King's assassination, Merton told them that the black leader had planned to visit him at Gethsemani but altered his plans to answer a call to Memphis. Merton saw in King a prophet and a suffering servant in the tradition of the biblical prophets.

"Fortunately the Negroes have a leader who is a man of grace, who understands the law of love, who understands the mystery of the greatest secret grace that has been *given to the Negro and to no other*. The grace which the people who first created the spirituals well knew about: the grace of election that made them God's chosen, the grace that elevated them above the meaningless and trivial things of life, even in the midst of terrible and unjust suffering."[45]

The struggle of the black in America was seen by Merton as an archetype of "colonial crisis" around the world.

The guilt of white America toward the Negro is simply another version of the guilt of the European colonizer toward all the other races of the world, whether in Asia, Africa, America or Polynesia. The racial crisis in the United States has rightly been diagnosed as a "colonial crisis" within the country itself rather than on a distant continent. But it is nevertheless closely related to the United States' problems in South East Asia and in Latin America, particularly with Cuba.[46]

The problem was rooted in an "I-it" view of the "have-nots" by the "haves," who exploit people as they exploit natural resources. Merton believed it impossible for whites to "think black." Merton's great empathy with the black man's struggle for freedom created for him an identity crisis of major proportions. "When I read about the race issue I have a tendency to identify with the Negro."[47]

Merton achieved what few white men have been able to in recent years, acceptance in the black community.

Eldridge Cleaver, the black radical, incorporated Merton's description of the Harlem ghetto in his Black Muslim lectures. While expressing mystification at Merton's voluntary incarceration in his monk's cell, Cleaver praised him as a "soul brother" and said, "Despite my rejection of Merton's theistic world view, I could not keep him out of the room. He shouldered his way through the door. Welcome, Brother Merton. I give him a bear hug."[48] Although Merton never condoned the use of violence, he interpreted the ghetto eruptions as symptomatic of deep-seated evil.

> . . . crime that breaks out of the ghetto is only the fruit of a greater and more pervasive violence: the injustice which forces people to live in the ghetto in the first place. The problem of violence, then, is not the problem of a few rioters and rebels, but the problem of a whole social structure which is outwardly ordered and respectable, and inwardly ridden by psychopathic obsessions and delusions.[49]

The anger of the white man was attributed to his need for a straw man to bolster his ego. "Blaming the Negro . . . gives the white a stronger sense of identity, or rather it *protects* an identity which is seriously threatened with pathological dissolution. It is by blaming the Negro that the white man tries to hold himself together."[50] Merton was convinced that the South was suffering from a fear psychosis objectified in the black.

> At the present time, the Southern pseudomystique of sexual and racist obsessions (and of course there have been rapes and seductions of Negroes by whites) now joins with the deeper and more universal fear of revolution. This combination results in a peculiarly potent climate of aggressive intolerance, suspiciousness, hatred and fear. When we consider that this self-righteous, pseudo-religious faith has its finger terribly close to

the button that launches intercontinental ballistic missiles, it gives food for thought.[51]

Racism was a morass that stifled both the subject and object. The Negro was incarcerated in the well-drawn stereotype, and the white man trapped in his superman image. Both the hater and the hated were dehumanized by the circumstances to which they had yielded.

Merton abhorred depersonalization of man, which he saw as the root of evil in our society. No man can be really free until all men are free. Millions are drowning in the "formless sea of irresponsibility which is the crowd"[52] to which they have fled for security. Merton believed that the structures of contemporary American society were so permeated with sin that only the most radical reordering held any hope of redemption.

> In the spiritual, social, historic crises of civilization—
> and of religious institutions—the same principle
> applies. Growth, survival and even salvation may
> depend on the ability to sacrifice what is fictitious and
> unauthentic in the construction and renewal. This
> task can be carried out only in the climate of faith, of
> hope and of love: these three must be present in some
> form, even if they amount only to a natural belief in
> the validity and significance of human choice, a deci-
> sion to invest human life with some shadow of mean-
> ing, a willingness to treat other men as other selves.[53]

In effect Merton was calling for a corporate spiritual pilgrimage. Illumination and reconciliation are possible only after purgation. The false images and values must be stripped away, the diseased tissue excised. The people have remained in darkness because they feared the light.

THE CHRISTIAN AND NONVIOLENCE

Long before the United States had become enmeshed in the quicksand of Vietnam, Merton had begun to publish his strong views on violence and to decry our national propensity for it as a means of solving problems.[54] He was repulsed by the official violent reaction to the civil rights movements. *Original Child Bomb* was an antipoem written in 1961 to satirize the American decision to drop the atomic bomb on Hiroshima and Nagasaki. Occasional news reports on unaccounted for or arrested Nazi war criminals inspired literary expressions of incredulity at their pragmatic explanation for their conduct. Merton provoked the ire of the American bishops and some of his own Cistercian superiors with his unmitigated condemnation of the United States involvement in Vietnam, which he termed "an overwhelming atrocity."[55] Some of his works on peace in the sixties were suppressed by the censors in response to the pressure of the American bishops, a situation that resulted in some "pacifistic bootlegging" on his part.[56] Many of the radicals wanted Merton to leave Gethsemani and join them in the streets; perhaps, eventually, in jail.[57] Although he did not condemn their efforts to transform society through demonstration and nonviolent resistance, he felt that the monk could speak most prophetically from the desert. He could not justify violence, even the destruction of draft cards and records, for any reason. The Christian could not hide behind an "end justifies the means" philosophy. Merton subscribed to the theory that those "who live by the sword shall perish by the sword"; therefore, everyone involved in a war ends up as a victim of war. He endorsed the wisdom of *Tao Teh Ching* in a lament of the tragic poetic justice of war.

> To rejoice over a victory is to rejoice
>   over the slaughter of men!
> Hence a man who rejoices over the slaughter of men cannot expect to thrive in the world of men.
> . . . Even victory is a funeral.[58]

Merton insisted that the contemporary Christian must follow the example of Jesus in these matters, even if it means a penultimate experience of a cross.[59] He cited the example of the martyrs who, he said, ". . . without forcible resistance, laid down their lives rather than submit to the unjust laws that demanded an official religious cult of the Emperor as God."[60] He inferred that those who bombed and executed women and children, not to mention opposing combatants, in the name of patriotism, enthroned their nation as God and made nationalism their creed. In 1962, he wrote that the policies of "hatred and destructiveness" that had inexorably plunged the world into two global wars in less than a quarter century were the products of "rabid, short-sighted, irrational and stubborn forces which tend to come to a head in nationalism."[61] Merton cited Origen's refutation of Celsus' charges that the Christians were subversive to Rome because of their refusal to bear arms as a basis for a contemporary Christian ethic. Origen synthesized in himself the best of the classical humanist tradition and a view that "human society has been radically transformed by the Incarnation of the Logos."[62] "No longer do we take the sword against any nations nor do we learn war any more since we have become the sons of peace through Jesus who is our author instead of following the traditional customs by which we were strangers to the convenant."[63] This is not to suggest an indifference to the *Polis* but a new relationship and a role that is spiritual and transcendent. Merton criticizes Augustine's "just war" concept on the basis of an "excessive naïveté with regard to the good that can be attained by violent means which cannot help but call forth all that is worst in man."[64] Man's addiction to war, maintained Merton, was like that of an alcoholic who knows that the drug is killing him but will not desist from its use. War inevitably includes good men working evil, and the best intentions are not enough.

> The tragedy of our time is then not so much the malice of the wicked as the helpless futility even of the best intentions of "the good." We have war-makers, war criminals, indeed. But we ourselves in our very

best efforts for peace, find ourselves maneuvered un-
consciously into positions where we too can act as
criminals.[65]

If Adolf Eichmann's actions to exterminate the Jews
were sane ones, then Christians must teach and practice
insanity. Merton contended that a theology that can focus
on and condemn individual violence while it "blesses and
canonizes the antiseptic violence of corporately organized
murder" is demented.[66]

Merton was not just antiwar, or even antiviolence; he
was prolove. War and violence were symptomatic of a
"whole social structure which is outwardly ordered and re-
spectable, and inwardly ridden by psychopathic obsessions
and delusions."[67] Nonviolence does not imply nonresist-
ance to injustice and evil but rather is the kind of resistance advocated in the Bible. "It combats evil as such by
doing good to the evildoer, and thus over-coming evil with
good (Rm. 12:21), which is the way our Lord Himself
resisted evil."[68] He had serious doubts about the efficacy
of burning draft cards and destroying property, which he
believed symbolized despair rather than hope. When two
young men, one of them associated with the Catholic
Peace Fellowship and the other a member of the staff of
the *Catholic Worker*, immolated themselves in protest of
the Vietnam war, Merton moved to remove his name
from the board of the Catholic Peace Fellowship. Only
after lengthy correspondence and a public clarification of
his relationship to the group was he persuaded to continue
public association. What Merton advocated was a theology of love without dissimulation, a claim on the promise
of blessing for the meek. Nonviolent resistance was for
him a manifestation of disinterested love in which self-in-
terest is nonexistent. ". . . he who practices nonviolent resistance must commit himself not to the defense of his
own interests or even those of a particular group: he must
commit himself to the defense of objective truth and right
and above all of man."[69] War is a cruel and evil task-

master that enslaves all it touches in one way or another. It is a mammoth obstacle to the realization of the goals of classical humanism as well as those of Christianity, the purpose of both being "to liberate man from the mere status of *animalis homo* (*sarkikos*) to at least the level of *rationalis* (*psychicos*) and better still, spiritual or pneumatic."[70]

Merton's social and political philosophy were rooted in a personalistic philosophy. Urban problems, racism, poverty, war, and peace all must be dealt with in the quest for the abundant life. Love that will overcome the massive problems that confront twentieth-century man transcends the individual but is possible only as the individual recognizes his own self-transcendence. "There is no real love of life unless it is oriented to the discovery of one's true, spiritual self, beyond and above the level of mere empirical individuality, with its superficial enjoyments and fears."[71] Mere activism even in good causes is not enough.

> He who attempts to act and do things for others or for the world without deepening his own self-understanding, freedom, integrity and capacity to love, will not have anything to give others. He will communicate to them nothing but the contagion of his own obsessions, his aggressiveness, his ego-centered ambitions, his delusions about ends and means, his doctrinaire prejudices and ideas.[72]

The pseudospirituality of activism must be distinguished from authentic Christian charity.

Personalism, the Christian Humanism of Thomas Merton

"Christian humanism" and "humanism" were synonymous terms to Merton. Humanity is possible only as the new man comes into being. Merton believed that the process of mystical transformation was a process of diffusion of the love of Christ in one's being. The love of Christ infused by the Holy Spirit elevates human faculties to a divine level and habit of action, uniting the new being with the essence of God: love.[73] Man's life is dependent on the transforming power of God demonstrated in Christ.

> True Christian humanism is the full flowering of the theology of the Incarnation. It is rooted in a totally new concept of man which grew out of the mystery of the union of God and man in Christ. . . . It is the full realization of man's dignity and obligations as son of God, as image of God, created, regenerated, and transformed in the Word made Flesh.[74]

The life that exists potentially in all men is a part of the divine mystery, which transcends the individual. Merton carefully distinguished personalism from individualism.

> Personalism and individualism must not be confused. Personalism gives priority to the person and not the individual self. To give priority to the person means respecting the unique and inalienable value of the other person, as well as one's own, for a respect that is centered only on one's individual self to the exclusion of others proves itself to be fraudulent.[75]

Individualism is treated as coterminous with the mass mentality of modern society. "Mass society is individualistic in the sense that it isolates each individual subject from his immediate neighbor, reducing him to a state of impersonal, purely formal and abstract relationship with other objectified individuals."[76] "Individualism" as understood in modern society is the epitome of ego-centricity. Since the renaissance, individualism has been an excuse for irresponsibility. Pseudospiritual, moralistic American "rugged individualism" divinizes material success and propagates the myth that every man has an equal opportunity to attain whatever goal he sets for himself; therefore, no one need feel responsible for others. The individual hides from his natural unity with all mankind. Conformism obliterates the singular traits of each being, which equip him to play his proper part in the concert of life. Many men are so conditioned for blank passivity that they have sacrificed their birthright and are incapable of authenticity. Man's hope is to some extent dependent upon his vulnerability to an experience of despair and concomitant dread. Sartre's *néant* is a philosophical expression of the void of the apophatic mystics. The ascent to knowledge begins when the fictitious images of life and carnal man's abilities are shattered. The capacity for experiencing pain is a gift of God to alert us to malfunctions of the flesh and the spirit. Contemporary Americans have been trained to believe that there are explanations for everything, that no problem is beyond "Yankee ingenuity." As long as man is dependent on the system, he resists dependence on God. But ". . . dread divests us of the sense of possession, of 'having' our being and our power to love, in order that we may simply be in perfect openness (turned inside out), a defenselessness that is utter simplicity and total gift."[77] Adam and Prometheus were both ensnared by the same fatal flaw, the desire to reconstruct themselves. "The fire Prometheus thought he had to steal . . . is his own identity in God, the affirmation and vindication of his own being as a sanctified creature in the image of God."[78] The sin that besets man is "liberation from his inordinate self-consciousness, his monumental self-awareness, his obsessions with self-affirmation, so that he may enjoy the freedom that goes with being simply what he is. . . ."[79] Today's society so constricts man that he never has an opportunity to give in to the creative impulse with which he is born. The experience of life for most of the progeny of the atomic era is not an experience of life as it is, but the illusion of life constructed according to their fathers' distorted vision. Man will not stumble on to the path to freedom. He must confront what is false in himself and the world and open himself to the creative energy at the core of his being. Merton did not wholeheartedly endorse the "new freedom" of the sixties. Freedom that permits or encourages people to be less than persons, that promotes baseness or stresses our earthbound animal dimension, is counterfeit. "Doing your own thing" sometimes means being a thing instead of a person. True freedom is freedom to be fully human, to actualize the divine image.

Merton's anthropology changed little over the years. Man is called to release the creative energy of life within him. The painful sense of inner division evokes a consciousness of the hard realities of history. If man will respond to God's call to freedom, he will be empowered to escape the abyss of greed and violence and to build for himself a world of love. Merton cites Eric Fromm as an authority on this point.

> Man is beset by the existential dichotomy of being within nature and yet transcending it by the fact of having self-awareness and choice; he can solve the dichotomy only by going forward. Man has to experience himself as a stranger in the world, estranged from himself, with his fellow man and with nature on a higher level. He has to experience the split between himself as subject and the world as object as the condition for overcoming this very split.[80]

Avoiding the pain of confrontation with himself, man has accepted the world as his progenitor and imprinted himself on its mold. However, he will never be completely comfortable in a form that doesn't fit. Human hope for true freedom can be realized in the natural orchestration of the parts. Modern man is frequently like a puzzle with all the pieces but not in their proper places. The paradigm for putting himself together is Jesus Christ. Integration of the person is the gift of Christ. One can find no peace, no reality, in the abstract. No gnosis can deliver him from the bondage of the pseudoself. "The summons to change, to man's creative self-realization and development in the spirit, as a child of God whom the truth shall make free, is a summons to permanent newness of life."[81] Those who respond, enter into an ongoing process of re-creation or transformation. The power within works incessantly, re-constituting spiritual man, who in turn participates in the remaking of all that is. The person's identity is es-tablished by the choices he makes and by a courageous commitment to hope in the countenance of anguish and risk. The process is one of divinization, which includes certain invariable concomitants. The gift of understanding opens the person's eyes to the ubiquitous presence of God in all creation. Few spiritual writers have expressed this ex-perience of revelation as simply as Julian of Norwich:

> Also in this He shewed me a little thing, the quan-tity of an hazelnut, in the palm of my hand; and it was as round as a ball. I looked thereupon with eye of my understanding, and thought: What may this be? And it was answered generally thus: It is all that is made. I marvelled how it might last for methought it might suddenly have fallen to naught for little(ness). And I was answered in my understanding: It lasteth, and ever shall (last) for that God loveth it. And so All-thing hath the Being by the love of God.[82]

The new relationship with God engenders a new rela-tionship with all things and all men. The shared identity with Christ manifests itself in concrete form; man in Christ as a form of Christ.

> When the encounter is real and complete, a new kind of relationship is established between our own free-dom and that ultimate freedom and spirit: the God who is love and who is also the "Lord of History." At the same time a new relationship with other men comes into being: instead of living for ourselves, we live for them. Ideally speaking, if we all lived in this kind of altruistic concern and engagement, human history would culminate in an epiphany of God in man. Mankind would visibly be "Christ."[83]

The Christian finds himself in union with Christ, which "implies the perfect integration of the whole human person,"[84] which means a being in God and like God whose nature is love. "This power to love another for his own sake is one of the things that makes us like God, because this power is the one thing that is free from all determination."[85] It is in and through love that the "new man" lays claim to all that is God's.

Every man is called to follow Christ, and those who respond, reproduce the likeness of Christ in their particular mode. The conduct of the new man toward and for others reflects new being. It is in respect to the social ramifications of man's new status with God that the evolution in Merton's thought is most noticeable, from his withdrawal period to his maturity, where he becomes a spiritual participant in the throes of history and a spokesman for the presence of God in the midst of individual and corporate turmoil. Active participation in God's creative freedom means sharing his concern for the freedom of others. ". . . trust in God cannot be completely divorced from a certain trust in man. The Christian knows that there are radically sound possibilities in every man, and he believes that love and grace always have power to bring out those possibilities at the most unexpected moments."[86] The disciple of Christ does the work that He did, imitating Him as precisely as possible. In a letter written in 1967, Merton stated the social dimension of his doctrine of divinization in lucid and succinct form.

> But indeed we exist solely for this, to be the place He has chosen for His presence, His manifestation in the world, His epiphany . . . if we once began to recognize, humbly but truly, the real value of our own self, we would see that this value was the sign of God in our being, the signature of God upon our being. Fortunately, the love of our fellow man is given us as the way of realizing this. . . . It is the love of my lover, my brother or my child that sees God in me, makes God credible to myself in me. And it is my love for my lover, my child, my brother, that enables me to

show God to him or her in himself or herself. Love is the epiphany of God in our poverty.[87]

"The Inner Experience"

In the early sixties, Merton began a statement of his theology in a treatise he called "The Inner Experience."[88] In the introduction to the French edition of *The Ascent to Truth*, published seven years after the American original, Merton wrote that if he were writing the book at that time, he would have relied less on the Scholastics and more on the Scriptures and the Fathers. This is generally the course he has taken in "The Inner Experience," which appears to be a confluence of the Fathers; the Scriptures; the Rhenish mystics; the English mystics; the Spanish mystics, especially John of the Cross; existential philosophy, and modern psychology, all synthesized within Merton. The treatise is a compendium of Merton's mystical theology, and serves as a kind of blueprint co-ordinating his many works, often characterized more by their vigor and vitality than by thoroughness or systematism. "The Inner Experience" provides an excellent matrix for the examination of Merton's thought; the diverse elements of this thought are laid succinctly alongside each other.

THE HUMAN DILEMMA

At the outset Merton asserts the personalist philosophy discussed in some detail above. Every man carries within himself heaven and hell. Modern psychology cannot dismiss the presence of evil in the world or man's deepest anxieties as figments of human imagination. Religion, too, may be only an evasion of the truth about authentic being. It is the illusionary self that paralyzes man and obscures reality. He is his own worst enemy. Dissolution of the false self is the answer to most problems. Man deludes himself into believing that this world is ultimate. His exile from paradise is self-imposed, and he has undertaken to save himself by creating the Utopia of his dreams. Adam

yielded to an impulse that told him he could do better on
his own and could construct a life and a world better than
God could. What Adam did not realize was that he was a
part of God and that he was abdicating a place in paradise
for a fool's paradise.

The story of Adam's fall from Paradise says, in
symbolic terms, that man was created as a contemplative. The fall from Paradise was a fall from unity.
The Platonizing Greek Fathers even taught that the
division of humanity into two sexes was a result of the
Fall. St. Augustine, in a more cautious and psychological application of the narrative, says that in the
Fall, Adam, man's interior and spiritual self, his contemplative self, was led astray by Eve, his exterior,
material and practical self, his active self. Man fell
from the unity of contemplative vision into the multiplicity, complication and distraction of an active,
worldly existence.

Since he was now dependent entirely on exterior
and contingent things, he became an exile in a world
of objects, each one capable of deluding and enslaving
him. Centered no longer in God and in his inmost,
spiritual self, man now had to *see* and *be aware* of
himself as if he were his own god. . . . And to compensate for the labors and frustrations of this estrangement, he must try to admire, assert and gratify
himself at the expense of others like himself. Hence
the complex and painful network of loves and
hatreds, desires and fears, lies and excuses in which
we are all held captive. In such a condition, man's
mind is enslaved by an inexorable concern with all
that is exterior, transient, illusory and trivial. . . .

So man is exiled from God and from his inmost
self. He is tempted to seek God, and happiness, outside himself. So his quest for happiness becomes, in
fact, a flight from God and from himself: a flight that
takes him further and further away from reality. In

the end, he has to dwell in the "region of unlikeness"
—having lost his inner resemblance [sic] to God in
losing his freedom to enter his own home, which is
the sanctuary of God [I.E., pp. 34–35].

Merton differentiates the "world," which infers secularity and a concept of temporal as ultimate, from the
cosmos, which is the true work of God. "Secular life is a
life of vain hopes, imprisoned in the illusion of newness
and change which brings us constantly back to . . . the
contemplation of our own nothingness" [I.E., p. 48].

Merton faults the neoplatonists for corrupting mystical
theology by introducing gnostic attitudes toward matter.
The universe was created good, and in its essence it
remains so. The world is the theater where man should act
out his proper role but where he must at least act. Man is
supposed to work in concert with the world rather than
fighting it. But man can lose himself in activity. The lesson of Ecclesiastes is a lesson for our age. What we do on
our own is "vanity and a striving after the wind," and
human wisdom is vaporous. Our knowledge only vexes
us and lays heavy upon us.

The quest for God evoked by the awakened consciousness of the emptiness of the *saeculum* is for a return to
the Father. Cast among the swine in the slough of despair, the prodigal remembered the loving father and
home. The Christian pilgrimage is a journey home.

It is a return to the infinite abyss of pure reality in
which our own reality is grounded, and in which we
exist. It is a return to the source of all meaning and
all truth. It is a return to the inmost springs of life
and joy. It is a rediscovery of paradise within our own
spirit, by self-forgetfulness [I.E., p. 35].

Monastic silence and solitude are not necessary prereq-
uisites for this experience. There are those who are "hidden contemplatives" who find God among the "little"
people they serve.

Christ has promised that the Three Divine Persons will manifest themselves *to all who love Him.* There are many Christians who serve God with great purity of soul and perfect self-sacrifice in the active life. Their vocation does not allow them to find the solitude and silence and leisure in which to empty their minds entirely of created things and to lose themselves in God alone. They are too busy serving Him in His children on earth. At the same time, their minds and temperaments do not fit them for a purely contemplative life: they would know no peace without exterior activity. They would not know what to do with themselves. They would vegetate and *their interior life would grow cold.* Nevertheless they know how to find God by devoting themselves to Him in self-sacrificing labours in which they are able to remain in His presence all day long. They live and work in His company. They realize that He is within them and they taste deep, peaceful joy in being with Him. . . . Although they are active labourers they are also *hidden contemplatives* because of the great purity of heart maintained in them by obedience, fraternal charity, self-sacrifice and perfect abandonment to God's will in all that they do and suffer. They are much closer to God than they realize. They enjoy a kind of "masked" contemplation.

Such Christians as these, far from being excluded from perfection, may reach a higher degree of sanctity than others who have been apparently favoured with a deeper interior life. Yet there is all the difference in the world between these hidden contemplatives and the surface Christian whose piety is merely a matter of externals and formal routine. The difference is: *These men live for God and for His love alone.* They cannot help knowing about Him.

It might be well to point out here that "masked contemplation" has its advantages. Since contemplation is communion with a hidden God in His own hiddenness, it tends to be pure in proportion as it is itself hidden. Obscurity and sincerity seem to go together in the spiritual life [I.E., pp. 62–63].

There is a form of activity that is energized by love, and it affirms reality, which is opposed to the hyperactivity into which some flee to hide from reality.

CALLED TO CONTEMPLATION

Any romantic fantasies that Merton may have entertained when he arrived at the Abbey of Our Lady of Gethsemani in 1941 had melted away by the sixties, when he wrote, ". . . it would be singularly unfeeling as well as dishonest for me to suggest that peace, joy and happiness are easily found along that most arid stretch of man's spiritual pilgrimage: the life of contemplation" [I.E., p. 2]. Contemplation is not a profession that one decides to enter. There are no maps for the journey, those who have traveled it say there is no certain way, and those who have decided to "become a contemplative" are doomed to frustration. Preconceived notions of what to expect will only accentuate the disappointment. On several occasions Merton expressed his conviction that contemplation is a vocation that requires a charism. ". . . we are called by the voice of God, by the voice of that ultimate being, to pierce through the irrelevance of our life. . . ."[89] The contemplative, like anyone else, must begin by discovering the "I" and separating it from the "we." The "I" must redeem itself from phony individualism and recover its natural organic unity.

> . . . [it] is not the "I" who can stand in the presence of God and be aware of Him as "Thou." For this "I" there is perhaps no clear "Thou" at all. Perhaps even other people are merely extensions of the "I," reflections of it, modifications of it, aspects of it. Perhaps for this "I" there is no clear distinction between itself and other objects: it may find itself immersed in the

world of objects, and to have lost its own subjectivity, even though it may be very conscious and even aggressively definite in saying "I" [I.E., p. 5].

The interior conflict between the real and illusionary self is no less acute for the monk than for the layman.

Nothing is more foreign to authentic monastic and "contemplative" (e.g., Carmelite) tradition in the Church than a kind of gnosticism which would elevate the contemplative above the ordinary Christian by initiating him into a realm of esoteric knowledge and experience, delivering him from the ordinary struggles and sufferings of human existence. . . .[90]

Indeed, the rarefied atmosphere of the monastery heightens the tension. The total corruption of mankind is demonstrated in the exterior self that attempts to manipulate even the spiritual. There is no technique by which the spirit may be appropriated or the inner man released.

The inner self is as secret as God and, like Him, it evades every concept that tries to seize hold of it with full possession. It is a life that cannot be held and studied as object, because it is not "a thing." It is not reached and coaxed forth from hiding by any process under the sun, including meditation. All that we can do with any spiritual discipline is produce within ourselves something of the silence, the humility, the detachment, the purity of heart and the indifference which are required if the inner self is to make some shy, unpredictable manifestation of his presence [I.E., p. 6].

The discipline and order of monastic life are designed to remove the scandal of self, so that the work of God may be effected. The purpose of monastic asceticism is to create an environment conducive to the inspiration of the Spirit.

Just as the monk has been called to abandon the ordinary circumstances of life, so he may also be called to transcend familiar and conventional patterns of religious thought and action. Rigid institutional circumstance may be a form of divine testing with a purpose of spiritual formation. The monk who knows inner turmoil in such a situation must test the spirits. The norms for such testing are "not the standards of books and manuals of piety, but the concrete inspiration of God . . ." [I.E., p. 75]. Merton knew from experience that even religious or monastic activities could be distractions for the contemplative.

> . . . ascetic practices which may be quite useful and even necessary in the active life can become, to persons who have been formed by silence, solitude, and monastic *conversatio*, a real obstacle to further progress. It may well confirm them in attachment to a willful and otiose exercise of their natural faculties and lead them to a morbid obsession with their own psychological reactions.[91]

This is not to suggest he ever denied the value of the monastic desert experience of purgation. Indeed, he feared that much that was worthwhile in the classical tradition was being carelessly abandoned. In one of the addresses on the fatal Asian tour, he expressed this concern. "But we do have to also admit the value of traditional monastic ways. In the West there is now going on a great upheaval in monasticism, and much that is of undying value is being thrown away irresponsibly, foolishly, in favor of things that are superficial and showy, that have no ultimate value."[92] Merton was afraid that the revolution of the sixties might sweep away forms almost sacramental in their import in the name of renewal. Just as theories and practices must not be preserved only because they are old, neither must they be destroyed for that reason. Merton's love for Cistercian simplicity and austerity was offended by the efficiency of many highly organized, profit-oriented contemporary monasteries constructed on a successful business mode. The well-oiled machinery and military regimentation of some of these inhibited contemplation. These developments are contrary to the ancient traditions and reflect an infusion of the Western mass mentality, which equates "its idea of" the work of the Holy Spirit with the common good. Well-meaning but visionless religious politicos have, in some instances, turned the religious life "into a procrustian bed on which potential saints and contemplatives have been so pulled apart and crippled that they have ended their lives as freaks" [I.E., p. 77b]. It is such perversion that has provoked the rebellion that has led to the collapse of many formal structures that were façades for "a traditionalism that was emptied of its truly living traditional content."[93] Unfortunately, the destruction of these structures has often included a "repudiation of genuine tradition, discipline, contemplation."[94] The monastery was far from a spiritual Utopia. The best one could hope for in this world is a community of sinners in the process of being redeemed and transformed.

> Even where the contemplative is not expressly forbidden to follow what he believes to be the inspiration of God . . . he may feel himself continually and completely at odds with the accepted ideals of those around him. Their spiritual exercises may seem to him to be a bore and a waste of time. Their sermons and their conversation may leave him exhausted with a sense of futility. . . . Their choral offices, their excitement over liturgical ceremony and chant, may rob him of the delicate taste of an interior manna that is not found in formulas of prayer and exterior rites. If only he could be alone and quiet, and remain in the emptiness, darkness and purposelessness in which God speaks with such overwhelming effect! But no, spiritual lights and nosegays are forced upon his mind, he must think and say words, he must sing Alleluias that somebody else wants him to feel. . . .

I am told that among certain Near Eastern people it is a mark of honor, at a feast, for the host to give a guest a morsel which he himself has partly chewed. To a contemplative, life in a community dedicated to prayer gets to be this kind of banquet all day long: you are always trying to swallow a dainty that has been chewed first by somebody else. The natural reaction is to spew it out of your mouth. But one does not dare, or if he does he feels intolerable guilt [I.E., pp. 77-78b].

Such notes point to his growing need for literal solitude. To generate and maintain the internal solitude he craved he needed physical insulation. Moreover, Merton thought that in many instances the essence of the monastic tradition was being preserved in paramonastic movements like the beats, hippies, and civil rights and peace movements. Their lives bore prophetic witness and constituted a dramatic renunciation of false values and decadent social patterns. Their personal sacrifices were far greater and, in many cases, more deeply rooted in spiritual values than those of many contemporary monks. On one particular occasion he spoke to the novices of some black visitors who had shared with him their plan to start a kind of ashrama in the inner city of Cleveland. He speculated that this might be the pattern for cenobitic monasticism of the future. But he never reached the point of giving up his own tradition; his formation in Cistercian piety was too deep for him to advocate disobedience. Neither anguish and despair nor useless acts of rebellion are acceptable reactions to stifling institutionalism. The grace of the Holy Spirit is sufficient to support the suffering meekness of the obedient monk.

The contemplative monk is one whose whole life is a continuous prayer for harmony with God. The call of God is to disengagement, detachment from all things in order that he may give himself without reservation, completely to God.

The monk is, or should be, a Christian who is mature enough and decided enough to live without the support and consolation of family, job, ambition, social position or even active mission in the apostolate. He is also mature enough and determined enough to use this freedom for one thing only: the love and praise of God and the love of other men.[95]

According to Merton, man's discovery of freedom and his encounter with God cannot be separated. The question for him is only one of degree. "Our encounter with God should be, at the same time, the discovery of our deepest freedom. If we never encounter him, our freedom never really develops."[96] God and self exist, together at the center of being. God's grace and Himself are experienced within. This is the experience of Ruysbroeck's "superessential" life, which is the life of the true contemplative.

Now the grace of God, pouring forth from God, is an inward thrust and urge of the Holy Ghost, driving forth our spirit from within, and exciting it towards all virtues. This grace flows from within, and not from without; for God is more inward to us than we are to ourselves, and His inward thrust or working within us, be it natural or supernatural, is nearer to us and more intimate to us, than our own working is. And therefore God works in us from within outwards; but all creatures work from without inwards. And thus it is that grace, and all the gifts of God, and the Voice of God, come from within, in the unity of our spirit; and not from without, into the imagination, by means of sensible images.[97]

Implicit here is the classical doctrine of infused contemplation to which Merton subscribed vigorously. No external work of the individual can penetrate the hiddenness of God. Even when one succeeds in boring into his inward being, his own efforts can bring him only into a void.

If you succeed in emptying your mind of every thought and every desire, you may indeed withdraw into the center of yourself and concentrate everything within you upon the imaginary point where your life springs out of God: yet you will not really find God. No natural exercise can bring you into vital contact with Him. Unless He utters Himself in you, speaks His own name in the center of your soul, you will no more know Him than a stone knows the ground upon which it rests in its inertia.[98]

Although the divine life exists within all men, not all men are conscious of it. Christians, even, are not all aware of the presence of the indwelling Christ to the same degree. Some men have been given a special grace that impels them to desire and seek a more conscious realization of the union with God, which has been effected by Christ and exists within them. The "hound of heaven" is on our trail, but we run with all of our energy in the wrong directions. The difficult thing to do is to stop and let ourselves be found. One is overwhelmed when he discovers he has been found, and in the process he comes to know the One by whom he has been found and is known. Where did He come from? Bernard of Clairvaux recorded his awe at this mystery.

By what way then did He enter? Can it be that He did not enter at all, because He did not come from outside? For He is not come of the things, that are without. Yet again, He did not come from within me, for He is good, and I know that *no good thing dwelleth in me*. I have gone up to the highest that I have, and behold, the Word was towering yet higher. My curiosity took me to my lowest depth to look for Him, nevertheless He was found still deeper. If I looked outside me, I found He was beyond my farthest; if I looked within, He was more inward still.[99]

The mind is boggled by the incomprehensibility of the person that is the experience. God is with us but ever before us; in us but beyond us. The Christian does not seek to be swallowed up in the divine, but he does want to be submerged in Him. To enter into the "heart" is to penetrate "the deepest psychological ground of one's personality, the inner sanctuary where self-awareness goes beyond analytical reflection and opens out into metaphysical and neopogical confrontation with the Abyss of the unknown yet present—one who is 'more intimate to us than we are to ourselves'!"[100] Again we are struck by the reality that He is both subject and object. The contemplative does not deal with ideas or concepts (except as they may serve as points of focus directing attention beyond himself). Spiritual progress fuels the desire for one objective, union with God. "We do not reason about dogmas of faith, or 'the mysteries.' We seek rather to gain a direct existential grasp, a personal experience of the deepest truths of life and faith, finding ourselves in God's truth."[101] The infinite absolute cannot be grasped or bound by human intelligence. The ineffable defies expression in human language. He cannot be verified by a laboratory test or checked against mathematical equations. The man who knows God in the full biblical and mystical sense loses interest in divine or self-objectification.

> I want to make it quite clear that the whole essence of contemplative prayer is that the division between subject and object disappears. You do not look at God as an object and you don't look at yourself as an object. You don't stand back and look at yourself, you are just not interested in yourself.[102]

Merton is resolute in his assertion that man can only clear away the obstacles and predispose himself for this union. Union is effected by God himself and remains always a mystery to the man.

> The monastic life has always had something of this element of "exploration" about it (at least in periods when it has been *alive*). The monk is a man who, in

one way or other, pushes to the very frontiers of
human experience and strives to go beyond, to find
out what transcends the ordinary level of existence.
Aware that man is somehow sustained by a deep mystery of silence, of incomprehensibility—of God's will
and God's love—the monk feels that he is personally
called to live in more intimate communication with
that mystery.[103]

This does not mean that there are no positive aspects to
the mystical experience. Although it cannot be reduced to
logical formulation or adequately expressed symbolically,
there is a conscious awareness of God, though it is ever
tenuous and tinged with doubt. It is futile for a man to
insist on a logical formulation of the process or the experience. It is not a matter of a theology of light or darkness,
affirmation or negation, immanence or transcendence. It is
"both," "either-or," and "neither-nor." It is faith and
hope; assurance and doubt.

> Does this knowledge admit of any doubt?
> Yes and no. On the conceptual level, where logic
> and rationality are in command, it may admit of
> doubt. In fact it may perhaps admit of nothing else
> but doubt. It is so unrelated to reason as to seem per-
> haps irrational. But on another level it admits of no
> doubt. What is this other level? It is a level of imme-
> diate intuition, in which an experience impresses itself
> upon us directly without ambiguity—a level on which
> we "experience" reality as we experience our own
> being. One does not have to prove that he exists: he
> knows it. He may doubt his ability to convince an-
> other of the fact. But one does not trouble to prove
> the obvious. Contemplative experience has about it an
> obviousness that is not arrived at through any step-by-
> step process. It is something you either "see" or don't
> see. It just bursts upon you, and is there [I.E., pp.
> 78–79].

This paradox extends to the creation of conditions conducive to the ultimate experience. Man's participation is both active and passive, but the control does not lie with him. At some point the reins are surrendered. Merton marshals strong support from classical mystical literature for his description of a passive state as prerequisite to an experience of infused contemplation. He cites his old ally John of the Cross, and buttresses John's testimony with that of John Ruysbroeck, the English anonymous treatise "The Cloud of Unknowing," Meister Eckhart, and Bernard of Clairvaux. Man's intelligence is incapable of comprehending God.

> Endeavor then when the soul is reaching this state to detach it from all coveting of spiritual sweetness, pleasure and delight and meditation, and disturb it not with care or solicitude of any kind for higher things, still less for lower things, but bring it into the greatest possible degree of solitude and withdrawal. For the more the soul attains of all this and the sooner it reaches this restful tranquility, the more abundantly does it become infused with the spirit of divine wisdom, which is the loving, tranquil, lonely, peaceful, sweet inebriator of the spirit. Hereby the soul feels itself to be gently and tenderly wounded and ravished, *knowing not by whom, nor whence, nor how*. And the reason for this is that *the Spirit communicates Himself without any act on the part of the soul.* [John of the Cross, *The Living Flame of Love*.] This purity is the dwelling place of God within us, nor can any but God alone act upon it. It is eternal, and in it is neither time nor place, neither before nor after: but it is ever present, ready and manifest to such pure minds as may be raised up into it. In it we are all one, living in God and God in us. This simple unity is ever clear and manifest to the intellectual eyes when turned in upon the purity of the mind. It is a pure and serene air, luccent with divine light; and

it is given to us to discover, fix and contemplate eternal truth with purified and illuminated eyes. Therein all things are one form and become a single truth, a single image in the mirror of the wisdom of God: and when we look upon and practice it in the divine light with these same simple and spiritual eyes, then have we attained to the contemplative life (John Ruysbroeck, *The Seven Steps of the Ladder of Spiritual Love*). But now you put a question to me asking: "How shall I think about Him, and what is He?" And to this I can only answer you, "I do not know." With your question you have brought me into that same darkness and into that same cloud of unknowing into which I would wish you to be in yourself. Through grace a man can have great knowledge of all other creatures and their works, and even of the works of God himself, and he can think of them all; but of God Himself no man can think. *I would therefore leave all those things of which I can think and choose for my love that thing of which I cannot think.*

And why is this so? He may well be loved, but He may not be thought of. He may be reached and held close by means of love, but by means of thought, never. And therefore even though it is good occasionally to think of the kindness and the great worth of God in particular aspects, and even though it is a joy that is a proper part of contemplation, nevertheless in this work it should be cast down and covered with a cloud of forgetting.

You are to step above it with great courage and with determination and with a devout and pleasing stirring of love, and you are to try to pierce that darkness which is above you. You are to strike that thick cloud of unknowing with a sharp dart of longing love; and you are not to retreat no matter what comes to pass (*The Cloud of Unknowing*, Ch. VI, trans. Ira Progoff, p. 72). Take care not to imagine that in this union of the Word with the soul we believe there to be some bodily element. . . . This union is in the spirit, because God is a Spirit. . . . The Spouse receives Him by a special gift in her inmost heart, coming down from heaven, and all at once possesses Him whom she desires, not under any definite form but obscurely infused; not appearing clearly but making His presence felt; and doubtless all the more delightful in that His presence is secret, and does not appear outwardly. This Word comes not sounding but penetrating; not speaking, but acting on the soul; not beating upon the ear but blandishing the heart. This is a Face that has no form, but impresses a form upon the soul; not striking the eyes of the body but making glad the countenance of the heart. (Bernard of Clairvaux, Sermon 31, *In Cantica*, n. 6). Know then that God is present at all times in good people and that there is a Something in the soul in which God dwells. There is also a Something by which the soul lives in God, but when the soul is intent on external things that Something dies, and therefore God does, as far as that soul is concerned. . . . The father speaks through this noble agent (the Something) and says to His only-begotten Son: "Get up, young man!" Thus God—and the unity of God with the soul—is so complete as to seem incredible, since He is so high Himself as to be beyond the reach of intelligence. Nevertheless this agent reaches farther than heaven, yes, farther than the angels. . . . We want to reach far—far beyond measure—and yet we find that all that is to be understood or to be desired is still not God, *but that where mind and desire end, in that darkness, God shines.* [*Meister Eckhart: A Modern Translation*, trans. Raymond B. Blakney (New York: Harper & Brothers, 1957), p. 133.]

These texts interlace Merton's discussion and argument on these points.

Like Moses on Mount Sinai, the mystic is blinded by the perfect holiness of God. The knowledge of God is an experience of love. According to Merton, ". . . we can . . . *attain directly to Him by love,* and we do in fact realize obscurely in contemplation that by love we 'reach Him and hold Him close'" [I.E., p. 80]. The attraction of love is such that the contemplative will endure the ordeal of God's apparent absence and the experience of existential dread in order to have that moment of intimacy, alone with the Alone. The perseverance of one who finds himself in the belly of the whale is a sign that he is being drawn by God Himself.

> The mere fact of seeking Him blindly, undauntedly, in spite of dryness, in spite of the apparent hopelessness and irrationality of the quest, is then the first sign that this pre-experiential contemplation may be infused. Another sign would be the forgetfulness of ordinary cares and of the routine level of life, in the darkness of prayer. Though the contemplative seeking for God may seem in a way quite senseless, yet in the depths of our soul it makes a great deal of sense, while on the other hand the seemingly rational preoccupations and projects of normal life now appear to be quite meaningless. This is important, because as a matter of fact a quite similar sense of meaninglessness is now prevalent everywhere, and more or less affects every intelligent man. Not that everyone who feels the futility of life is *ipso facto* a contemplative. But the fact that secular existence has begun to clearly manifest its own meaninglessness to everyone with eyes to see, enables all sensitive and intelligent people to experience something akin to one of the phases of pre-contemplative purification. . . .
>
> Finally, a third sign that pre-experiential contemplation may have an infused character is the very definite and powerful sense of attraction which holds the soul prisoner in mystery. Although the soul is filled with a sense of affliction and defeat, *it has no desire to escape from this aridity.* . . .
>
> Sometimes this attraction is so powerful that it can-

cels out all the suffering felt by the soul, which counts
its own pain and helplessness as nothing and becomes
totally absorbed in this inexplicable desire for peace
which it thinks can somehow be found in solitude
and darkness . . . [I.E., p. 83].

The experience of union is a transforming one affecting
every particle of one's being, every attitude, every act. All
that has passed for knowledge and love is blown away; the
new man is a reality.

> The soul has entered a new world, a world of rich ex-
> perience that transcends the level of all other knowl-
> edge and all other love.
>   From then on its whole life is transformed, al-
> though externally sufferings and difficulties and
> labours may be multiplied, the soul's interior life has
> become completely simple. It consists of one thought,
> one preoccupation, one love: GOD ALONE. . . . It
> is perfect prayer, perfect worship. It is pure and sim-
> ple love, that love which, as St. Bernard says, draws
> and absorbs every other activity of the soul into itself:
> "Amor caeteros in se omnes traducit et captivat
> affectus" (Sermon 83, In Cantica.). This love, in-
> fused into the soul by God, unifies all its powers and
> raises them up to Him, separating its desires and
> affections more and more from the world and from
> perishing things. Without realizing it, the soul makes
> rapid progress and becomes free, virtuous and strong:
> but it does not consider itself. It has no eyes for any-
> thing or anyone but God alone.
>   It has entered into the mystery of the spiritual life,
> the illuminative way, and is being drawn on towards
> complete union with God [I.E., p. 84].

This is the particularization of the resurrection motif. In
union with God that is symbolized in baptism is realized
in the "final integration" of human personality; Paul's carnal man, temporal man, is transformed into spiritual man.

The idea of "rebirth" and of life as a "new man in Christ, in the Spirit," of a "risen life" in the mystery of Christ or in the Kingdom of God, is fundamental to Christian theology and practice—it is after all the whole meaning of baptism. All the more so is this idea central to that peculiar refinement of the theology of baptism which is the monastic *conversatio* —the vocation to a life especially dedicated to self-renewal, liberation from all sin, and the transformation of one's entire mentality "in Christ."[104]

There is a sense in which the monastery or hermitage is a tomb and at the same time a womb. "Seen from the viewpoint of monastic tradition, the pattern of disintegration, existential moratorium and reintegration on a higher, universal level, is precisely what the monastic life is meant to provide."[105] Merton borrows a description of the spiritual man and the totality of the transformation, "whether he eats or drinks or whatever else he does, does all for the glory of God" (1 Co. 10:31). Such a person is free to act "freely, simply, spontaneously, from the depths of his heart, moved by love."[106] The preoccupation of Merton's life became simply to turn "to Him daily and often, preferring His will and His mystery to everything that is evidently and tangibly mine."[107] To be free is to be transformed by God and to have His love and the love of His new creation become identical. The office of the contemplative is "to go beyond death even in this life . . . to be . . . a witness to life. . . ."[108] The contemplative must ever remain alert, moving upward, sloughing off the old man. The struggle of Jacob with the angel is the archetype for the spiritual ascent (Gn. 32:24–29). The battle is not with God but with the exterior self. The power of God's love is sufficient to overcome the adversary and to transform Jacob into Israel, "He who sees God."

The struggle is not an easy one, and it takes its toll in the human economy.

The battle is with "man" and yet it is with God, for it is the battle of our exterior self with the interior self, the "agent" which is the likeness of God in our soul and which appears at first sight to be utterly opposed to the only self we know. It is the battle of our own strength, lodged in the exterior self, with the strength of God which is the life and actuality of our interior self. And in the battle, which takes place in the darkness of night, the angel, the inner self, wounds a nerve in our thigh so that afterwards we limp. Our natural powers are restricted and crippled. . . . Yet we have power over our antagonist to the extent that though we cannot overcome him, yet we do not let him go until he blesses us. This power is more than our own strength, it is the power of love, and it secretly comes from within, from the antagonist Himself. . . . It is the power by which he is "reached and held close" according to the *Cloud of Unknowing*. It makes us "strong against God" and merits for us a new name, Israel, which means "He who sees God." And this new name is what makes us contemplatives—it is a new being and a new capacity for experience. Yet when we ask the name of our antagonist we cannot know it, for even our own inmost self is unknown, just as God Himself is unknown [I.E., p. 88].

The results more than compensate for the pain. A new name is appropriate for the new man. This new being shares in the very essence of God, love.

The true contemplative is not one who has the most exalted visions of the Divine Essence but one who is most closely united to God in faith and love and allows himself to be absorbed and transformed into Him by the Holy Ghost. To such a soul everything becomes a source and occasion of love [I.E., p. 93].

Merton illustrates this new relationship to the world with a metaphor from Bernard, "Even as the bee extracts from all plants the honey that is in them and has no use for them for aught else save for that purpose, even so the soul with great facility extracts the sweetness of love that is in all things that pass through it. IT LOVES GOD IN EACH OF THEM, WHETHER PLEASANT OR UN-PLEASANT" [I.E., p. 93].

One must guard against self-deception with regard to the contemplative experience. An ever-present danger in the life of the contemplative is the intrusion of a narcissis-tic preoccupation with self. The end of such a detour is a self-indulgence that is indifferent to others. Such an atti-tude is a religious twin to the hyperindividualism of self-centered materialism. It is a form of religious fundamen-talism, that focuses on personal salvation and ignores the human family.

> Now it is easy to understand that an unwise and manichean type of asceticism can give a person a pathological attitude towards reality. In such case there is great danger of his becoming a pseudo-mystic who flees into his own inner darkness and tries to wall himself up inside his own silence. There he seeks to enjoy the false sweetness of a narcissistic seclusion, and does indeed enjoy it for a while until he learns too late that he has poisoned himself with the fruit of a tree that is forbidden [I.E., p. 105].

Merton labels such pseudocontemplation as idolatry as seductive as any imaginable, with ruin an almost inevita-ble end. A lack of concern for the world or an inability to "bear the burden of others" and share in their suffering is a sign that one shares neither the mind nor the heart of God.

The curriculum of monastic life was designed to liberate a man from fixation upon himself, freeing him to cherish the divine image in others. "The place of the mystic and the prophet in the twentieth century is not totally outside of society, not utterly remote from the world."[109] The monk is something of a sacrament in that he should be a witness to the possibility of freedom. He is a martyr who lays down his life as a sign of hope to man crushed and alienated by the senselessness and injustice of a society with splendid hopes but also with agonizing problems. The monk's life is a comment on the superficiality of contemporary secularity. ". . . the monk's chief service to the world [is]: this silence, this listening, this questioning, this humble and courageous exposure to what the world ignores about itself—both good and evil."[110] His life can be a mirror that reflects what is true and what is false in the world. The monk empties himself that God may be seen through his transparency.

The benefits of contemplation are not the exclusive possession of those who have put on the monk's cowl. Life in the industrialized West is like living in a pressure cooker. In such a society, quiet and stillness have become luxuries. Forests and parks throughout the United States become weekend and summer metropolises as Americans flee the concrete and steel of the city, seeking some peace. Church camps and retreats have becomes a regular part of American church life. However, the true seeker can establish a modified contemplative existence for himself in the urban manswarm. Time and again Merton made the point that contemplation is not synonymous with any "place." Even monasteries frequently become beehives of useless activity —not to be excused by the fact that it is religious activity.[111] On the other hand, a man may have inner peace and be an authentic contemplative in the heart of Manhattan. It is not easy, but it can be done if one is willing to pay the price and adopt poverty for Christ's sake. Merton noted two requirements:

> First he must as far as possible reduce the conflict and frustration in his life by cutting down his contact with the "world" and his secular subjections. This means reducing his needs for pleasure, comfort, recreation, prestige and success, and embracing a life of true spiritual poverty and detachment. Secondly, he must learn to put up with the inevitable conflicts that

remain—the noise, the agitation, the crowding, the lack of time, and above all the constant contact with a purely secular mentality which is all around us everywhere and at all times, even to some extent in monasteries [I.E., p. 131].

The determining factor is one's relationship to the world, in particular to systems and things. Support groups can be formed to function in the role of the monastic community. Participation in the liturgy and meditation on the Scriptures assist in focusing the attention and directing the energies of those who would grow in "the grace and knowledge of our Lord Jesus Christ." Merton believed that the monasteries should function as schools of the spirit, accepting groups and helping to form them into spiritual cells. He suggested five possibilities for groups interested in experiencing the grace of contemplation:

1. A move to the country or a small town might offer a slower pace, with time for spiritual pursuits with no apparent utilitarian value. An isolated job such as that of a forest ranger might be an alternative for a few.

2. Recognize and use those parts of the day that the world does not value. The early morning hours probably offer the most opportune period for peace and solitude.

3. Sunday might be restored to the dignity of the "Lord's Day" and used as a special opportunity for meditating on the "mystery of the resurrection."

4. A spiritual discipline should be adopted, but the possibilities in the secular world are limited, and such a person should accept the fact and live with the fact that he or she will most likely remain a "hidden contemplative."

5. The married Christian should recognize that the very nature of nuptial love makes it a sacred and symbolic act. His marriage must be an integral part of the contemplative experiment.[112]

Merton applauded the "active contemplatives" who have penetrated the secular world to bear witness to the love of God as they have experienced it.

The most significant development of the contemplative life "in the world" is the growth of small groups of men and women who live in every way like the lay-people [sic] around them, except for the fact that they are dedicated to God, and focus all their life of work and poverty upon a contemplative center. Such is the life of the Fraternities of the Little Brothers of Jesus, the most typical of twentieth-century innovations in the contemplative life. The Little Brothers do not form a religious Order in the strict sense of the word. They have no special religious habit, they do not live in enclosed monasteries. Though some of them are priests, they do not exercise a formal apostolic ministry among the faithful, do not have parishes or missions. Priests and brothers alike wear ordinary civilian clothing, and work at ordinary jobs, in factories or on farms, availing themselves of the normal opportunities for work open to the poor among whom they live. . . . They seek only to *be* with them, to share their lives, their poverty, their sufferings, their problems, their ideals: but to be with them in a special way. For as members of Christ, they *are* Christ. And where they are present, Christ is present. Where He is present, He acts. Their being, their presence, is then active, dynamic. It is the leaven hidden in the measure of meal. This of course is a strictly contemplative view of the Christian life, and unless it implies a complete sacrifice of oneself, of all one's ambitions and worldly desires, it cannot be effective [I.E., pp. 138–39].

The contemplative life, regardless of its environs, is essentially a life of unity. "A contemplative is one who has transcended divisions to reach a unity beyond division" (I.E., p. 143). Contemplation does not necessarily imply abstraction or withdrawal.

The true contemplative is not less interested than others in normal life, not less concerned with what goes on in the world, but *more* interested, more concerned. The fact that he is a contemplative makes him capable of a greater interest and of a deeper concern [I.E., p. 144].

The contemplative has discovered himself in the dialectical movement of history, and he enters into conscious dialogue with history. By entering into God, he enters into history, for God is the interior of history.

For the Christian too has a mystique of history. He too is committed by his faith to a contemplative view of man, in which history is oriented to a final discovery and revelation of Man in God and God in Man at the *Parousia*. And a rediscovery of the inner meaning of the New Testament may perhaps startle him with the realization that this revelation of the Mystery of God and Man in Christ, the Mystical Body, is not something we can passively anticipate. It is something that we are called to *bring about by the action of our creative freedom* [I.E., p. 145].

The new man is a part of the new creation. The transformation of a single man is a sign of the coming transformation of the whole universe. A contemplative is a person who has taken seriously the words attributed to Jesus by the writer of Matthew that one should not be concerned about the material needs of life and should not fret about an earthly existence that shall fade away; rather should the Christian "seek first his kingdom and his righteousness, and all things shall be yours. . . ."

It is precisely because the Christian view of history has lost too many of its contemplative and mystical elements, that it has become something inert and passive, a mere reactionary obscurantism that tolerates injustice and abuse on earth for the sake of a compensation in the afterlife. Marxism pours scorn on this kind of religion, and takes advantage of its deficiencies to caricature it without mercy. In this way the Marxist is able to steal from Christianity one of its most potent and characteristic claims: that it has come to divinize the freedom and the spirit of man. Christians, hearing this for the first time, forgetting that their baptism is a new birth as children of God, with a vocation to the highest creative responsibilities, have not understood the hidden implications of this claim make blasphemous only by its separation from its true context. . . .

All this is to say that Christian contemplation cannot consist merely in a dark withdrawal into subjective peace, without reference to the rest of the world. A contemplation that merely hides in subjectivity and individualism is a by-product of the bourgeois spirituality we have discussed above. It is a comfortable negation of the life which is not really a negation of anything but only an evasion of responsibility in order to enjoy interior comfort [I.E., p. 146].

It would be wrong to react against this with sheer activism. That is the danger of the more extreme endeavors that have attempted to integrate Christianity into working-class movements. They have allowed themselves to be carried away by political delusions and have put more trust in the words and tactics of pressure-groups than in the Spirit of God. But this is precisely the age-old temptation of the People of God, the idolatry that was lashed by Moses and the Prophets, the hardness of heart that called forth Christ's tears over Jerusalem [I.E., pp. 146–47].

The contemplative's life is his profession of faith, and words should not really be necessary to explain or convey it. He seeks no kind of mastery except the mastery of self, no kind of knowledge except the intuitive knowledge of God at the depths of the contemplative's being. All else is superfluous. The life of prayer establishes contact with the source of all life and with the only source of authentic peace. The contemplative life has no inherent value but derives its importance from its sign value, its revelation of the possibility of freedom.

> . . . freedom is a spiritual thing. It is a sacred and re-
> ligious reality. Its roots are not in man, but in God.
> For man's freedom, which makes him the image of
> God, is a participation in the freedom of God. Man is
> free insofar as he is like God. His struggle for freedom
> means then a struggle to renounce a false, illusory au-
> tonomy, in order to become free beyond and above
> himself. In other words, for man to be free he must
> be delivered *from himself*. . . .
>
> Before there can be any external freedom, man
> must learn to find the way to freedom within himself.
> For only then can he afford to relax his grip on others,
> and let them get away from him because then he does
> not need their dependence. It is the contemplative
> who keeps this liberty alive in the world, and who
> shows others, obscurely, and without realizing it, what
> real freedom means [I.E., pp. 148–49].

The new man, the free man is the man whose whole life is theonomous, whose life is dominated by the spirit as op-posed to human reason or sentimentality. The trans-formation is effected by the recovery of the lost image of God.

CHRISTOLOGY

A crucial question to be directed to the Christian mystic who seeks an immediate, direct experience of the Absolute is, "What is the meaning of the Christ, and what role does He play in the mystical experience?" Merton's works are not saturated with orthodox discourses on the person and nature of Christ, or, for that matter, with any ex-tended discourses on Christ's nature. But to fault Merton too strongly for this omission would be like condemning the works of a medieval theologian for not including long discussions of the "problem of God." The medieval theologian had no "God problem," and implicit in Merton's work is an a priori assumption of Christ as the foundation and model for mystical theology. "The Inner Experience" provides the most complete statement of Merton's Christology, although other works include important allusions, which will be interspersed in this discussion.

The preoccupation of the early Fathers with the nature of Christ was essential to the development of Christianity. Had they not focused on this fundamental problem, the results would have been disastrous for Christian spiritual life. Merton contends that Christ is the means of union with God, and, if He is not God, all hopes of union are in vain; "all mystical experience is communicated to men through the man Christ."[113]

Christ is the new Adam in whom the original divine image of man is restored and the possibility of the natural divinization of man recovered.

> One of the main reasons why St. Athanasius so stubbornly defended the divinity of Christ against the Arians . . . was that he saw that if Christ were not God, then it followed that the Christian hope for union with God in and through Christ was a delusion. Everything, as St. Paul himself had declared equivalently, depended on faith in Christ as the true Son of God, the World Incarnate. "For if Christ be not risen again then our preaching is vain, and your faith also is vain. Yea and also we are found false witnesses of God, because we have given testimony against God" [1 Co. 15:14–15].
>
> It may perhaps not be clear at first sight what this belief in the Resurrection might have to do with contemplation. But in fact the Resurrection and Ascension of Christ, the New Adam, completely restored human nature to its spiritual condition and made possible the divinization of every man coming into the world [I.E., p. 36].

The perfect blending of the divine and human in Jesus makes possible the transformation of all men into true sons of God. Jesus is the uttered Word who breaks through the silence of alienation.

> If the Word emerged from the depths of the unknowable mystery of the Father "whom no man hath seen at any time," it was not merely in order to have mankind cast itself down at His feet. He came to be a man like ourselves, and, in His own Person, to unite man to God. As a result of this union of God and Man in the one Person of Christ it was possible for every man to be united to God in his own person, as a true son of God, not by nature but by adoption [I.E., p. 37].

Merton does not subscribe to a theory of transactional atonement. Christ's mission was to reveal God to man and to reveal to man his own potential for life.

> If the "Son of Man came to seek and to save that which was lost" this was not merely in order to re-establish man in a favorable juridical position with regard to God: it was to elevate, change and transform man into God, in order that God might be revealed in man, and that all men might become One Son of God in Christ [I.E., p. 37].

Christ was the perfect "God-conscious" man whose transparence allowed God to shine through as perfect love. In Christ, man has a dramatic portrayal of human transcendence effected by the actualization of being. There is no excuse for man's continuing alienation and fragmentation; all things can be reconciled in Christ, including human and divine natures.

> If in Christ the assumed human nature, which is in every respect literally and perfectly human, belongs to the Person of the Word of God, then everything

human in Christ is by that very fact divine. . . . In Him, we see a Man in every respect identical with ourselves as far as His nature is concerned, thinking and feeling and acting according to our nature, and yet at the very same time living on a completely transcendent and divine level of consciousness and of being. For His consciousness and His being are the consciousness and being of God Himself. Of course, the Living Christ, now enthroned at the right hand of the Father in eternity (according to the metaphorical language of the Scriptures) is indeed in a state of being in which He lived on this earth. Though the two natures were not confused in any way, they were still completely one in Him, as completely as our own body and Soul are one in us [I.E., p. 38].

The function of the Christian life is to move toward the completion of that work begun in the believer by the Spirit, metamorphosis from man to spiritual man—divinization. The universal was particularized in Christ, but that particularization must be personally appropriated, actualized in each of us. Jesus made God present to us; the cosmic Christ makes God present in us. Christ is our theology-incarnate in us. Merton shared with Paul a belief that Christ is God's agent of creation, and it is He in whom "all things hold together." In Jesus Christ, all things are supernaturalized and are being transformed.

He not only says that we will be transformed, but that *we are being transformed*. The degree and intensity of our transformation depends precisely on our union with the Holy Spirit, on the purity of the image with us.[114]

Man is called to a higher nature and is to cast off any aspect of his being that is ignoble and unworthy of being divinized. Our vocation is not merely the imitation of Christ, but also to become Christ and reproduce as much as possible the life of Christ on earth. Without qualification, Merton categorically affirms that contemplation "is a deep participation in the Christ-life, a spiritual sharing in the union of God and Man which is the hypostatic union" (I.E., p. 41). Merton's theology and anthropology are synthesized in his incarnational Christology. Christians are "the Second Adam," he says, "because we ourselves are Christ."[115]

The image of God is potentially complete and whole in every individual soul. The destination that lures the mystic through darkness and poverty of spirit is the consummation of the mystical formation in which the subject and object become one and the disciple is perfectly conformed to the Master. "We will be 'the New Man' who is, in fact, one Man—the One Christ, Head and Members."[116] The mystic meditates on Jesus and the images of Him stirred by the historical witness because he is what the mystic believes he is becoming. The Christian mystic stakes his existence on the veracity of the witness of the evangelist that the Father and Son are one, that He is the dispeller of darkness, and that those who believe are given the power to become sons of God.

Merton found in the Gospel of John texts he interpreted as affirming the mystery of the perfection of the Christian through the indwelling Christ.

> These texts are clear enough. . . . Christian contemplation is based on faith in this mystery. If Christ came into the world as the Son of God, and if the Father was present in Him: if Christ has left the world and gone to the Father, how do we "see" Him, or bridge the gap that remains between us and the transcendental remoteness of His mystery in heaven? The answer is that the Word, in the Father, is not only transcendentally removed at an infinite distance above us, but also and at the same time He is immanent in our World, first of all by nature as the Creator of the world, but then in a special dynamic and mystical presence as the Savior, Redeemer and Lover of the

world . . . in order to become the sons of God we
have to receive Christ, then how do we receive
Christ? The answer is, *by faith* . . . not simply by an
intellectual assent to certain authoritative dogmatic
propositions, but . . . by *the commitment of our
whole self and of our whole life to the reality of the
presence of Christ in the world*. This act of total surrender is not simply a fantastic intellectual and mystical gamble . . . it is an act of love for this unseen Person who, in the very gift of love by which we
surrender ourselves to His reality, also makes himself
present to us. The union of our mind, spirit, and life
with the Word present within us is effected by the
Holy Spirit" [I.E., p. 41–42].

This is a mystery that defies human science but points
to the consummation of creation as all things are drawn
back into their source. The mystic is not infrequently
charged with pantheism, but panentheism more accurately
depicts immanent transcendence. It is in and through
Christ the Holy Spirit that one is transformed in Christ.
The New Testament makes clear (Jn. 16:7, 14; 1 Co. 2:7,
10–12; 1 Jn. 2:20, 27) that the Holy Spirit, *Donum Dei
altissimi*, is given "as a personal principle of love and activity in the supernatural order, transforming us in Christ"
(I.E., p. 43). It is the dynamic spirit of Christ that in-
sures the nontemporality of the Gospel. It is the spirit
that clears the mind's eye, enabling the contemplative to
be incarnated with the *Zeitgeist* of his epoch in history.
The light of the Spirit instills in man the capacity for discerning what is authentic in the characteristic movements
of his age, e.g., in the seventies some which might be considered are the so-called "third-world," the Jesus movement, the youth rebellion. The Christian absorbs into
himself that which is real and universal and synthesizes
it in a form that transcends transient cultures and political
entities.

In the revision of *Seeds of Contemplation* that appeared

in 1961, Merton was extremely explicit in stating that there is no way station along the mystic course where one graduates from a need for Christ. "No one can dismiss the Man Christ from his interior life on the pretext that he has now entered by higher contemplation into direct communication with the Word."[117] His stress on Christ as the heart of the Christian life and only focal point for the Christian contemplative never diminished. The centrality of Christ in Christian experience was the central focus of an address to a group of nuns delivered at Calcutta on the first leg of the Asian journey. Christ is the ruler of the kingdom of the heart, whose power lies not in force or law but in love. The Christian is defined by the love of Christ. The Christian's worth is affirmed not by any talent he has nor by any act he performs, but by the fact that he is loved by Christ. In return for this love, He expects nothing more than that the subject love Him and all mankind. A general letter written by Merton to his "friends" from New Delhi only a month before his death closes with the comment that his contacts in Asia had deepened his sense of consolation in his faith in Christ and in the inward presence of Christ. He concluded with a statement of his hope in Christ, "for in my contacts with these new friends I also feel consolation in my own faith in Christ and His indwelling presence."[118]

WEST MEETS EAST

The Merton of *The Seven Storey Mountain* was a Catholic bigot with disdain for other expressions of Christianity as well as for other religions. His language suggested a lack of respect, if not outright disgust, for Protestantism. By 1966, in an apology to non-believers, he cited the openness of Christians to others as a hopeful sign of religious renewal. True catholicity requires a willingness to enter into a lived, theological dialectic and a free dialogue with all that is true and humane in every culture. "I will be a better Catholic," he wrote in *Conjectures of a Guilty Bystander*, "not if I can *refute* every shade of Protes-

tantism, but if I can affirm the truth in it and still go further. So, too, with Muslims, the Hindus, the Buddhists,
etc."[119] Merton's consciousness of the grace of God and the
efficacious life of Christ had by the sixties expanded to
cosmic proportions. It was now a guarded, qualified admission in 1961, that "God lives in the souls of men who are
unconscious of Him,"[120] and only a few years later, it
had become a confident declaration: "Every man at some
point in his life encounters God, and many who are not
Christians have responded to God better than Christians."[121] Merton's experience of God had magnified to
such an extent that to confine His reality, grace, and love
to a spiritual ghetto would be tantamount to primitive
henotheism. Moreover, Merton's understanding of the
unity of reality led him to the idea that he could apprehend this reality only as it was particularized and per-
sonalized in him.

> If I can unite *in myself* the thought and the devotion
> of Eastern and Western Christendom, the Greek and
> the Latin Fathers, the Russians with the Spanish mys-
> tics, I can prepare in myself the reunion of divided
> Christians. From that secret and unspoken unity in
> myself can eventually come a visible and manifest
> unity of all Christians. If we want to bring together
> what is divided, we can not do so by imposing one di-
> vision upon the other or absorbing one division into
> the other. But if we do this, the union is not Chris-
> tian. It is political, and doomed to further conflict.
> We must contain all divided worlds in ourselves and
> transcend them in Christ.[122]

Merton had fought desperately to be a good Thomist
and to conform himself to the Scholastic tradition, which
he had thought during his early training was Catholic
truth; in a sense, this had been his own Jacobian bout
with the angel. The problem for him at that time was the
problem that blurs the vision of many earnest spiritual pil-

THE DESERT OF THE HEART 191

grims: the problem of a preconceived idea of God and truth.

> The earnest seeker after truth has usually decided in advance what kind of truth he is looking for. That is to say, his views are dictated in advance by the needs of the illusory image he has constructed of himself. In his estimate of other people and of their ideas, truth will be manipulated to correspond with his estimate of himself.[123]

Merton's reversal on the issue of those religions that he had earlier facilely dismissed as "pantheism" was another stage in his ongoing conversion. His change of mind with regard to the higher religions was not the result of tedious comparison and contrast or even concerted analysis. It was an outgrowth of his experience of the Absolute.

> Since in practice we must admit that God is in no way limited in His gifts, and since there is no reason to think that He cannot impart His light to other men without first consulting us, there can be no absolutely solid grounds for denying the possibility of supernatural (private) revelation and of supernatural mystical graces to individuals, no matter where they may be or what may be their religious tradition, provided that they sincerely seek God and His truth. Nor is there any a priori basis for denying that the great prophetic and religious figures of Islam, Hinduism, Buddhism, etc., could have been mystics, in the true, that is, supernatural, sense of the word.[124]

A quarter century of monastic experience and study of the monastic tradition brought him to see certain universal characteristics "common to solitaries and recluses in all ages and in all cultures."[125] He had come to the realization that Christian truth is not propositional but personal. It is not something to be learned and possessed by a devout votary but by someone who knows and possesses his creation. Mystical experience is that single intuition *given* by God and uniting all creeds and doctrines in the presence of Light.

Merton was a member of that rather large contingent of Christians who have tremendous admiration for what they see as Christian virtues in the life of Gandhi. As Merton's contact with non-Christian monks increased, his suspicions about the implicit Christianity in their religious experience were confirmed. The sincerity and truth of the Eastern religious quest was embodied in the persons he encountered. In his description of his first meeting with D. T. Suzuki, Merton said he felt as if he had met the "True Man of No Title," about whom the Zen masters speak. Merton's tone was joyful as he recalled his feeling that he had arrived at his own home. Merton was deeply moved by the depth and spirituality of the Vietnamese Buddhist poet-monk Nhat Hanh, who inspired him to declare in a brief article that "Nhat Hanh Is My Brother."[126] Merton was no less impressed by his meeting with the Dalai Lama on his Asian trip. Enthusiastically he wrote of the Dalai Lama's dedication, intelligence, high mysticism (marked by its simplicity), and his openness and frankness. Merton spoke favorably of encounters with Tibetans, Cambodians, and Sufis. He expressed a desire to immerse himself in the wisdom he encountered in order to share it with his brothers who had remained at home. The authentic humanism of these Asians and the intensity of their devotion to the quest for truth were to Merton signs of God's reaching out to all men. The existence of the conflict between the "spiritual and the gross" and "the beautiful and the obscene" were evidence to him of a universal religious consciousness. He warned readers not to dismiss the religions of the East too quickly because of their primitiveness, reminding Christians of their own heritage and the richness of primitive (perhaps pristine) Judaism. "If on the one hand there are Bacchic orgies of drunken women, and if temple prostitution substitutes, in certain fertility cults, for the discovery of our own intimate contemplative secret, on the other hand there are pure and sublime mysteries and, especially in the Far East, utterly sophisticated and refined forms of spiritual contemplation. The religion of Abraham indeed was primitive, and it hovered, for a terrible moment, over the abyss of human sacrifice. Yet Abraham walked with God in simplicity and peace and the example of his faith (precisely in the case of Isaac) furnished material for the meditations in the most sophisticated religious thinker of the last century, the Father of Existentialism, Sören Kierkegaard" (I.E., p. 27). The universal appearance of contemplation as ordinary or at least *de jure* in all the higher religions attests its integrity for the ascent to God. "Everywhere," Merton observed, "we find at least a natural striving for interior unity and intuitive communion with the Absolute" (I.E., p. 110).

William James analyzed the Buddhist ascent ("descent" might be a more precise term here) as a series of "fields of consciousness"; a journey through subfields, "which figures as focal and contains the excitement, and from which, as from a centre, the aim seems to be taken."[127] It is not difficult to see how such a pattern might be applied as a paradigm for the stages of the mystical ascent. The Buddhists scorn human speculation and ridicule abstract philosophical discussion. The goal of the Buddhist contemplative is

> . . . to penetrate the ground of Being and of knowledge . . . by the purification and expansion of the moral and religious consciousness until it reaches a state of super conscious or meta-conscious realization in which subject and object become one.[128]

Zen training is designed to liberate the disciple from dependence on logic and sentimentality. The aim of the student of Zen is to graduate from a "consciousness of" to a state of pure consciousness.[129] This presents a problem of the greatest magnitude to the Westerner, whose entire education has been oriented toward problem-solving via the discovery of the logical and right answer.

But is all this totally foreign to the West? It is certainly alien to the Cartesian and scientific consciousness of modern man, whose basic axiom is that his "cogitation" consciousness ("clothed with ideas of objects") is the foundation of all truth and certitude.[130]

The Westerner is threatened by the suggestion that his detached objectivity may be misleading and that he must involve himself in the spiritual "problem." America is a nation of spectators whose fears drive them to the false security of empiricism. Merton believed the following Rilke verse to be an apt description of our condition.

And we, spectators, always, everywhere, looking at, never out of, everything! It fills us. We arrange it. It collapses. We rearrange it, and collapse ourselves.[131]

Merton grew more and more convinced that Christians have substituted the attributes and concomitants of religion and religious experience for the reality that "God is" and "I am-in God."

. . . what really matters in spiritual experience is not its interiority, or its natural purity, or the joy, light, exaltation, and transforming effect it may seem to have: these things are secondary and accidental. What matters is not what one feels, but *what really takes place* beyond the level of feeling or experience. In genuine contemplation, what takes place is a contact between the inmost reality of the created person and the infinite Reality of God. The *experience* which accompanies this contact may be a more or less faithful sign of what has taken place. But the experience, the vision, the intuition, is only a sign, and is, furthermore, capable of being dissociated from any reality and being a mere empty figure (I.E., p. 102).

Zen is instructive for the Christian in its insistence that "pure consciousness" excludes "self-consciousness."[132]

It is at the point of self-transcendence that Merton found the clearest affinity between Zen and Christianity, especially the apophatic tradition.

> Zen has provided us with a deadly weapon against pious illusions, because Zen (which grew up in a highly formalized, hierarchial and traditionalist civilization) makes a point of exploding all forms of spiritual self-importance. So too, as a matter of fact, does Christianity. Or have we forgotten the Gospels?[133]

Merton felt that Christians were too often mired down in self-obsession. The empiricist Westerner frequently has become lost in a maze of self-analysis and the consequence of biological and psychological reductionism. The modern Western mind seemed to Merton to be entangled in the web of illusion in the state called *maya* by Zen masters. Modern man hides from spiritual reality behind his rational and scientific knowledge. The Christian expedition in search of the image of God, Merton's "true self," is likened to the Zen plunge in search of one's "original face" or "mind."[134] Merton suggests a parallel to Paul's "having the mind of Christ" (1 Co. 2:16) and being "of one spirit with Christ" (1 Co. 6:17), though conceding the Buddhist includes no idea of a "supernatural order." He might also have cited Ph. 2:5, "Let this mind be in you which was in Christ Jesus. . . ." Christianity and Buddhism share a common point of departure, the simple fact of human existence and human anxiety. William James similarly noted that both religions are "religions of deliverance," built on a motif of death and resurrection, dying to inauthentic existence and being born to authentic life. Merton noted the common ground of the "rebirth" motif in Sufism, Zen Buddhism, and in other religions, translating the idea as it exists in these various spiritual traditions into a modern idiom; each challenges their adherents to "become someone that one already (potentially) is, the person one is truly meant to be."[135]

Christian and Zen masters appeared to Merton to be in agreement with regard to the first step toward reality, the destruction of the false self. Being must free itself from all nonbeing. The numinous hidden essence of the soul is realized in self-knowledge, but this is only possible in proportion to the degree to which it rids itself of selfish I-ness. Zen teaches that the real self can be experienced only in the void left by the dissolution of the temporal ego. The Zen contemplative is challenged "To thoroughly purify the heart: This is the teaching of the Buddhas."[136] He must exorcise the egocentric consciousness that pollutes the mind and blocks out truth. Merton (and Suzuki, for that matter) found a true expression of Zen in Meister Eckhart, in passages such as the following:

> If it is the case that man is emptied of all things, creatures, himself and god, and *if god could still find a place in him to act* . . . this man is not poor with the most intimate poverty. For God does not intend that should have a place reserved for him to work in since true poverty of spirit requires that man shall be emptied of god and all his works so that if God wants to act in the soul *he himself must be the place in which he acts* . . . [God takes then] responsibility for his own action and [is] himself the scene of the action, for God is one who acts within himself.[137]

Merton's crisis theology affirms the moment of greatest desolation as the *kairos* moment when God is known. In utter poverty, when everything has been taken away—God is found where the husk has been stripped away and only the seed of the person remains. Purgation frees the individual to go to the center. Merton points to the cross as a model for the handling of the egocentric self. To follow Christ means being nailed to the cross with him. "To receive the word of the Cross means the acceptance of a complete self-emptying, a *Kenosis,* in union with the self-emptying of Christ 'obedient unto death' [Ph. 2:5–11]. It is essential to true Christianity that this experience of the Cross and of self-emptying be central in the life of the Christian so that he may fully receive the Holy Spirit and know (again by experience) all the riches of God in and through Christ [Jn. 14:16–17, 26; 15:26–27; 16:7–15]."[138] Without reference to any Absolute person beyond the self, Zen aims at the discernment of the ontological source of one's own existence, an intuitive experience that is at the same time incontrovertible and beyond linguistic expression. Merton was attracted by the Zen mode of spiritual enlightenment, *Satori*, "a spiritual enlightenment, a bursting open of the inner core of the spirit to reveal the inmost self" (I.E., p. 7). This enlightenment is invested with no extraordinary or supernatural elements, but is rather a natural occurrence within the inner self, which has disposed itself to the experience by the opening of itself to reality. When the false self has been conquered, "the monk experiences a kind of inner explosion that blasts his false exterior self to pieces" (I.E., p. 7). Little imagination is required to see the Zen *Sunyata* (void) as a natural analogue of the "unknowing" of the Christian apophatic tradition where God is experienced. Christian mystics would not be uncomfortable with the description of the phenomenon by Shen Hui, who said, "The true seeing is when there is no seeing." Merton likens the ecstasy of *Satori* with the terrifying encounter with the Absolute. "It is like the wonderful, devastating and unutterable awe of humble joy with which a Christian realizes: 'I and the Lord are One,' and when, if one tries to explain this oneness in any way possible to human speech—for instance as the merging of two entities—one must always qualify: 'No, not like that, not like that.'" It brings to one's mind the proclamation of Job at the end of his ordeal: "I have uttered what I did not understand. . . . I had heard of thee by the hearing of the ear, but now my eye sees thee" (Jb. 42:3, 5) (I.E., p. 9). Zen does not set up any priorities with regard to the many facets of man. Zen is not oriented toward any thing or person beyond the truth of self lived in existential awareness; its design is to liberate from all forms of bondage, including spiritual exercises, philosophies, and social systems. Matter is not renounced except as sensual gratification dominates life.[139] Merton's own journey had taught him that denial of the flesh, religious exercises, the most scrupulous study of religious literature, no activity or plan can guarantee spiritual fulfillment. He had observed the futility of religious simony in those who attempted to bargain for God's grace, offering their piosity and pharisaical practices in return for His gifts. With this background, Merton's admiration for a spirituality that expends no energy in apologetics and will say little more than that "it is" is readily understandable.

> Zen is not a "method of meditation." . . . It is a "way" and an "experience," a "life," but the way is paradoxically "not a way." Zen is therefore not a religion, not a philosophy, not a system of thought, not a doctrine, not an ascesis.[140]

Language is inadequate to convey its theory or practice or even to define it. Zen is a calibration of life for the purpose of evoking intuitive awareness.

> Buddhist meditation, but above all that of Zen, seeks not to *explain* but to *pay attention*, to *become aware*, to *be mindful*, in other words to develop a certain *kind of consciousness that is above and beyond deception by* verbal formulas—or by emotional excitement.[141]

The spiritual guide is as essential to Zen mysticism as the guru is to Hinduism; indeed, in both instances the master is a "dispeller of darkness" rather than a teacher. Zen literature consists primarily of accounts of dialectic between disciple and master. The "koans" have as their purpose the diffusion of false images. The master does not attempt to rescue the inquirer from his anxiety and confusion, but, on the contrary, the spiritual director often intentionally exacerbates the novice's malaise as an effort to drive him from self-consciousness to deeper levels of consciousness.

> . . . led by the spiritual master the disciple who can't possibly know quite what is going on is completely led into a trap; he is led almost to a point of collapse where he flips and this near-flip in Zen is a very, very fruitful thing because it simply brings the person to realize the total insufficiency of all systems, the Zen system included, of all organizations, all disciplines, and forces him, if he is any good, to make a break-through beyond all disciplines, all organizations, all systems, after which he is able to function in the organization, in the systems, etc. with perfect freedom.[142]

On another occasion, Merton suggested that a Christian monastery should be a *schola caritatis*, where teachers of love point their students in the direction of freedom. While not explicit as to what the mode of Christian monastic direction should be, the function that Merton assigns to Christian spiritual directors bears strong resemblance to the function of the Zen master described above. ". . . it is the function of the human teacher to help the novice to listen to the authentic voice of the spirit. . . ."[143] Whatever method is used, the aim is to stimulate or provoke an inexorable ingress into Being. The successful master gently (sometimes ruthlessly) urges his pupil to move from dependence to independence and ultimately to interdependence. Merton looked with favor on the paradoxical vitalism of Zen that bore witness to reality that was nonobjective, elusive, concrete, dynamic, in constant flux, perpetually renewing itself in the newness of the moment, reality that should not be studied but lived.

But when one has penetrated the mist and "sees," even through a smoky glass, what is the nature of the reality within? Buddhism speaks of Nirvana beyond experience, a state of "full realization" and "total awakening" to Being itself. Merton said it was a matter of "pure presence," but in the Buddhist mind it is only the realization of "being fully present."[144] The Zen master's "explosion" is an awakening to the "ground of our being, a ground which is not only entitative but enlightened and aware, because it is in immediate contact with God."[145] In this instance, Merton has imposed a Christian doctrine on oriental thought. Buddhist mysticism does not include a principle of a personal God external to the human person. The Buddhist mystical vocabulary does not include "communion," for the word denotes intercourse between two separate entities. For the Zen Buddhist, there is only the convergence of a multiplicity of thoughts and acts into the undifferentiated unity of Being. The "enlightenment" of Buddhism consists of an ontological awareness of the evaporation of subject-object delusion in pure void. However, Merton seems to interpret the apparent conflict as a problem of semantics. The apogee of the contemplative journey is the recollected perfect image of God and the assimilation of the "I" into the "Thou." Merton fortified his contentions with the unorthodox commentary of Meister Eckhart, who seems to have anticipated Bonhoeffer, Altizer, Hamilton, and other theologians of this century in opting for an experience of the absence of God in order that all the false ideas of God can be blotted out.

Man's last and highest parting occurs when for God's sake he takes leave of god. St. Paul took leave of god for God's sake and gave up all that he might get from god as well as he might—give together with every idea of god. In parting with these he parted with god for God's sake and God remained in him as God is in his own nature—not as he is conceived by anyone to be—nor yet as something yet to be achieved, but more as an is-ness, as God really is. Then he and God were a unit, that is pure unity. Thus one becomes that real person for whom there can be no suffering, any more than the divine essence can suffer.[146]

Rest becomes a reality for the contemplative only when he is able to lose himself in the Absolute. The self must be negated in order to realize divine identity. The mystic scales the peaks so that on the mountain he can vanish into "the pure unknowable, ineffable and mysterious good which is God. . . ."[147] John Ruysbroeck uses the popular mystical metaphor of marriage to describe the intimacy of the divine union. Without intermediary, naked, in darkness and nothingness, man immerses himself in God.

> In this darkness, the man is enveloped and he plunges in a state without modes, in which he is lost. In nakedness, all consideration and distraction of things escape him, and he is informed and penetrated by a simple light. In nothingness he sees all his works come to nothing, for he is overwhelmed by the activity of God's immense love, and by the fruitive inclination of his Spirit he . . . becomes one spirit with God.[148]

Such statements as these are anathema to orthodox theologians and tend to arouse hostility along the whole religious spectrum. Individuals without competent guidance can destroy themselves in the pursuit of this absorption. On face value, these ideas easily point in the direction of Merton's old specter, Quietism. Such statements are pregnant with the seeds of world negation and pathological introversion.

David Steindl-Rast reports in the narrative of his last conversation with Merton that the Cistercian told him that he could see no contradiction between Christianity and Buddhism and that he had determined "to become as good a Buddhist as I can."[149] This statement requires some amplification to put it into proper perspective. It does not necessarily imply that Merton had elected the route of syncretism instead of his usual mode of synthesis.

In the diary of the Asian trip he records a dream in which he saw himself wandering the countryside of the knobs of Kentucky wearing a Tibetan Zen habit. But only a few pages later he writes that the stimuli of his ecumenical conversation evoked thoughts of Irenaeus, Gregory of Nyssa, Cyril of Jerusalem, the early Christian liturgy, Baptism, the Eucharist, and the Paschal Christ. He had not become indiscriminate in his acceptance of the new or non-Christian. Christianity had nothing to fear from genuine dialogue with other religions or even with nonreligious movements. The Scriptures declare that the truth is what makes men free, and the Christian must devote himself to ferreting out truth in whatever form or place God chooses to incarnate it. Just as the pagan world influenced the development of the early Church, so now the Church must be informed by the non-Christian and non-Western world. In Merton's opinion, openness to other cultures and philosophies poses no threat to what is authentic and essential in Christian life and theology.

> First of all, it is quite clear that no non-Christian
> religion or philosophy has anything that Christianity
> needs, in so far as it is a supernaturally revealed reli-
> gion. Yet from the point of view of the "incarnation"
> of revealed Christian truth in a social and cultural
> context, in man's actual history, we know how much
> Greek philosophy and Roman law contributed to the
> actual formation of Christian culture and even Chris-
> tian spirituality.[150]

The slower industrialization of the East has permitted at least pockets of unexploited wilderness. The efficient mechanization of all life has not yet suppressed the innate creative impulse or the sense of metaphysical reality. As much as anything else, Merton appreciated the quiet sense of personhood and the sense of human, natural, and cosmological unity. He was, however, disappointed to find on his Asian pilgrimage that there was little quiet and peace in the East. Even where mechanization was undeveloped, there was the noise of routine commerce and the same hyperactivism so characteristic of Western society.

Merton identified some striking dissimilarities between Christian and Buddhist mysticism. Both set out in search of the true self, but the latter group is content to go no farther than the inner self, whereas Christianity views this as only a preliminary stage. The Christian mystic presses on through his personal center to God. Emphasis on the experience as opposed to God, who comes to us in the experience, leads to a subjective simulation of the breaking-in of the Holy One. The contemplative is not ossified by the presence of God. The dynamic ground of man's being will not tolerate a cessation of the quest, for to do so would invite stagnation and atrophy. The soul is ever drawn on by love to the ultimate goal, God. As John of the Cross noted, it is He who draws us to our inner ground.

> The soul's center is God. When it has reached God with all the capacity of its being and the strength of its operation and inclination, it will have attained to its final and deepest center in God; it will know, love and enjoy God with all its might. When it has not reached this point . . . it still has movement and strength for advancing further and is not satisfied. Although it is in its center, it is not in its deepest center for it can go deeper in God.[151]

God is His own agent, encouraging and leading on through and beyond the human "I." Augustine stresses the fact that the surrender of the soul is only a crossing of the boundary, a mere adumbration of the joy and fulfillment to come. The soul cannot rest in itself, for to do so would be to evade being apprehended by God. According to Augustine, throughout the entire experience a sense of over-againstness remains.

> When would my soul attain to that object of its search, which is "above my soul," if my soul were not

to pour itself out above itself? For were it to rest in itself, it would not see anything else beyond itself, would not, for all that, see God. . . . I have poured forth my soul above myself and there remains no longer any being for me to attain to save my God. . . . His dwelling place is above my soul; from thence He beholds me, from thence He governs me and provides for me; from thence He appeals to me, calls me and directs me; leads me in the way and to the end of my way.[152]

Guided by the spirit, Augustine found in his inward being, perceived by the soul's eye, the tremendous fascination of the Numinous.

And being by them (that is by the Platonists) admonished to return to myself, I entered even to my inmost self, Thou being my guide. I entered and beheld with the eye of the soul, above the same eye of my soul, above my mind, the Light unchangeable. . . . And Thou didst beat back the weakness of my sight, streaming forth Thy beams of light upon me most strongly, and I trembled with love and awe.[153]

Merton observed the separation of the self and God in an article written only a year before his death, "The self is not its own centre and does not orbit around itself: it is centered on God, the one centre of all, which is 'everywhere and nowhere' in whom all are encountered, from whom all proceed."[154] The awakened soul intuits the ground of its existence and becomes conscious of that which it is and yet which lies beyond it. But being in search of Being is not detoured by the poverty of human language and thought: "It does not consider God as Immanent or as Transcendent but as grace and presence, hence not as a 'Centre' imagined somewhere 'out there' or within ourselves."[155] Nonetheless, He is beyond us, drawing us on to Him even while he dwells within us. This personal, transcendent God who makes himself known in the inner man is also the Creator and the Lord of history. The "I-Thou" may be hyphenated, but it is still "I-Thou." Merton further distinguishes Christianity from Buddhism on the basis of Christian eschatology. Man's newfound harmony with God makes man a participant in the ongoing process of creation. The establishment of the Kingdom of God in the heart of man transforms him into a theandric person who shares in the work of the mystical Christ. The new Adam is called to manifest the presence of Christ in his life by submitting himself as an agent for the transformation of the cosmos.

In what sense did Merton boast that he was going to become a "good" Buddhist? In every period of his life and in every major title published over his name, he attacked the problem of the real and illusory selves. The enthronement of self, and the self-conscious attempt to make all men over in self's image were, Merton believed, the root problems of human existence. Selfishness is the original sin that infects man, isolates and estranges him from God, and places him in conflict with his brothers. Buddhism, especially Zen Buddhism, attacks this problem with incredible ruthlessness and vehemence. No quarter is given. All defenses—physical, emotional, and intellectual—are devastated, leaving the subject naked and vulnerable. Stripped of his ignorance (which to many, including himself, may have appeared to be knowledge), he is left empty, void of delusion, and in a receptive state for enlightenment. Merton felt to this point that there is no better approach to purification and, when the "explosion" of consciousness occurs, the Christian mystic can plunge deeper into the mystery of God. The absolute humiliation inherent in the Zen mode of living is not, he thought, subject to the subverting transactionalism and self-righteousness that so often undermine Christian religious life.

Virtually all the elements of Merton's theology in the last eight years of his life are sketched in "The Inner Experience." No title could be a more apt umbrella under which every aspect of his ministry could appropriately be gathered. Every significant event and decision of those last years was put through the crucible of the heart. He became more and more convinced that civilization tottered on the brink of self-destruction and that the majority of men did not hear the call of God or see His judgment or mark the manifestations of His love only because they did not want to see or hear. He admired the work of Camus and Ionesco and responded positively to their depiction of the world as absurd.[156] Men were living in a bubble of illusion created and maintained by their own blurred vision and distorted self-images. Zen demands that a man confront himself. One appeal of Zen for him was its aloofness to speculation, explanation, and rhetoric. It was no longer a question of a theology of darkness or a theology of light. Man can neither affirm nor deny; he can only exist and derive his essence from that existence. Zen's aversion to particular forms and structures and its zealous resistance to suprainstitutionalism invests it with a special measure of freedom.

> It neither denies them (forms and structures) nor affirms them, loves them nor hates them, rejects them nor desires them. Zen is consciousness unstructured by particular form or particular system, a trans-cultural, trans-religious, trans-formed consciousness.[157]

The aim of Zen is to free the mind to grasp the principle of life. The masters do not dispense right or wrong answers, but they act out their lives in word and deed in such a way as to let the truth shine through, to let the simple truth break through and grasp the subject.

> When the spirit of Zen is grasped in its purity, it will be seen what a real thing that (act—in this case a slap) is. For here is no negation, no affirmation, but a plain fact, a pure experience, the very foundation emptiness one might desire in the midst of most of our being and thought. All the quietness and

active meditation lies therein. Do not be carried away by anything outward or conventional. Zen must be seized with bare hands, with no gloves on.[158]

Such ideas grasped Merton because they gave form to his experience of God for which the analogies of symbolic theology were unsatisfactory. The "nonapparent" theology of the mystical tradition required mythological formulation or silence. From the fourth century, Merton pointed out, the Fathers had taught that a finite declaration that "God is," "indicating that in Him is the fullness of all that we can conceive of a Being," must be completed, "by saying also 'God is not' to indicate that the fullness of his Being is far beyond anything we can conceive of as existing (since all existents we know are limited and circumscribed by their existence)."[159] The apophatic school derived its name from the attempt to dramatize the limitlessness, ineffability, incomprehensibility, and mystery of God by refuting all efforts to define or describe Him. Influenced by the existentialists and absurdists, Merton showed signs of fascination for the idea of "God's absence." God is transcendent and immanent, absent and present. The only knowledge available to the spiritual life is intuitive and personal. God is experienced only as He chooses to be; love speaks to sleeping love.

> For silence is not God, nor speaking is not God; fasting is not God, nor eating is not God; loneliness is not God nor company is not God; nor yet any of all the other two such quantities, He is hid between them, and may not be found by any work of the soul, but all only by love of thine heart. He may not be known by reason, He may not be gotten by thought, nor concluded by understanding; but he may be loved and chosen with the true lovely will of thine heart. . . . Such a blind shot with the sharp dart of longing love may never fail of the prick, the which is God.[160]

The intellect only sorts and reflects and is subdued by the incomprehensibility of the Absolute. Implicit in this analysis is a Tillichian understanding of the demonic. Anthropological categories are unsuitable for contemplation of the divine or the demonic, i.e., that which has not yet come to be. God is form-creating, but he is also form-destroying. Merton's pilgrimage appears to have moved from a dependence on form, e.g., a strong liturgical orientation in the first dozen years at Gethsemani, to an awareness of reality that transcends form. By the early sixties, Merton had begun to question certain common presuppositions with regard to the "ideal" world as well as the ideal man, e.g., he decided that perhaps disorder is a more accurate key to the perception of the world than order, which man has established as the ideal.

> The real order of the cosmos is an apparent disorder, the "conflict" of opposites which is in fact a stable and dynamic harmony. The wisdom of men is the product of willfulness, blindness, and caprice and is only the manifestation of his own insensibility to what is right before his eyes. But the eyes and ears tell us nothing if our minds are not capable of interpreting their data.[161]

Wisdom cannot be acquired by interrogation nor truth established by debate. Man is inclined to dissipate his strength, flailing about in a sea of trivia. *Wu Wei* is a phrase shared by the Taoist and Zen adherents that has been transliterated "non-ado," and is a prescription for treatment of Western man's propensity for making "much ado about nothing." True contemplation will mean an end to competition within and with others. The unity of love in Christ extends to fellowship with all men and transcends the need for individual definition.

> . . . the inner self sees the other not as a limitation upon itself, but as its complement, its "other self," and is even in a certain sense identified with that

other, so that the two "are one." This unity in love is one of the most characteristic works of the inner self, so that paradoxically the inner "I" is not only isolated but at the same time united with others on a higher plane, which is in fact the plane of spiritual solitude. Here again, the level of "affirmation and negation" is transcended by spiritual awareness which is the work of love. And this is one of the most characteristic features of Christian contemplative awareness. The Christian is not merely "alone with the Alone" in the neo-platonic sense, but he is One with all his "brothers in Christ" [I.E., p. 19].

The new man shares in the unity of the Father through the Son, and in this relationship shares in the "I am" of God. In the words of Eckhart:

> For in this breaking through I perceive what God and I are in common. There I am what I was. There I neither increase nor decrease. For there I am the immovable which moves all things. Here man has won again what he is eternally and ever shall be. Here God is received in the soul.[162]

Man's simple temporal identity is established not in verbalogical analysis but in naked silence. The "I" caught in the bursting through of reality needs no identification beyond being. The experience of the anonymity of silence affirms the gift of His presence. Merton believed that Zen can teach the Christian to live in the tension between a sense of having been deserted and the ebullience of being discovered and grasped by absolute reality.

> Look at the empty, wealthy night
> The pilgrim moon!
> I am the appointed hour,
> The "now" that cuts
> Time like a blade.
> I am the unexpected flash
> Beyond "yes," beyond "no,"
> The forerunner of the Word of God.

Follow my ways and I will lead you
To golden-haired suns,
Logos and music, blameless joys,
Innocent of questions
And beyond answers:

For I, Solitude, am thine own self:
I, Nothingness, am thy All.
I, Silence, am thy Amen![163]

Silence and loneliness are the true teachers; words are deceivers. Merton's notebooks reveal a growing disenchantment with the feeble efforts of humans to communicate.

SPEAKING THE UNSPEAKABLE

Merton the mystic-poet was beginning to occupy the center ring of his literary circus. Didactic tone and vocabulary, already rare in his better works, disappeared almost completely in his works of the second half of the sixties.[164] Merton increasingly assumed a role as a terminal through whom the wisdom of others was relayed. Perhaps "mirror" is a more appropriate metaphor with respect to his social commentary, in which he reflected the interior conditions he believed were the root causes of the human predicament. Merton enunciated what he considered to be the peculiar function of the contemplative social critic. "A contemplative will . . . concern himself with the same problems as other people, but he will try to get to the spiritual and metaphysical roots of these problems, not by analysis but by simplicity. . . . I will . . . hazard a few conjectures that are subjective, provisional, mere intuitions . . . to be completed by the thinking of others."[165] His personal journals in the sixties reflect a growing concern that the steady stream of articles for various periodicals were accomplishing little. In those pages he agonized over the nuisance of an ever larger number of activists, religious leaders, and editors of religious and secular periodicals who wrote, called, and came to Gethsemani for his counsel or to get him to write an article on some important issue or pot-boiler. His fellow monks and friends confirm the journal accounts of his literally hiding in the woods to avoid visitors. His turmoil grew as he questioned how much good he was accomplishing in proportion to the time taken away from the central purpose of his life, contemplation. I believe that Merton would have written less and less as a spiritual adviser or with any rhetorical purpose. There were several reasons for this movement away from a use of rhetoric to effect social change. First, Merton had always harbored a distrust of human language and logic and had always worried about time spent on popular literary enterprises. Second, there was disappointment that the flood of peace literature and civil rights propaganda had accomplished so little. Finally, there was always lying just beneath the surface his apocalyptic faith that only God could right the wrong in the world. This mood was reflected in a September 1968 circular letter.

> It is understandable that I cannot undertake to answer any requests about writing articles, prefaces, or to give out statements on this or that. It will be impossible for me to think of keeping in touch with political issues, still less to comment on them or to sign various petitions, protests, etc. Even though the need for them may be even greater: but will they by now have lost any usefulness? Has the signing of protests become a pointless exercise?[166]

One of the outgrowths of his interest in the East was his turning to the Eastern art of calligraphy. In 1964, he published the first of a series of Zen calligraphies to come from his pen, another example of a nonlogical form of expression. Language itself was so prescribed by the culture that produced it as to impede personal universal communication. He was now looking for ways to convey metaphysical and transcultural experience. The writing that

now excited him was that which poured freely and spontaneously out of his contemplative experience.

Cables to the Ace and The Geography of Lograire
(published posthumously) mark an important turning
point in his writing style. These works mirror his literary
and spiritual state of mind. Just as traditional liturgical
forms were being called into question, and new forms were
being developed by experimentation, so should all modes
of communication, and linguistic forms in particular. The
mystic has always been confronted with the problem of expressing the inexpressible. One of the characteristics of
mystical experience arrived at by William James' study is
that the episode "defies expression, that no report of its
contents can be given in words."[167] A second conclusion
attributes a noetic quality to the mystical state, noting
that the insights erupt from "depths of truth unplumbed
by the discursive intellect."[168] These insights are "illumi-
nations, revelations, full of significance and importance, all
inarticulate" but with a lingering sense of authority for
the subject.[169] How does one communicate "the mysteries
of theology" that are infused?

> . . . in the dazzling dark of the welcoming silence
> lie hidden, in the intensity of their darkness
>   all brilliance outshining,
>   our intellects, blinded—overwhelming,
>   with the intangible and
>   with the invisible and
>   with the illimitable.[170]

When the communicative task of the mystic is assayed,
one is not surprised to find so many poets interwoven in
the mystic mosaic. The mixed metaphors and contra-
dictory expressions one finds in mystical literature demonstrate that "not conceptual speech, but music rather, is
the element through which we are best spoken to by mystical truth."[171] Poetry, with its primary appeal to the affective rather than the cognitive faculties, is a form of music.
Just as contemporary musicians have achieved effect and

evoked response through experimental forms, including overt dissonance, the modern poet has launched out to find ways of breaking through the walls of pseudosophistication, even resorting to nonform (e.g., Merton's "antipoems"). Merton the poet did not yield to possible conceptualization, but resorted to literary techniques designed to expand the reader's consciousness (perhaps a kind of *Satori*). The effect of a poem is like that of a pebble tossed into a pond that sets in motion ever-widening circles spiraling out from the point of surface contact. A poem may "mean" something, but it also has the power to transmit something beyond meaning. Luke Flaherty describes *Cables to the Ace* as

> . . . long prose-poem, [which] begins explosively, projecting neon-like images before the reader with kaleidoscopic effect. The result is a mosaic of humor, meditation, irony, and fast-paced allusion; the whole moves, though with hints of ambivalence, from the center of Merton's mysterious mind.[172]

Merton incorporates the thought of others into his mosaic, enriching their thought and his own by crossfertilization. The work affirms the unity of creation and declares that "I-Thou" and "I-you" are intrinsic to humanity.

I am the incarnation of everybody and the zones of reassurance.
I am the obstetrician of good fortune, I live in the social cages of joy.
It is morning, afternoon or evening. Begin.
I too have slept here in my stolen Cadillac.
I too have understudied the Paradise swan.[173]

The desert hermit, Merton once told the novices, can have confidence that everything around him is doing the will of God, every single minute. His wooded sanctuary embraced him and fed his silence. They were "cables," medium and message to him. The summer morning drove away his inner chill, and he reveled in being "delicately eaten by an entirely favorable day."[174] Nature was a visible part of the all, a part that could consume and be consumed. Even a small wilderness reservation like his retreat was a sacrament affirming pristine natural beauty as yet unspoiled by the bulldozers of civilization intent on "developing" it into "something."

Gelassenheit:
Desert and void. The Uncreated is waste and emptiness to the creature. Not even sand. Not even stone. Not even darkness and night. A burning wilderness would at least be "something." It burns and is wild. But the Uncreated is no something. Waste. Emptiness, Total poverty of the Creator: yet from this poverty springs *everything*. The waste is inexhaustible. Infinite Zero. Everything comes from this desert. Nothing. Everything wants to return to it and cannot. For who can return "nowhere?" But for each of us there is a point of nowhereness in the middle of movement, a point of nothingness in the midst of being: the incomparable point of nothingness in the midst of being: the incomparable point, not to be discovered by insight. If you seek it you do not find it. If you stop seeking, it is there. But you must not turn to it. Once you become aware of yourself as seeker, you are lost. But if you are content to be lost you will be found without knowing it, precisely because you are lost, for you are, at last, nowhere.[175]

The role of the contemplative is neither to flee from history nor to create it, but to stand in it with "The Lord of History" who "weeps into the fire."[176] Even form must be put aside because it is temporal, therefore, transient.

Form: the flash of nothingness. Forget form, and it suddenly appears, ringed and reverberating with its own light, which is nothing. Well, then: stop seeking. Let it all happen. Let it come and go. What? Everything: i.e., nothing.[177]

If *Cables to the Ace* is "neon lights flashing," then *The Geography of Lograire* is electronic impulses out of a majestic, spontaneous spring storm. The text, published in 1969, is only a "tentative first draft of a longer work in progress."[178] One has the feeling that, had he lived another fifty years, it would have remained his "unfinished symphony." It was his attempt to communicate himself and his sense of being a part of the whole in "authentically personal images."[179] The poem is an effort to give dynamic form to his perception of life. It suggests a fugue in which the parts are interwoven, with alternating dominant themes, but orchestrated into one whole. Existence and nonexistence are both imagined; only Being is. Time and space limit and deceive man, and it is only when he is able to become oblivious to them that he can be illuminated. The work rotates between the true and the false. Man has constructed a superhighway that is the broad path to destruction, and he passes by the narrow trail that must be walked to truth. "No one," Merton wrote, "who travels a bad road ever arrives."[180]

The Turn in the Road

Life as a journey is one of the great universal themes in literature, and yet, on first glance, it does not seem an appropriate analogue for a man who spent almost his entire public life on a relatively small reservation, geographically remote from the mainstream of life. However, the reader of Merton feels that he is following Merton on an unending journey through labyrinths, Elysian fields, and through hell itself, first one, then the other. He was guided by a navigator other than himself. It was in a restricted environment and a self-imposed form of exile that he discovered and exercised freedom. He found abiding presence in solitude and the universe in himself.

The free man is not alone as busy men are
But as birds are. The free man sings

Alone as universes do. Built
Upon his own inscrutable pattern
Clear, unmistakable, not invented by himself alone
Or for himself, but for the universe also.[181]

Merton's death, as his life, was surrounded by ironies.
The decision to travel to the East had not come easily.
This was the only extended trip he had made in twenty-
seven years as a Cistercian monk. Then for him to die the
victim of a faultily wired electric fan on the anniversary of
his entrance into the order seems the ultimate irreverence
for a hermit. However, the most striking of that strange
series of events was that his body would be flown back to
the United States on an American bomber returning from
service in Vietnam. Merton once wrote that "the free
man's road has neither beginning nor end."[182] That certainly seems true in his own life. Talking with his friends,
one gets the distinct impression that "Tom" is just away,
at another level on his "ascent to Truth."

CHAPTER VI

The Unfinished Journey

Thomas Merton's life and thought are indivisible. The mystic's theology is lived out, and his writings are a record of his life, the "working out of his salvation." His more mature works are almost entirely dialogic in nature. They are nearly devoid of finality and dogma. The principles enunciated are couched in heuristic form suggesting incomplete knowledge, a journey in process. A reader has the feeling that he is in conversation with the author, but Merton's life and style indicate that the reader is more likely reading the interior dialectic of the author. The ambiguity, sometimes patent contradiction, that has drawn the attention of a number of his interpreters was the manifestation of this continuing synthesis. Merton was aware of his logical inconsistency and noted the paradoxical nature of his life on occasion, e.g., the Preface to *The Thomas Merton Reader*. Brother Patrick Hart once humorously commented to this writer that had Merton lived long enough, he would have rebutted everything he ever wrote. Merton continually posited a new antithesis for each synthesis in his own works, as well as those of others. He did not feel bound to produce irrefutable logic enshrined in perfect systems. The evolution of Thomas Merton's thought is the unfolding of his life. There were no moments in his life that he would have frozen, no plateau so pleasurable that he would forsake seeing the next peak. He was content with the "winged life" celebrated by his poet-theologian Blake in *Auguries of Innocence*:

> He who binds to himself a joy
> Does the winged life destroy;

But he who kisses the joy as it flies
Lives in eternity's sunrise.

Merton never sought to stop time and never allowed himself to be imprisoned by it.

Merton's spiritual formation began almost from his conception, although some would question his heritage and early environment as conducive to religious development. The exceptional intellect and rare aesthetic sensitivity of his parents bred into him a rare and hybrid genetic strain. He was in many ways always a man without a country, free from the nationalistic bias that distorts the vision of many; he had no national womb to which to cling. The environment of austere intellectualism and respect for the creative impulse undoubtedly instilled in him a conditioned appreciation for nature and beauty. The nonconformity of his parents may well have impressed him with a certain distrust for the mundane and routine. Even the unfortunate absence of normal, overt familial affection had a part in his evolution as a mystic lover of mankind ever drawn on by love. He was unsure of himself with regard to love on a personal, one-to-one basis; the scars of his lonely childhood and unexpressed parental love were too deep. A day of recollection in 1965 stirred those doubts and prompted him to write with remorse for "his lack of love, or rather his selfishness and glibness, springing from his deep shyness and need of love. . . ."[1] A year later he recorded his fear that he might be numbered among those nominal Christians who persuade themselves that they love God because of their inability to love anyone or anything.[2] His happy penance was to know God fully and to experience His love in such a way as to be an embodiment of that love. Merton lived an insular existence all his life, during the years with relatives, in boarding schools, at college, even in the cenobitic community. His closest friends, men like Dan Walsh and John Howard Griffin, respected his need for solitude, physical and spiritual, the interior private places he reserved from all inspection. Henri Nouwen expresses well this characteristic of Merton.

> . . . it is indeed a very important aspect of Merton's contemplative spirit that he remained detached from his environment, even from his good friends. He loved them, but didn't use them, he was intensely thankful for everything he received from them, but he didn't attach himself to them. More and more he learned to see his friends as signposts toward God.[3]

Loneliness was forever a part of Merton's life, sometimes a liability with which he finally learned to live and that he learned to use in his quest for union with God. Tom had been driven inward at a very young age, compelled to explore and suppress his deepest feelings. For years he sustained himself on the anticipation of sharing life with his father, but, just as it appeared his dream would come to pass, death struck. It is not difficult to understand his doubts about risking himself in an intimate personal relationship. The love that dominated his life was genuinely disinterested love.

Ruth Merton, in spite of her brief time with Tom, instilled in him a sense of self-reliance; a propensity for attention to detail (at least in matters he considered important); and strong self-discipline, which was slow to emerge but enduring once actualized. From his father, Merton seemed to inherit the clear vision of the artist. Merton's journals are replete with references to nature. The unity of all creation could be detected in the order and beauty of nature. Merton's sensorial woods meditations evoke an awareness of man's bond with nature, and the dynamic stillness of his photography provides a contemporary hermeneutic for the exhortation of the Psalmist to "be still and know that I am God." Merton demonstrated that it is possible to revel in the experience of God's "good" creation in a hypertensive, frenetic age. The cycle of nature, and the mysteries of fire, water, and the seasons were symbols of resurrection. Merton's appreciation of the revelatory value of nature rivaled that of the nineteenth-century transcendentalists. "The old creation," he wrote, "is made solely for the new creation. The new creation . . . springs from the old. . . ."[4]

Merton's education and early cosmopolitan life prepared him in a unique way to reflect upon and critique international events and situations from the rural knobs of Kentucky. Ironically, even the wild seeds sown in his adolescence seemed to bear good fruit, although he almost certainly would never have admitted it. He knew from firsthand experience the emptiness of sensual, intellectual, and Machiavellian exploits. The secular world had been unable to sate his appetite for life. By the time he was twenty-five years old, Merton had traveled widely throughout Europe, in Cuba, and in the United States. He had been in school in three countries, and had visited the great galleries and museums of the world. His autobiography of those early years and the parallel account of Ed Rice corroborate Merton's ravenous hunger for life. But rather than consuming, he was consumed. No sensual experience, no philosophy, no cultural enrichment fulfilled him. Merton was driven to the spiritual dimension in search of the ultimate experience that neither reason nor the flesh had been able to deliver. What gratification of the senses had failed to produce, he sought by subduing them. A life that had followed a course of yielding to the passions now turned into the classical way of *apatheia*, suppression and complete control of the sensual instincts. Merton's appreciation for nature and his proclivity for intuitive knowledge cultivated by his parents were nurtured by the experience of his Columbia days, especially by the influence of Mark Van Doren. Merton's poetic sense and comprehension of symbolic, even mythological, form as a means of expressing non-rational experience provided him outlets as well as means of communication.

Merton's early encounter with mystical religion and mystical literature made an impression that never faded. The ideas that struck him in his student days in Gilson,

Huxley, John of the Cross, Meister Eckhart, and Augustine remained prominent in his thought, enriched by the interaction and support of others. The significance and ramifications of their legacy were worked out in the crucible of his own soul. When they emerged in the contemporary idiom of his vigorous poetry and poetic prose, they remained the universal wisdom they had always been, yet were enhanced and enriched by the imprint of Merton's personality. A number of authors who have addressed themselves to Merton have commented on his cyclic development. It is not difficult to see how they have arrived at this conclusion, but such a metaphor fails to differentiate between the cocoon and the butterfly. One may attribute the beautiful performance of a musician to his natural gifts, but the years of training and discipline that have refined those gifts cannot be dismissed. A more apt description of Merton's growth would be a spiral evolving from a narrow cone to a bountiful cornucopia. Out of the seed of himself, the complex organism, spiritual, physical, and mental that was Thomas Merton, evolved.

Brother Louis began his monastic career with all the seriousness a human being can muster. He left the world as had the early desert fathers, with complete disdain for its delusive powers and a firm resolution to be forever done with it. He was determined to bury Thomas Merton through severe ascesis. His rigorous practice of monastic self-denial led to two periods of incapacitating illness during his first decade at the Abbey at Gethsemani, one at the end of his novitiate and the other following his ordination. During his apprenticeship, Merton put his trust in the structure, in asceticism, in the liturgy. He kept waiting for a spiritual breakthrough that never came. His books and articles written during those years are pious and dogmatic, void of the spontaneity and spiritual vigor that characterize his later works. Merton's total commitment to the strictest observance of the monastic rule, to life regulated by the hours of the office and the liturgical cycle, and to conscientious preparation for the priesthood did not yield the peace he sought. By the 1950s Merton's priorities had shifted, with a concern for interior spiritual experience taking precedence over the *Opus Dei*. After the early fifties, only one work was published under his name that could really be called liturgical, and it was an abortive attempt to reinterpret the liturgy in the spirit of Vatican II. Merton's intense study of theology and his complete immersion in worship led him to the realization that dogma and ritual are not the same thing as spirituality. It is interesting to note that in the twenty-four volumes of *Collected Essays*, covering most of his published and unpublished writings over the last seventeen years of his life, there is little that deals with liturgy from a religious viewpoint and nothing that explicitly deals with the priesthood, a primary focus in *The Sign of Jonas* covering the years from 1941 to 1949. In the nearly two hundred tapes of his conferences, which date from 1962, none deals explicitly with the priesthood or with the liturgy as more than a springboard into discourses on the need for interior spirituality. This does not mean that the liturgy and his priesthood were not important to him. He apparently took great delight in the daily exercise of the office and bore in his heart a strong sense of responsibility to pray and suffer with and for the world as a priest of Christ and the Church. Only two years before his demise he advised:

> It is precisely in familiarity with liturgical worship and moral discipline that the beginner finds his identity, gains a certain confidence from his spiritual practice and learns to believe that the spiritual life has a goal that is definitely possible of attainment.[5]

The change in emphasis only infers an enlightened view of the meaning of sacrament and how it may be abused by false conceptions of its purpose and power.

This period served to instruct Merton in the unity of man as flesh, mind, and spirit. The subjection of the flesh, the purification of the senses do not insure spirituality. His ascesis evoked in him a clear vision of the illusion of the world, of self-illusion, and of religious illusion. These discoveries drove him deeper into himself. Also, he was able to glean much from his broadened study of the Fathers, whose ideas he absorbed and made a part of himself. He came out of this period able to discriminate between tradition and convention. The timeless truths formulated by the Fathers would always be a living tradition, but the propositional interpretations of those truths and the lifeless structures and rules constructed to impose and preserve them are anathema to the spiritual man. He compared and contrasted "tradition" and "convention," often passed off as tradition, in a treatise, "Art and Worship": "Tradition is living and dynamic, convention is passive and inert. Tradition constantly renews the everlasting newness of revelation. Convention merely surrenders to the paralyzing grip of the past."[6] It was evident to Merton by 1950 that no system or structure could do more than provide a temporary haven or a conduit for one who aspired to union with God. Merton's development followed almost exactly Bernard's three degrees of experience, with the first third of his career being marked by personal misery, the searing of the soul by the penetrating light of truth, the experience of *vertias in nobis*.

The expedition into the inner self led to the discovery that, fundamentally, Tom Merton and Father Louis were not in conflict but were only aspects of the same man, and that as a man, Merton was inextricably bound to mankind, and as such must share in the anxieties and hopes of the whole human race. In a sense he had rediscovered the world in himself and intuited spiritual reality at the core of the world. He realized that the world from which he had fled was a world of illusion, obscuring from him and others the presence of the Ultimate. In this period, during which he was charged with the responsibility of being a spiritual director for others, he shared in the experience of the misery of his brothers, the experience of truth in fraternal love, *veritas in proximo*. In his study of the Fathers, he had found the seeds of a high Christian anthropology, a view of man as bearing in himself the potential of divinity. Merton believed that the clearest disclosure of God is in the love of Christ. Therefore, his search for union led through God's infinite love for man, and His love is the *fons et origo* of man's divinization. Merton's involvement in contemporary social problems was the inevitable outgrowth of his belief that his freedom to share in God's being was indissolubly linked to the freedom of all men. He began in the fifties to expose those forces that obscure the *imago Dei* in man.

Merton's social criticism evolved out of his experience with the unmasking of personal illusion. The articulation of these ideas achieved polished form in the treatises published in the sixties. Merton pleaded for the redirection of man from almost certain self-destruction. Vigorously he campaigned against all forms of totalitarianism. Christian duty requires that every effort be made to "preserve the human person in his integrity, his freedom and his individuality. . . ."[7] Merton's humanism was void of the uncritical optimism that so often characterizes personalists. Man must view with uncluttered vision his devastated and desperate condition and face reality about himself and his world. The pathway to freedom is strewn with obstacles that man lacks the power to remove or overcome. The pearl of great price is obtainable only via the intervention of God.

> Now there is no fulfillment of man's true vocation in the order of nature. Man was made for more truth than he can see with his own unaided intelligence, and for more love than his will alone can achieve and for a higher moral activity than human prudence ever planned.[8]

The so-called political democracy of the West is but an illusion of freedom. The contemporary American is free only to gradually die and disappear into the formless mass. Human wholeness is dependent on man's acceptance of

God's acceptance and the inherent worth implied in that acceptance.

Freedom, Love, Union

James Baker observes that "the thread that runs through all Merton's works . . . is this theme of unity: unity of man with God and of man with man."[9] The individual's ability to accept others is directly proportionate to his acceptance of himself. One must escape the false self to experience the authentic self with a unique role in the orchestra of mankind. No price is too great to break out of the pseudotogetherness of mass culture and to reassert one's right to be a person. The truly religious man is free to be ordinary, free from the false props of "success."

> Freedom from domination, freedom to live one's own spiritual life, freedom to seek the highest truth, uabashed by any human pressure or any collective demand, the ability to say one's own "yes" and one's own "no" and not merely to echo the "yes" and the "no" of state, party, corporation, army, or system. This is inseparable from authentic religion. It is one of the deepest and most fundamental needs of man, perhaps as such: for without recognizing the challenge of this need no man can truly be a person, and therefore without it he cannot fully be a man either.[10]

It is only when the creature asserts his freedom that he becomes person with all the privilege and burden that word implies. "To be a person implies responsibility and freedom . . . a sense of one's own reality and of one's ability to give himself to society. . . ."[11] Reconciliation is the discovery of self, but, more than that, it is the discovery of selves. "We all need one another, we all complete one another. God's will is found in this mutual interdependence."[12] When treasured prerogatives, special privileges, prejudices, and platitudes are laid aside, one discovers they were not really needed at all.

Man is not meant to resolve all contradictions but to live with them and rise above them and see them in the light of exterior and objective values that dwarf them. To discover what it means to be fully human is to discover God. Each of us "works out his own salvation with fear and trembling," but the task is made easier when we help one another along the way. Redemption means wholeness, completion, health. It means seeing the light at the end of the tunnel. As Merton put it in the Prologue to *No Man Is an Island*, "No matter how ruined man and world may seem to be, and no matter how terrible man's despair may become, as long as he continues to be a man his very humanity continues to tell him that life has a meaning."[13] If man, a man, has inherent value simply because he is man and for no other reason, then every man is endowed with value because of his manliness. There is within each member of the race authentic man waiting to be born. "The Christian knows that there are radically sound possibilities in every man, and he believes that love and grace always have power to bring out those possibilities at the most unexpected moments."[14] Each man who submits to the living Christ within him becomes a new man in whom Christ is made visible. Each man experiencing the new birth is called to be a midwife to others.

Merton's indirect involvement in campaigns against technological dehumanization and social injustice continued into the sixties. The escalation of the Vietnam conflict made terrific demands on Merton, as he anguished over what he considered to be an immoral act on the grandest scale. Opponents of the war were anxious to include his trenchant indictment and the influence of his national recognition as a spiritual leader. Merton was appalled by the American government's policies and indifference to what he considered to be clear-cut moral issues. He was further incensed by the indifference and callous response of the national leadership of the crusaders against the war. He never ceased to be concerned about the war and other forms of unconscionable injustice and indifference to human suffering, but there is some evidence that he believed his personal involvement had gone too far and was interfering with his prior commitment to a life of prayer. There is some hint of this reassessment in the final pages of *Faith and Violence:*

> My own peculiar task in my Church has been that of a solitary explorer, who, instead of jumping on all the latest bandwagons at once, is bound to search the existential depths of faith in its silences, its ambiguities, and in those certainties which lie deeper than the bottom of anxiety. In these depths there are no easy answers, no pat solutions to anything. It is a kind of submarine life in which faith sometimes mysteriously takes on the aspect of doubt.[15]

These horrible sores on the corporate body of man were only symptoms of an inward disease that must be arrested before the human race annihilates itself.

Merton accepted suffering and anguish as necessary concomitants of the experience of the love of God. This world, and man as a part of it, is becoming in God. It is not a matter of forcing the issue but of being liberated in the grace of His spirit and being open to the unpredictable working of God. Man's hope of freedom lies in the communion of his freedom with God's ultimate freedom. Merton seemed to have a vision of union with God. The union of men will occur as a coincidence of the experience of union with the Absolute. The hope for man is the hope of the experience of Truth in itself, *veritas in seipsa*— union with God by pure love. It was at this point that Merton's preoccupation with Buddhism took over. Tradition was for him a root from which to grow—not a chain by which he was bound. The "true vine" was of such strength and purity that branches that for centuries had been rejected by Christians as deciduous and blighted, fit only to be cast into the fire, could be safely engrafted. Christians had too often been inhibited by cultural accretion to the gospel. Merton increased his efforts to obtain solitude where he might probe into the divine abyss. Merton believed that once an institution like a monastic order had set a man on the road to freedom, it could withdraw as a wise parent withdraws when a child is equipped and ready to assume responsibility for himself. Merton shared Leclercq's view that ". . . the hermit is a person who has become sufficiently obedient to be able to obey without a superior."[16] In this solitude he hoped to experience final integration. Only this total integration held the prospect of true universality.

> Final integration is a state of transcultural maturity far beyond mere social adjustment which always implies partiality and compromise. The man who is "fully born" has an entirely "inner experience of life." He apprehends his life fully and wholly from an inner ground that is at once more universal than the empirical ego and yet entirely his own. He is in a certain sense "cosmic" and "universal man." He has attained a deeper, fuller identity than that of his limited ego-self which is only a fragment of his being. He is in a certain sense identified with everybody: or in the familiar language of the New Testament . . . he is "all things to all men." He is able to experience their joys and sufferings as his own, without however becoming dominated by them. He has attained to a deep inner freedom—the freedom of the Spirit we read of in the New Testament. He is guided not just by will and reason, but by "spontaneous behavior subject to dynamic insight."[17]

Merton set out on the Asian journey in search of men who were *catholic* because of an inner experience, men with whom he could converse in the language of the spirit. Anticipating his trek, he wrote for *Forum* in August, before his death in December.

> I am looking to a wider horizon, to something more than adjustment to the western—or the American—

way of life. What I am "for" is the idea of the fully integrated "universal man" who is not merely adjusted to western urban and technological life-styles but wise in the classical sense of the word. I *hope* one can be both—I'm not sure.[18]

His last notes and correspondence indicate that in some of those he encountered, he found evidence of the work of the cosmic Christ, an unspoiled dedication to Truth unclothed in patriotic flags, economic systems, or religious conventions. He went to the East not as a preacher to proclaim "the truth" but as a seeker to discover truth—or at least to get a new vision of it. He went looking not for artifacts but for living witnesses.

I come as a pilgrim who is anxious to obtain not just information, not just "facts" about other monastic traditions, but to drink from ancient sources of monastic vision and experience. I seek not only to learn more (quantitatively) about religion and about monastic life, but to become a better and more enlightened monk (qualitatively) myself.[19]

He was not enthralled with all that he found in Asia. The Orient turned out not to be a primitive paradise; indeed, the ugliness and suffering were more visible there than that cleverly hidden in many American cities, and the signs of "progress" prompted him to speculate on the possibility of the technological corruption of Buddhism, or the emergence of a "secular Nirvana." There was a difference, he soon realized, between the "real" India and the "ideal" India. It was, he observed, another of those illusions "that needed to be dissolved by experience."

Certainly not all his experience was negative or disappointing; with joy he reflected upon the examples of living faith that enriched his experiences. Merton did find the spiritual brothers he had expected to find in Asia. He felt especially comfortable with the Tibetans, who impressed him with their intellect and spiritual depth. A planned interview with the Dalai Lama multiplied to three lengthy conversations over several days in which the two masters confirmed a genuine spiritual affinity. Another Tibetan monk concluded their meeting by designating Merton a "natural Buddha." The journey affirmed for Merton the mystical theology implicit and explicit in his earlier writings, i.e., that matters of the spirit have little to do with geography, culture, or language. His dialogues supported his opinion that the function of diverse religious traditions is to give direction and form to the mystic, but that there is little, if any, difference in the essence of authentic religious experience. However, he seems to have been no less convinced that to ignore the differences in religious tradition would be to demean the authentic spirituality of holy men who have dedicated their lives to the search for the Divine. The experience of God can not be programmed, promoted, or discovered.

> The door without wish. The undesired. The unplanned door. Not a joke, not a trap door. Not select. Not exclusive. Not for a few. Not for many. Not FOR. Door without aim. Door without end. Does not respond to a key—so do not imagine you have a key. Do not have your hopes on possession of the key.[20]

His whole life had been one of release and acceptance and, at least for him, that was the way.

The Witness of His Life

Merton's life is a model for total commitment to the spiritual quest. In his maturity, he was not so much "detached" from the world as he was "unattached" to it. He was not aloof and unconcerned for the world of commerce, education, domestic life, culture, religion, and politics; he was deeply concerned about it. He was not, however, attached to it, i.e., the world and its goods did not define him or determine the course of his life. His errors or excesses were the product of misguided zeal, not unlike that which one detects in the vibrant characters of the Bible.

The matter of Merton's psychology and the effect of the disorientation of his early life remain open to question. No thorough psychological study has yet been attempted, but there will almost certainly be one. One can only hope that it will be undertaken by a writer competent in the field of psychology and knowledgeable in matters of the spirit. Merton's close acquaintances are quick to point out that a highly competent psychiatrist judged him to be the most balanced person he had ever known. Nevertheless, Merton's early traumas and emotional deprivation, combined with a highly active dream life (recorded in his notebooks) and with his personal doubts about his ability to relate on the level of human love, make this a subject worthy of study. Such a study can be extremely positive and of great benefit to all those interested in the spiritual life. Certainly all the evidence now available would indicate that his was a healthy religion. Those who search for pathological explanations for his life enlist in the army of unbelieving critics who would "expose" all who subscribe to notions of spiritual reality and who seek to imitate the life of Christ, who has had his own detractors and analysts. Thomas Merton's life was marked by radical commitment and self-abandonment, but it was done in the belief that the stakes were the honor of God and his own life. Men and women like Thomas Merton discredit those who ridicule Christianity as an untried, unlived philosophy.

Merton's approach to social problems was a simple one; so is the Bible's. Merton's analysis is marked by a beautiful naïveté that tends to ignore the complexity of social and political structures. It is this complexity behind which whole generations hide and explain away their apathy. Did not the prophet declare the requirements of God in the simple words "do justice . . . love kindness and walk humbly with your God?" Merton took these words and the example of Jesus seriously and implored the rest of the world to do the same. Merton could speak a word of judgment because he was willing to stand under judgment. He identified with the oppressors, and repented of his part in the system that seemed to him so indifferent to human needs. At the same time, he bore in himself the suffering of the victims and empathized with their frustration and bitterness. The real heart of the problem as he perceived it lay in the fact that the offenders were as much, or more, the victims of their greed, hate, and cruelty as the offended. Repentance meant more than a confessional formula; it meant for him remorse and sacrifice in the hope of reconciliation.

Merton's early spiritual writings reveal a certain naïveté in these matters as well. Those who accused him of writing propaganda for mysticism for the masses were not without grounds for their charges.[21] He tended to make broad generalizations about the appropriateness of mysticism and contemplation for all persons. One of his important contributions was the calling of all men to examine themselves and unmask their humanity in order to discover their spiritual nature, but in the early years he was not always clear as to what that meant, and often left the impression that there was room in the desert for everyone. However, his later works distinguish different forms of contemplation, e.g., the "hidden contemplatives," whose lives are lives of prayer uttered in secular activity and service. Discourses in the sixties acknowledge the diversity of God's gifts and concede that not everyone has the same capacity for mystical experience. All men, then, are called to spirituality, but the form of that spirituality differs according to God's will and grace.

Merton's writings on Eastern mysticism are tempered by repeated allusions to traditional Christian symbols. His diaries written in the last months he spent at the hermitage record his preference for the Fathers for reading in the cottage and for the works of the Zen masters in the fields. However, his published works are not always instructive as to how Zen experience is to contribute to the Christian experience or how the study of Eastern religions or the practice of oriental techniques engender or complement the Christian experience. Some of his published remarks might well be interpreted as syncretistic and might leave the reader with the impression that it does not matter what religious expression one's spirituality takes as long as one has broken through the façade of the illusionary self. Published discourses excerpted from continuing dialogue between or among two or more spiritual masters do not always mean the same thing to the general reader as to the dialogue participants. Few Westerners are endowed with the ability to think "oriental" or to translate their Western experience into Eastern modes. Some are deluded by teachers who interpret oriental and occidental religious concepts as univocal when in fact the differences are profound. The casual reader might overlook the fact that Merton spent half his life disciplining himself and reaching a level where he could think and write in terms of the "universal" man and transculturation. Even then, he considered himself a beginner who had much to learn. The ease with which he accepted the potential worth of Eastern spirituality at this stage was undoubtedly due in part to his "Augustinian bent." Augustine refused to differentiate "truth," contending that all truth is of God, and, therefore, revelatory.[22] An accurate impression of Merton or understanding of his thought cannot be gained from any single work bearing his name. He is open to abuse and distortion by one using his writings as proof texts for a position on almost any theological question. Because of the revelatory nature of his work, i.e., the record of personal dialectic, there is a certain danger in isolating any one work or phase of his work as definitive of him or his philosophy.

Merton contended vigorously against the image of Buddhism as a "world denying" religion. He argued that the discovery of the "real" self would be the discovery of a compassionate self. Some of these arguments, like his earlier attempts to disassociate "infused contemplation" from "Quietism," lack persuasive force. The Zen practitioner aims at a "self-sustaining independence."[23] The danger of acute self-consciousness is present in all forms of mysticism but is especially strong in Buddhism, where "enlightenment" may be as individualistic as "salvation" in fundamentalist Christianity. Both religions in their purest forms are committed to radical and unconditional transcendence of the individual ego. Mystics, whether Christian or non-Christian, strive for "an experience of metaphysical or mystical self-transcending and at the same time an experience of . . . 'the absolute . . . not so much as object but as subject.'"[24] Merton noted a difference in the Christian and Zen interpretation of this experience of ontological union.

> In the Christian tradition the focus of this "experience" is found not in the individual self as a separate, limited and temporal ego, but in Christ, or the Holy Spirit "within" this self. In Zen it is self with a capital S. . . .[25]

Merton's mounting stress on union, in language, suggestive of Eastern absorptionism, combined with his growing election of nonlogical forms of expression, suggest that he may have been on the brink of a new period of withdrawal. If not, there still remains the problem that the course he seems to have been laying out was subject to the pitfall of an inordinate preoccupation with self. The novice should take seriously Merton's frequent allusions to false religious experience and the martyr's syndrome. The support and discipline of a community are imperative for most.

This study will appear to many to be as much an anachronism as its subject. Piety and speculative theology have both fallen into disrepute in the twentieth century. Popular theology today has a distinctive sociological and psychological cast to it. The past eight years have been characterized by a mass exodus from "religious" professions and the ridicule of traditional religious practices.

Merton, in spite of his unorthodox monastic life style, stood in a tradition as old as the Christian Church. Moreover, he maintained that no amount of social involvement could take the place of spiritual discovery and transformation. On the one hand, he pointed out that hyperactivism, even in a good cause, could be a flight from humanity, and, therefore, from spiritual authenticity. On the other hand, he contended that wherever the demonic was being attacked and overcome in corporate society, the spirit of the Lord was present. Many who admired the power of his pen and his incisive analysis of the inherent corruption of contemporary social and political structures could not understand his self-imposed exile in the monastery or his continuing submission to the rule of obedience. Merton was committed to a concept of man as spiritual being and to the principle that no man could be fully human and consequently fully free without the cultivation of his spiritual nature. Merton's diagnosis of human society was "fragmentation" as a result of personal "brokenness," i.e., interior-exterior separation. His prescription was reconciliation through union with Jesus Christ. Merton's prognosis was a new man in a new creation. He was almost the perfect blend of the theological (not in the sense of dogmatics but in the sense of concentration on and intimacy with God) and the ethical, i.e., a life in which the presence of God is concretely manifest.

Merton believed that man subconsciously yearns for "spirituality," the clue that will put man and his world back together. The only hope for decaying Western civilization is to attain the spiritual life as defined by Christian Duquoc, "the lived unity of human existence in faith."[26] William James observed more than half a century ago that no explanation of the universe that ignores spiritual consciousness can be considered complete.[27] Paul Tillich affirmed in our own time that religion is a universal and necessary experience of man and that the nature of religion requires a sense of the ultimate, which imposes a mystical category upon the memory and consciousness of man.[28] Merton advocated a bold search for reality in the deepest recesses of human consciousness, where he believed the authentic self, in the true image of God, lay waiting to be discovered and released.

Three motifs surface in every period of Merton's life. Freedom, love, and union form a thread that holds together the different stages of Merton's development. These are the essence of life, the source of a spontaneous and creative life. The basic question to which man should address himself is not, "Am I happy?" but, "Am I free?" Alienated man is imprisoned in the Babelian process. The individual has sold his birthright to live in collective illusion. Modern man has settled for "freedom of choice," which Merton believed was no real freedom at all, but only modified dependence. He enjoined man to be satisfied with nothing less than freedom of spontaneity, the freedom to respond with the whole self to ultimate reality. "The freedom you have when everything has been taken away," he said, "is the real freedom."[29] The *imago Dei* within man is the principle of the uninhibited, spontaneous, and creative life. This freedom is the consequence of resurrection, and energizes the new man. As a result of the transformation from the false to the real, the person's living experience reveals truth. This deepest freedom occurs in the *kairos* moment of existential encounter with God. The identity that is found in the encounter with God is an image of love.

Love is both form and substance, intuition and action. The Christian's freedom is the freedom to love.

> Love is an act of surrender and the intuition of a freedom beyond life and death, but of a freedom which can only be attained by self-surrender in the midst of self-contradiction. Love becomes perfect in a dialectic of action and intuition, culminating in the mysterious presence of Someone who is invisible but who *is love*.[30]

Merton came to understand that love, the need for it, the catharsis of its infusion, the fulfillment of its experience, the motivating power of its indwelling, was at the center of his entire life and pilgrimage. Love was the ultimate experience he pursued beyond the senses. Love was what cleared his distorted vision and gave him a new view of the world. Love was the source of his identification with the suffering of the oppressed. Love was the presence of God that he found at the core of his being. Merton came to believe that the grace of God could be "known" only by immersion into His love. The Christian becomes Christ the incarnate Word as he becomes a pure manifestation of love. Love is the center that unifies all creation.

> Rooted in the biological riches of our inheritance, love flowers spirituality as freedom and as a creative response to life in a perfect encounter with another person. . . . It responds to the full richness, the variety, the fecundity, of living experience itself: it "knows" the inner mystery of life. . . .[31]

There was a sense in which Merton fell in love with love, not in the sense of puerile romanticism but in the mode of pure consciousness of perfect love. Merton became more and more absorbed with spiritual mind-expansion, the *Satori* explosion that opened one to the rapture of being "alone with the Alone."

The language is modern. Merton's expression and concerns are those of the twentieth century and are not foreign to modern concepts of psychology, energy, organism, process, and complementarity. His vision, particularly before Vatican II, is set in the matrix of traditional Catholic moral and dogmatic theology. But the overarching feel of his biography and writings is the classical dynamism of mystical union with God. Freedom and love are subsidiary motifs of the obsession of his life, to know God as he was known by Him, to be transformed totally through and in Him. Union with the Absolute, the void of the convergence of transcendence and immanence in being one with the One, was the *experimentum crucis* of his existence. He spent the majority of his life attempting to remove all obstacles to the infusion of God's gift of Himself. Union is the leitmotif that subsumes all others in His thought.

Thomas Merton was endowed with special ability to synthesize the traditional and the transient. He was an Erasmian humanist who could speak universal truths in contemporary terms. Distinctly eclectic in his reading, he refused to become the preserver or spokesman of any school. The thoughts and words of others pervade all his works but are always modified by their fusion with Merton. Merton served his own Catholic tradition in a special way by restoring respectability to personal religious experience and establishing it as a viable alternative for disoriented modern man, even those caught up in institutional reform and revolution. Within him there was always a radical tension among his identification with suffering and sinful humanity, his own desire for solitude and the uninterrupted life of prayer, and his own psychology. He was perplexed by the paradox of the authentic Catholic tradition, which he perceived to be contemplative and dynamic, and the static form that encrusted that living organism. These ambiguities could be neither explained nor resolved; they could be only absorbed in living the life of the spirit. Thomas Merton was not a reformer, though he contributed much to reform; he was not a teacher, though many made him their mentor; he was not a prophet, though he often spoke prophetically; he was not a philosopher, though his life reflects a definite philosophy; he was not a theologian, though his work is rich in theological insight. Thomas Merton was a Christian poet-mystic whose life was his message. Raymond Panikkar might have had Merton in mind when he described a special spiritual breed whom he calls "theandric" persons:

> They realize the rhythm of the universe and discover inside their beings a constant call to surpass the self

and possess a certain universal prophetic awareness, not so much in the concrete and particular as in the totality of the Mystical Body of Christ, which is none other than the Universe—insofar as it is on the way up—and I am not saying returning—to the bosom of the Father.[32]

Thomas Merton's life was a living parable of one who was willing to give up all that he had, to take up his cross, to seek the pearl of great price, that he might be a joint heir with Christ and be one with the Father. And yet, he testified until the end that he only saw through a glass darkly.

Notes

CHAPTER I

1. Thomas Merton, "The Captives—A Psalm," *The Tears of the Blind Lions* (Norfolk, Conn.: New Directions, 1949), pp. 20–21.

2. Thomas Merton, *Seeds of Contemplation* (Norfolk, Conn.: New Directions, 1949), p. 2.

3. Aelred Graham, "The Mysticism of Thomas Merton," *Commonweal* 62:155 (May 13, 1955).

4. E. Glenn Hinson, "The Catholicizing of Contemplation: Thomas Merton's Place in the Church's Prayer Life," *Perspectives in Religion* 1:2 (Summer 1973). John Higgins came to a similar conclusion in his study of Merton's philosophy of prayer; see *Thomas Merton on Prayer* (Garden City, N.Y.: Doubleday & Company, 1973), p. 11.

5. Thomas Merton, "Extemporaneous Remarks," *The World Religions Speak on "The Relevance of Religion in the Modern World,"* ed. Finley P. Dunne, Jr. (The Hague: Dr. W. Junk N.V. Publishers, 1970), p. 81. The idea expressed here is one that was frequently repeated by Merton in his writings, conversation, and lectures. The particular occasion of this quotation was an international conference at Calcutta six weeks before his death. In his teaching notes on "Vows," delivered in the 1950s, he wrote, "Our Job in life is . . . to be what we are supposed to be." *Introduction to the Vows*, Vol. XIV, *Collected Essays* (Trappist, Ky.: Abbey of Gethsemani, n.d.), p. 3.

6. Hal Bridges, *American Mysticism: From William James to Zen* (New York: Harper & Row, 1970), p. 1.

7. Thomas Merton, "Christian Culture Needs Oriental Wisdom," *Catholic World* 195:77–78 (May 1962).

8. Dom Edward Cuthbert Butler, *Western Mysticism* (2d ed.; London: Constable, 1951), p. 4.

9. Butler and Bouyer sought to dignify the mystical tradition

among Catholic scholars by de-emphasizing the affective elements and stressing intellectual aspects. Both have demonstrated a preference for "contemplation," which they seem to feel lacks the negative connotations of "mysticism." Merton commented on the terms in his teaching notes on mystical theology. "For the Greek Fathers—'Mystical Theology' and 'Contemplation' are two ways of saying the same thing. The term 'contemplation' is borrowed from Greek philosophy. Both terms mean the hidden knowledge of God by experience, the 'passive' illumination of the soul by the divine light 'in darkness.' To be precise, *theology* (theologia) refers to the highest contemplation of God, in Himself, the triune God. *Contemplation* (theoria) refers rather to the contemplation of God in creatures, and in the action of His Providence in the world, in the 'economy' of man's salvation. (Therefore, above all in the Scriptures)." *Cistercian Fathers*, Vol. XX, *Collected Essays*, p. 55. *Collected Essays* are twenty-four volumes of Merton's writings, some unpublished, others published, compiled and bound by the Abbey of Gethsemani. There is a set in the Abbey and one in the Bellarmine Collection.

10. Stace quoted by Kenneth Wapnick in "Mysticism and Schizophrenia," *Journal of Transpersonal Psychology* 1:50 (Fall 1969).

11. Evelyn Underhill, *Mysticism* (New York: E. P. Dutton & Co., 1961), p. 81.

12. Ibid., p. 82.

13. Raymond Panikkar, "The Theandric Vocation," *Monastic Studies* 8:71–72 (Spring 1972).

14. Underhill, p. 455.

15. Bridges, p. 4.

16. Merton, *Cistercian Fathers*, p. 55.

17. R. E. Welsh, *Classics of the Soul's Quest* (New York: George H. Doran Company, 1923), p. 155.

18. Merton, "Extemporaneous Remarks," p. 73.

19. Merton, *Cistercian Fathers*, p. 55. Cf. Butler, "Afterthoughts," *Western Mysticism*, pp. xxi ff. He states that, "Only by a comparative method, by the analysis and synthesis of the accounts given by a wide circle of mystics, and viewed from the standpoints alike of theology and of modern psychology, can a broad enough foundation be laid for such a superstructure of mystical theology as will satisfy all desires."

20. William R. Inge, *Studies of English Mystics* (Freeport, N.Y.: Books for Libraries Press, n.d.), p. 5.

21. F. C. Happold, *Mysticism: A Study and An Anthology* (Baltimore: Penguin Books, 1964), p. 69.

22. An example of the very early use of this account in an allegorical fashion may be found in Gregory of Nyssa's *The Life of Moses.*

23. Gregory quoted in Robert L. Simpson, *The Interpretation of Prayer in the Early Church* (Philadelphia: The Westminster Press, 1965), p. 50.

24. Etienne Gilson, *The Mystical Theology of Saint Bernard* (New York: Sheed & Ward, 1940), p. 19. Cf. Simpson, pp. 50ff.

25. Several centuries later, Bernard discussed four degrees of love in the *De Diligendo Deo.* Prior to illumination man loves himself for his own sake. He is then turned to love God for his own sake, but this love grows to love of God for God's sake, thus freeing man to love himself for God's sake. It is possible to trace Merton's self-actualization to these stages. His discussion of the degrees can be found in *Cistercian Fathers,* pp. 18ff.

26. Merton, "Extemporaneous Remarks," p. 72.

27. Happold, p. 250.

28. See Butler, pp. 142ff, 220ff; Happold, pp. 101ff; Underhill, p. 101, et al. Underhill, p. 459, underscores the influence of the mystics in Germany and Italy: ". . . it appeared in a more startling form: seeking, in the prophetic activities of St. Hildegarde of Bingen and the Abbot Joachim of Flora, to influence the course of secular history. In St. Hildegarde and her fellow Benedictine St. Elizabeth of Schonau (1138–65) we have the first of that long line of women mystics—visionaries, prophetesses, and political reformers—combining spiritual transcendence with great practical ability. . . . Exalted by the strength of their spiritual intuitions, they emerged from an obscure life to impose their wills, and their reading of events, upon the world."

29. Thomas Merton, "The Spiritual Father in the Desert Tradition," *Cistercian Studies* 3, 1:8 (1968).

30. Thomas Merton, *Contemplation in a World of Action* (Garden City, N.Y.: Doubleday & Company, 1971), p. 154.

31. Wapnick, p. 53.

32. William James, *The Varieties of Religious Experience* (New Hyde Park, N.Y.: University Books, 1963), p. 242.

33. Underhill, pp. 81ff.

34. Wapnick, p. 53.

35. Tarcisius Conner, "Merton, Monastic Exchange and Renewal," *Monastic Exchange* 1:2 (1969).

36. Jean Leclercq, "Introduction," *Contemplation in a World of Action*, p. xi.

37. Merton, *Contemplation in a World of Action*, p. 145.

38. The middle four divisions were suggested by Merton in "First and Last Thoughts: An Author's Preface," *A Thomas Merton Reader*, Revised Edition. Ed. by Thomas P. McDonnell (New York: Image Books, 1974). Cf. James Thomas Baker, *Thomas Merton, Social Critic* (Lexington: The University Press of Kentucky, 1971). The missing years were periods of poor health and relative inactivity.

CHAPTER II

1. This assessment, like many to follow, grew out of conversations with John Howard Griffin (and in some cases lectures). Mr. Griffin, currently engaged in writing the official Merton biography, has been most generous in his assistance through conversations and correspondence. Griffin has had access to certain personal notebooks and materials that will not generally be made available to scholars for some years in the future. Material based on these contacts will be cited J.H.G., Conversations.

2. Thomas Merton, *The Seven Storey Mountain* (New York: Harcourt, Brace & Company, 1948), p. 3. The first half of Merton's life is presented in detail in this autobiography, covering his life from birth to his entry into the Abbey of Gethsemani in 1941. In later years he referred to his first popular success as "callow," and it certainly is characterized by a kind of romanticism and pious fervor. Nevertheless, it records in the style of Augustine's *Confessions* a man's search for meaning and his traumatic discovery of the transcendent. Future references from this work will be indicated *SSM*.

3. Ibid., p. 11.

4. "Tom's Book," his mother's account of his first two years, is included in the Merton Collection at Bellarmine College.

5. *SSM*, p. 23.

6. Ibid., p. 287.

7. Thomas Merton, *Conjectures of a Guilty Bystander* (Garden City, N.Y.: Image Books, 1968), p. 200. Hereafter indicated as *CGB*.

8. *SSM*, p. 14. These passages exude the anguish and anxiety of a young man's memories of loneliness and yearning for affection.

9. Ibid.

10. J.H.G., Conversations.

11. *SSM*, p. 51.

12. Ibid., p. 73.

13. Ibid., p. 53. The spirit as well as the language here call to mind Bonhoeffer's notion of "cheap grace." Merton was searching for the ultimate: ultimate experience, ultimate reality. The forms of Protestantism to which Merton had been exposed lacked vigor and were too compromised for him to stake his integrity, his very life on. He was looking for that pearl of great price for which a man will abandon everything to possess. The honor of God had to demand more than quiet acquiescence.

14. Thomas Merton, "The White Pebble," *Sign* 29:26 (Jul. 1950).

15. Ibid.

16. *SSM*, p. 85.

17. Thomas Wolfe, "The Story of a Novel," *The Thomas Wolfe Reader* (New York: Charles Scribner's Sons, 1962), p. 28.

18. Thomas Wolfe, *Of Time and the River* (New York: Charles Scribner's Sons, 1935), pp. 869–70.

19. *CGB*, p. 244.

20. Mark Van Doren, "Thomas Merton." *America* 120:22 (Jan. 4, 1969).

21. J.H.G., Conversations.

22. *SSM*, p. 198.

23. Edward Rice has vividly recounted his friend's libertine days at Columbia in *The Man in the Sycamore Tree: The Good Times and Hard Life of Thomas Merton* (Garden City N.Y.: Doubleday & Company, 1970). Dan Berrigan has said that Merton never overcame the "bum" style of life begun in Europe and perfected at Columbia. Berrigan describes him as an "inspired bum." Tape, Thomas Merton Life Center, New York.

24. Thomas Merton, *Poetry and Poets*, Vol. II, *Collected Essays* (Trappist, Ky.: Abbey of Gethsemani, n.d.), p. 173.

25. Thomas Merton, "Christian Hope and Relatedness," Tape 63 (Louisville, Ky.: Thomas Merton Collection, Bellarmine College).

26. *SSM*, p. 140.

27. Ibid.

28. Thomas Merton, *The Secular Journal of Thomas Merton* (Garden City, N.Y.: Image Books, 1969), pp. 268–69.

29. "The White Pebble," p. 26.

30. E. T. Starbuck, quoted in Evelyn Underhill, *Mysticism* (New York: E. P. Dutton & Co., 1961), pp. 176–77.

31. Thomas Merton, *My Argument with the Gestapo* (Garden City, N.Y.: Doubleday & Company, 1969), p. 138. This was his second novel, which he later described as "full of double talk and all kinds of fancy ideas that sounded like Franz Kafka." Naomi Burton Stone, "Thomas Merton's Mountain," *The Sign* 44:46 (Oct. 1964).

32. "The White Pebble," p. 27.

33. *SSM*, p. 229.

34. Ibid., p. 221.

35. Ibid., p. 225. The circumference reference is borrowed from Eucherius, who described the immersion of the soul into God, "a circle whose center is everywhere and whose circumference is nowhere."

36. John of the Cross, *The Complete Works of St. John of the Cross*, trans. and ed. E. Allison Peers, I (Westminster, Md.: The Newman Bookshop, 1946), p. 61.

37. *SSM*, pp. 238ff.

38. *SSM* is the best source for biographical information on the first twenty-six years of Merton's life, but the theology of *SSM* is more that of the first years in the monastery, and the anguished thought of those crucial first Christian years are recorded in the *Journal*. In the Preface to the latter work, he was to apologize for "the callow opinions, careless style, and youthful sarcasms" of the *Journal* (he made similar assessments of *SSM* in *The Sign of Jonas*), but the fervency of the rhetoric reveals the intensity of conviction with which he approached the questions posed by his commitment to the will of God.

39. Robert McAfee Brown, *The Spirit of Protestantism* (New York: Oxford University Press, 1965), p. 118.

40. *Journal*, p. 34.

41. Ibid., p. 43.

42. Ibid., p. 135.

43. Ibid., p. 109.

44. Ibid., p. 88.

45. Ibid.

46. Ibid., p. 100. From the vantage point of the literature of

Bonhoeffer, Father Delp, Frankel, etc., the prophecies of Merton and his informants appear extremely accurate.

47. *SSM*, p. 292.

48. *Journal*, p. 167.

49. Ibid.

50. It is interesting that in addition to *My Argument with the Gestapo*, he wrote during this period a work that was never published, entitled "The Labyrinth," the title of which, at least, must have expressed his own sense of wandering down dead-end paths.

51. *Journal*, p. 209. Cf. *SSM*, pp. 340ff.

52. *SSM*, pp. 345ff.

53. Thomas Merton, "Commentary on the Meditations of Guigo the Carthusian," *Life and Truth*. Tape 7A, *The Thomas Merton Tapes*, ed. Norm Kramer (Chappaqua, N.Y.: Electronic Paperbacks, 1972).

54. *Journal*, p. 218. Merton used the Latin, *"Nam quantum unusquisque est oculis tuis, tantum est et non amplius, ait Sanctus Franciscus."*

55. Ibid., p. 219.

56. Ibid., p. 240.

57. "The White Pebble," p. 27.

58. *SSM*, p. 88.

59. Thomas Merton, *William Blake*, Vol. X, *Collected Essays*, p. ii.

60. Ibid., pp. 79ff.

61. Ibid., p. 71.

62. Ibid., p. 63. See Michael Polanyi, *Personal Knowledge: Toward a Post-Critical Philosophy* (New York: Harper & Row, 1964).

63. Ibid., p. 89.

64. Quoted in ibid., p. 84.

65. Thomas Merton, "Blake and the New Theology," *Poetry and Poets*, pp. 156–67. The book reviewed was Thomas J. J. Altizer, *The New Apocalypse: The Radical Christian Vision of William Blake* (East Lansing: Michigan State University Press, 1967). The review appeared in the April 1968 issue of *Sewanee Review*.

66. Ibid., p. 160.

67. Ibid., p. 166.

68. Sister Mary Julien Baird, "Blake, Hopkins and Thomas Merton," *Catholic World* 183:48 (Apr. 1956).

69. E. Glenn Hinson, "The Catholicizing of Contemplation: Thomas Merton's Place in the Church's Prayer Life," *Perspectives in Religion* 1:4 (Summer 1973).

70. Jacques Maritain, *Art and Scholasticism*, trans. J. F. Scanlan (London: Sheed & Ward, 1939), p. 80.

71. Lawrence Binyon, quoted in Underhill, p. 74.

72. Wilhelm Dilthey, quoted in H. A. Hodges, *The Philosophy of Wilhelm Dilthey* (London: Routledge & Kegan Paul, 1952), p. 113.

73. G. W. E. Hegel, quoted in Underhill, p. 21.

74. Thomas Merton, "Art and Worship," *Art and Literature*, Vol. IV, *Collected Essays*, p. 22.

75. Humbert Wolfe, quoted in E. I. Watkin, *Poets and Mystics* (New York: Sheed & Ward, 1953), p. 14.

76. Irwin Edman, *Arts and the Man* (New York: W. W. Norton & Company, 1939), p. 26.

77. William James, quoted in *Arts and the Man*, p. 15.

78. Karl Rahner, "Priest and Poet," *The Word: Readings in Theology* (New York: P. J. Kenedy & Sons, 1964), p. 3.

79. Thomas Merton, *No Man Is an Island* (Garden City, N.Y.: Image Books, 1967), p. 41.

80. Thomas Merton, *The Sign of Jonas* (Garden City, N.Y.: Image Books, 1953), p. 56.

81. Thomas Merton, *A Thomas Merton Reader*, ed. Thomas P. McDonnell (New York: Harcourt, Brace & World, 1962), p. 443.

82. Thomas Merton, *New Seeds of Contemplation* (New York: New Directions, 1961), p. 102

83. Thomas Merton, "Answers on Art and Freedom," *Raids on the Unspeakable* (New York: New Directions, 1960), p. 175.

84. Ibid., p. 160.

85. Henry David Thoreau, quoted in Wilfred A. Peterson, *Adventures in the Art of Living* (New York: Simon & Schuster, 1968), epigraph.

CHAPTER III

1. Thomas Merton, "First and Last Thoughts: An Author's Preface," *A Thomas Merton Reader*, ed. Thomas P. McDonnell (Garden City, N.Y.: Image Books, 1974), p. 15.

2. Thomas Merton, *No Man Is an Island* (Garden City, N.Y.:

Image Books, 1967), p. 118. Comments such as this one reflect a later evolution of his formation as a monk.

3. Thomas Merton, *Contemplation in a World of Action* (Garden City, N.Y.: Doubleday & Company, 1971), p. 16.

4. George H. Williams, *Wilderness and Paradise in Christian Thought* (New York: Harper & Row, 1962), p. 5.

5. Ibid., p. 18. Cf. Eric Voegelin, *Israel and Revelation*, Vol. I, *Order and History* (Baton Rouge: Louisiana State University Press, 1956); Ulrich Mauser, *Christ in the Wilderness* (Naperville, Ill.: Alec R. Allenson, 1963).

6. Thomas Merton, *What Are These Wounds? The Life of a Cistercian Mystic, Saint Lutgarde of Aywieres* (Milwaukee: Bruce, 1950), p. 120. Cf. *Monastic Orientation* (1950–52), Vol. XVI, *Collected Essays* (Trappist, Ky.: Abbey of Gethsemani, n.d.), p. 61.

7. Thomas Merton, "Wilderness and Paradise: Two Recent Studies," *Cistercian Studies* 2:84 (1967). The books reviewed were Mauser and Williams; see notes 4 and 5 above.

8. Ibid.

9. Thomas M. Gannon and George W. Traub, *The Desert and the City* (London: The Macmillan Company, 1969), p. 18.

10. "Epistle XLIII" in Williams, p. 39.

11. Thomas Merton, "Preface," Jean Leclercq, *Alone with God*, trans. E. McCabe (New York: Farrar, Straus & Cudahy, 1961), pp. xxi–xxii.

12. Thomas Merton, *The Waters of Siloe* (New York: Harcourt, Brace & Company, 1949), p. 340.

13. Thomas Merton, *Seeds of Contemplation* (New York: New Directions, 1949), p. 48.

14. Thomas Merton, "The Landfall," *Selected Poems* (New York: New Directions, 1959), p. 73.

15. *Thoughts in Solitude* (Garden City, N.Y.: Image Books, 1968), pp. 20–21.

16. A. Bertholet, quoted in Karl Barth, *Church Dogmatics*, trans. G. W. Bromiley, IV, 2 (Edinburgh: T. & T. Clark, 1958), p. 12.

17. Thomas Merton, "The Contemplative Life," *Dublin Review* 223:31 (Winter 1949).

18. Thomas Merton, *The Living Bread* (New York: Farrar, Straus & Cudahy, 1956), p. 92.

19. "*Omnis qui ad Dominum convertitur contemplativam vitam*

desiderat." Gregory the Great, in Thomas Merton, "Poetry and the Contemplative Life," *Figures for an Apocalypse* (New York: New Directions, 1947), p. 96.

20. Merton, "Poetry and the Contemplative Life," p. 96.

21. Thomas Merton, "Ecumenism and Monastic Renewal," *Journal of Ecumenical Studies,* V (Nov. 1968), p. 271.

22. Thomas à Kempis, "The Royal Road of the Holy Cross," *The Imitation of Christ,* in F. C. Happold, *Mysticism: A Study and an Anthology* (Baltimore: Penguin Books, 1964), pp. 269, 274.

23. Thomas Merton, "Introduction," Shirley Burden, *God Is My Life* (New York: Reynal & Co., 1960), p. 1.

24. Thomas Merton, *The Sign of Jonas* (Garden City, N.Y.: Image Books, 1953), p. 20. Future references from this work will be indicated *SJ*.

25. Thomas Merton, *New Seeds of Contemplation* (New York: New Directions, 1961), pp. 260–61. This is a revised edition of *Seeds of Contemplation,* published in 1949.

26. One of the speculations that continues to circulate after Merton's death is that he did not plan to return to Gethsemani. Edward Rice argues this position in *The Man in the Sycamore Tree: The Good Times and Hard Life of Thomas Merton* (Garden City, N.Y.: Doubleday & Company, 1970), p. 124. In this further respect there was a kinship with Merton's spiritual patron, John of the Cross, about whom Peers reported, ". . . he thirsted for a stricter rule than as yet he had found and . . . had thoughts of leaving the Order of Carmel to become a Carthusian." E. Allison Peers, I *Studies of the Spanish Mystics* (2d ed.; London: S.P.C.K., 1951), p. 187.

27. Bernard, Canticle 31:6, in Merton, *Waters of Siloe,* p. 294.

28. Merton, "Introduction," *God Is My Life,* p. 3.

29. *SJ,* p. 65. Cf. pp. 31, 115.

30. Ibid., p. 38.

31. The writer is indebted to Brother Patrick Hart and Father Tarcisius Conner, both monks of the Abbey of Gethsemani, for discussion and confirmation of this material. Father Patrick Reardon, formerly a monk of the Abbey, was also generous with his time and assistance in discussing these matters. Father Conner was a student under Merton's direction when the latter was master of scholastics, and Father Louis was Father Reardon's novice master. Brother Patrick Hart was Father Louis' secretary at the time of the latter's death.

32. William James, "The Religion of Healthy-Mindedness," Chaps. IV and V; "The Sick Soul," Chaps. VI and VII, *The Varieties of Religious Experience* (New Hyde Park, N.Y.: University Books, 1963), pp. 78–165.

33. Thomas Merton, *Ascent to Truth* (New York: Harcourt, Brace & Company, 1951), p. 250.

34. *Waters of Siloe*, p. 21.

35. Father Dan Berrigan said in a speech at the Cathedral of St. John the Divine in New York City that Merton once wrote him that if he had it to do over again, he would not be a monk, but since he was, he would never leave. Such a specific statement this writer was unable to find in their correspondence, although he may have said such a thing without thinking or in an unguarded moment. In a letter on this subject, John Howard Griffin expresses the opinion that if he wrote such a thing, "It is rather like the musings of a married man who sometimes feels he should not have married, which is no serious impediment to any marriage really. . . . To the very end . . . he wrote that this was where he belonged, this was his place in the Church; and at the very end, that he had found no place better. . . ."

36. Matthew Kelty, "Reflections from Oxford," (Oxford, N.C.: mimeographed letter circulated at Gethsemani, Feb. 1973).

37. Ibid.

38. Ibid.

39. Merton, *The Seven Storey Mountain*, *A Thomas Merton Reader*, p. 145.

40. Thomas Merton, trans., *The Wisdom of the Desert: Sayings from The Desert Fathers of the Fourth Century* (New York: New Directions, 1960), p. 6.

41. Newman, "Historical Sketches," pp. ii, 452, in Herbert B. Workman, *The Evolution of the Monastic Ideal* (2d ed.; London: The Epworth Press, 1927), p. 12.

42. Merton, *Waters of Siloe*, p. 293.

43. *New Seeds of Contemplation*, p. 1.

44. Thomas Merton, "First Christmas at Gethsemani," *Catholic World* 170:171 (Dec. 1949).

45. He wrote in his journal in March 1947, ". . . they seem to me to be the most detailed and concrete and practical set of rules arriving at religious perfection that I have ever seen." *SJ*, p. 40.

46. Thomas Merton, "The White Pebble," *The Sign* 29:27

(Jul. 1950). In the medieval period, the assumption of the monk's cowl was considered a second baptism; it seems to have had a similar meaning for Merton.

47. William R. Inge, *Studies of English Mystics* (Freeport, N.Y.: Books for Libraries Press, n.d.), p. 108.

48. Aldous Huxley, *Time Must Have a Stop* (New York: Harper & Brothers, 1944), pp. 293–94. The concept of the empty void of the human soul is especially important in Zen, and the Zen theoria on the subject had great appeal to Merton in his last years.

49. Eckhart, in Raymond B. Blakney, *Meister Eckhart: A Modern Translation* (New York: Harper & Brothers, 1957), p. 131. In another passage he again stresses this theme as he writes: "So long as anything is still object of our gaze we are not yet one with The One. . . . Every creature is as a "beam" in the soul's eye since, by its very nature as creature, it is an obstacle to union with God. Thus, so long as anything remains in the soul, it must get outside of itself. Nay more, it should reject even the saints and angels, yes, and the nakedness, without any needs, for God is thus in nakedness and without any need. In other words, it is stripped of matter that the soul attains to God. It is only thus that it succeeds in uniting itself to the Blessed Trinity." "*Expedit vobis*," Gannon and Traub, p. 119.

50. *SJ*, p. 74. Cf. "The Gift of Understanding," *The Tiger's Eye* 1:43–45 (Dec. 16, 1948); "Poetry and the Contemplative Life," p. 106.

51. Evagrius, "On Prayer," in Elmer O'Brien, *Varieties of Mystic Experience* (New York: Holt, Rinehart & Winston, 1964), p. 62. Cf. Gannon and Traub, pp. 12ff, 42ff.

52. Bonaventure, *De Itineraria Mentis in Deo*, cap. vii, in Evelyn Underhill, *Mysticism* (New York: E. P. Dutton & Co., 1961), p. 124.

53. Merton, "First Christmas at Gethsemani," p. 169. Cf. "The Contemplative Life," p. 34.

54. Pseudo-Dionysius, de. div. Nom. vii. 3, in Edward Cuthbert Butler, *Western Mysticism* (2d ed.; London: Constable, 1951), p. 6.

55. Merton, "First Christmas at Gethsemani," p. 30.

56. Thomas Merton, *The Secular Journal of Thomas Merton* (Garden City, N.Y.: Image Books, 1969), p. 173.

57. "The Contemplative Life," p. 27.

58. *Journal*, p. 42.

59. Thomas Merton, "Contemplation in a Rocking Chair," *Integrity* 2:19 (Aug. 1948).

60. "Poetry and the Contemplative Life," p. 105.

61. Theresa, "Vida," Chapter II, in Peers, p. 123.

62. Paul Tillich, *Systematic Theology*, II (Chicago: University of Chicago Press, 1968), p. 84.

63. Merton, *Waters of Siloe*, p. 349.

64. Thomas Merton, *Introduction to the Vows*, Vol. 14, *Collected Essays*, p. 3.

65. *The Living Bread*, pp. xii–xiii.

66. "Poetry and the Contemplative Life," p. 108.

67. Thomas Merton, *The Seven Storey Mountain* (New York: Harcourt, Brace & Company, 1948), p. 169.

68. Ibid.

69. "Poetry and the Contemplative Life," p. 103.

70. Athanasius, I, "Contra Arianos," in Louis Bouyer, *The Spirituality of the New Testament and the Fathers* (New York: Desclee Company, 1960), p. 418.

71. Ibid., pp. 416ff.

72. Underhill, p. 419.

73. Ibid., p. 420.

74. In those early years Merton avoided Eckhart, electing to study the safer, Church-approved models of John, Teresa, Ailred, Bernard, etc.

75. *SJ*, p. 26.

76. Augustine, "Treatise on John," in Merton, *The Living Bread*, p. 95.

77. *The Living Bread*, p. 4.

78. Tillich, p. 88. The thought of Merton and of Tillich have some clear affinities, and Merton's allusions to Tillich in later works show that Merton was acquainted with his work.

79. Alfred Lord Tennyson, *The Poetic and Dramatic Works of Alfred Lord Tennyson* (Cambridge ed.; Boston: Houghton Mifflin Company, 1898), p. 498.

80. Merton, "Contemplation in a Rocking Chair," p. 18.

81. "The Gift of Understanding," p. 42.

82. *Waters of Siloe*, pp. 22–24.

83. *The Living Bread*, p. 30. Cf. *Waters of Siloe*, p. 279; "Is Mysticism Normal?," p. 94.

84. Thomas Merton, *What Is Contemplation?* Paternoster Series, No. 7 (London: Burns, Oates & Washbourne, 1950), p. 15.

85. *What Are These Wounds?*, p. 117.

86. *The Living Bread*, p. 12.

87. Ibid., pp. ix–x.

88. Ibid., p. 28.

89. *SJ*, pp. 30–35.

90. "The White Pebble," p. 28. He wrote in the same place that the grace of monastic profession fell far short of that of the priesthood.

91. *SJ*, p. 109 (dated May 30, 1948).

92. "The White Pebble." Anticipation of this experience had been recorded in his diary eleven days before his ordination (ordained May 26, 1949). *SJ*, p. 187.

93. Ibid., p. 221. Cf. *The Living Bread*, pp. 142ff.

94. Ibid., p. 7.

95. Merton, quoted in Rice, p. 130.

96. Ibid., p. 372.

97. Thomas Merton, "Address to the Special General Chapter," Sisters of Loretto (Aug. 1967), p. 8.

CHAPTER IV

1. Thomas Merton. "Preface," *A Thomas Merton Reader*, ed. Thomas P. McDonnell (New York: Harcourt, Brace & World, 1962), p. ix.

2. Thomas Merton, *The Sign of Jonas* (Garden City, N.Y.: Image Books, 1953), p. 247. Hereafter cited *SJ*.

3. John Howard Griffin, Conversations.

4. Thomas Merton, "Poetry and the Contemplative Life," *Figures for an Apocalypse* (Norfolk, Conn.: New Directions, 1947), pp. 110–11. There has been a great deal of discussion as to why Merton continued to write if he felt so strongly that it was a digression from his vocation. He often gave the impression that he had written under orders from his superiors (e.g., *SJ*, 23ff). On the basis of conversations with the abbots, John Howard Griffin concludes that Merton was never coerced to write but was encouraged and thus motivated by a desire to please his spiritual superiors.

5. Thomas Merton, *What Is Contemplation?*, Paternoster Series, No. 7 (London: Burns, Oates & Washbourne, 1950), pp. 9–10.

6. He comments on this problem in a number of places including *SJ* and the "Preface" to *A Thomas Merton Reader*.

7. *SJ*, p. 47.

8. Ibid., p. 65. E. Glenn Hinson, "Merton's Many Faces," *Religion and Life* 42:165 (Spring 1973).

9. Thomas Merton, "Preface," *Nanal No Yama (The Seven Storey Mountain)*, trans. Tadishi Kudo (Tokyo: Chuo Shuppansha, 1966), p. 6.

10. Drawing upon a large number of personal interviews with the monks at Gethsemani, Frederic Joseph Kelly in his book *Man Before God* (Garden City, N.Y.: Doubleday & Company, 1974), pp. 58–59, reviews Merton's efforts to transfer: "He had written to the Cardinal Prefect of the Congregation of Religious asking to transfer to the Camaldolese Order of hermit-monks. He received an eight page letter in reply, quoting canonical and legalistic reasons why the permission was to be refused. He was both amused and disappointed that one of the supposedly 'telling arguments' for the refusal was a quotation from one of his own books in praise of Trappist life (cf. Shannon, "Thomas Merton's New Mexico," p. 21, also personal recollection). He had also written to the Archbishop of Milan, Cardinal Montini (later Pope Paul VI), asking his intervention to expedite the transfer. Cardinal Montini wrote a short letter in reply, while on retreat near the ruins of an ancient Camaldolese monastery. The implication of Cardinal Montini's warm personal reply by his reference to the 'ruins' was: 'Don't go on beating a dead horse' (personal recollection)."

11. Merton, *SJ*, p. 111.

12. The material on this subject has been drawn from conversations with several of Father Louis' friends who are aware of the details. It was all pulled together in dialogue with John Howard Griffin, who was gracious enough to share the fruits of his study of Merton's journals and interviews with the parties involved. Griffin's analysis of the episode is recorded on a tape in the Merton Collection at Bellarmine College, Louisville, Kentucky.

13. Thomas Merton, *Ascent to Truth* (New York: Harcourt, Brace & Company, 1951), p. 258.

14. His friend and longtime correspondent, Dom Jean Leclercq, faults Merton's early works with being too much a restatement of the ideas of others and not enough of Merton. In a conversation with this writer in May 1973, he said that Merton was stung by the response of theologians he respected to *Ascent*. John Howard Griffin says Merton recorded his disappointment in

Ascent's unfavorable reception in his personal journals. In 1967, Merton ranked all his books and described *Ascent* as only "fair." In the 1960s Merton wrote something of a systematic exposition of his own mystical theology, but he never submitted it for publication, and his will expressly forbids its publication, although it does allow its study by "qualified scholars." This work, entitled "The Inner Experience," will be dealt with in Chapter V.

15. Evelyn Underhill, *Mysticism* (New York: E. P. Dutton & Co., 1961), p. 115.

16. Tauler, "Third Instruction," in Underhill, p. 115.

17. Merton, *Ascent*, p. 94.

18. Walter Hilton, *The Ladder of Perfection*, in F. C. Happold, *Mysticism: A Study and an Anthology* (Baltimore: Penguin Books, 1964), p. 286.

19. Dionysius the Areopagite, "The Mystical Theology," in Happold, p. 212.

20. Merton, *A Thomas Merton Reader*, p. 531.

21. John of the Cross, *Ascent of Mount Carmel*, i, I and ii, in *Ascent*, p. 52.

22. John of the Cross, *Ascent of Mount Carmel*, Book II, c. IX, in Edward Cuthbert Butler, *Western Mysticism* (2d ed.; London: Constable, 1951), p. xiii.

23. Merton, *Ascent*, p. 114.

24. Thomas Merton, *New Seeds of Contemplation* (New York: New Directions, 1961), pp. 134-35.

25. *Ascent*, p. 109.

26. John of the Cross, *The Complete Works of St. John of the Cross*, trans. and ed. E. Allison Peers (Westminster, Md.: The Newman Bookshop, 1946), p. 69. A part of the "safety" of John can be seen in his use of the "safe" Thomistic language of ratiocination.

27. Thomas Merton, *Seeds of Contemplation* (Norfolk, Conn.: New Directions, 1949), p. xv.

28. Upon reading Cardinal Newman on the advice of a superior, Merton noted that he could find nothing in common between them (*SJ*, p. 57), although his appreciation of Newman did increase; see *Conjectures of a Guilty Bystander*, p. 24. According to Father Dan Walsh, in the last year, Merton could not even sit through one of his old friend's lectures on Scholastic theology.

29. *Conjectures of a Guilty Bystander*, pp. 203-8.

30. *SJ*, p. 208.

31. Ibid.

32. Augustine, *De utilitate credendi*, 25, in Happold, p. 26.

33. Nicholas of Cusa, "On Learned Ignorance," in *Late Medieval Mysticism*, ed. Ray C. Petry, Vol. XIII, *The Library of Christian Classics*, ed. John Baillie, John T. McNeill, and Henry P. Van Dusen (London: SCM Press, 1957), p. 364.

34. John of the Cross, *Ascent of Mount Carmel*, Book II, in Merton, *Ascent*, p. 83.

35. Meister Eckhart, "Sermon I," a sermon preached at Christmastide, in Happold, p. 247.

36. David Steindl-Rast, "Recollections of Thomas Merton's Last Days in the West," *Monastic Studies* 7:9 (1969). Merton explicitly taught such an understanding in the afternoon of his life. At the spiritual conference in Calcutta, he said, "Faith means doubt. Faith is not the suppression of doubt. It is the overcoming of doubt and you overcome doubt by going through it. The man of faith who has never experienced doubt is not a man of faith." "Extemporaneous Remarks," *The World Religions Speak on "The Relevance of Religion in the Modern World,"* ed. Finley P. Dunne, Jr. (The Hague: Dr. W. Junk N.V., 1970), p. 80.

37. Merton, *SJ*, p. 292.

38. Thomas Merton, *Thoughts in Solitude* (Garden City, N.Y.: Image Books, 1956), p. 113. Cf. Merton, "The Night Spirit and the Dawn Air," *New Blackfriars* 46:690 (1965); *CGB*, p. 19; *Ascent*, p. 114.

39. *Ascent*, p. 88.

40. Thomas Aquinas, *De Potentia*, in *Boetium de Trinitate*, in *Ascent*, pp. 100–1.

41. Merton, *Thoughts in Solitude*, p. 62.

42. Ibid., p. 75.

43. Ibid., p. 29.

44. Augustine Baker, *Holy Wisdom*, in Butler, p. xiii. Baker's *Holy Wisdom* was one of the works Merton kept on his bookshelf at the hermitage.

45. Merton, *Ascent*, p. 255.

46. Thomas Merton, "The Person of Christ in Prayer," *Life and Prayer*, Tape 3A, *The Thomas Merton Tapes*, ed. Norm Kramer (Chappaqua, N.Y.: Electronic Paperbacks, 1972).

47. Thomas Merton, *The Seven Storey Mountain* (New York: Harcourt, Brace & Company, 1948), pp 16, 203. Cf. E. Glenn

Hinson, "The Catholicizing of Contemplation: Thomas Merton's Place in the Church's Prayer Life," *Perspectives in Religion* 1:5, 6, 13, 14 (Summer 1973).

48. *Ascent*, p. 66.

49. Ibid., p. 219. An entire chapter is devoted to "Intelligence in the Prayer of Quiet"; see pp. 217–39.

50. John of the Cross, *Living Flame*, in *Ascent*, p. 238.

51. John of the Cross, *Dark Night*, Book ii, n. 5, in *Ascent*, p. 272. In brackets Merton defines "The Dark Night" as "pure faith."

52. Merton, *Ascent*, p. 162. The interpolation is Merton's.

53. *What Is Contemplation?*, p. 5.

54. Ibid., pp. 11–12.

55. Ibid. My italics.

56. Ibid., p. 28.

57. *Ascent*, p. 76.

58. *What Is Contemplation?*, p. 20.

59. Ruysbroeck, "*L'Ornement des Noces Spirituelles*," Book II, c. 74, in Merton, *Ascent*, p. 228.

60. Merton, *Ascent*, p. 274.

61. This test certainly does not exclude all Quietists. No other religious group has expressed more concretely their experience of love than the Quakers, avowed Quietists.

62. *SJ*, p. 269.

63. In *No Man Is an Island* (Garden City, N.Y.: Image Books, 1967), p. 152.

64. Thomas Merton, "The Contemplative Life," *Dublin Review* 223:32 (Winter 1949). In the same place he invokes the opinion of Aquinas "that the only really effective teaching and preaching is that which flows from the fullness of contemplation: *ex plenitudine contemplationis derivatur.*" (*Summa Theologica*)

65. Arnold J. Toynbee, *A Study of History* (New York: Oxford University Press, 1961), p. 263.

66. Herbert B. Workman, *The Evolution of the Monastic Ideal* (2d ed.; London: The Epworth Press, 1927), p. 336.

67. *No Man Is an Island*, p. 40.

68. *SJ*, pp. 97–98.

69. Thomas Merton, *New Seeds of Contemplation* (New York: New Directions, 1961), p. 51.

70. Merton included an essay on "The English Mystics" in *Mys-

tics and Zen Masters (New York: Farrar, Straus & Giroux, 1967), pp. 128–54. About the English mystics generally he wrote, "There is every reason for interest in the English mystics. They have a charm and simplicity that are unequaled by any other school. And they are also, it may be said, generally quite clear, down-to-earth, and practical, even when they are concerned with the loftiest of matters. They never seem to have thought of their life with God as something recondite or even unusual. They were simply Christians" (p. 128). He was especially fond of Lady Julian, about whom he said, "The theology of Lady Julian is a theology of the all-embracing totality and fullness of the divine love. This is, for her, the ultimate Reality, in the light of which all created being and all the vicissitudes of life and of history, cosmos and history are unreal: but their reality is only a revelation of love" (p. 141). See William R. Inge, *Studies of English Mystics* (Freeport, N.Y.: Books for Libraries Press, n.d.); Julian of Norwich, "Revelations of Divine Love," Happold, pp. 291–301.

71. Merton, *New Seeds of Contemplation*, p. 21.

72. Ibid., p. 24.

73. Ibid., p. 125. Cf. *No Man Is an Island*, p. 90. The idea of sin as vaporous illusion was not a new one to him. In 1941, he had written in his *Secular Journal* (Garden City, N.Y.: Image Books, 1969), p. 179, "To say we are born in sin, is to say we are born in illusion and blindness, and this blindness makes us fall into every other evil."

74. *No Man Is an Island*, p. 11.

75. Ibid., p. 125.

76. Ibid., p. 59. Cf. *Ascent*, p. 305.

77. *No Man Is an Island*, p. 158.

78. *Thoughts in Solitude*, p. 46. Cf. *No Man Is an Island*, p. 95.

79. *No Man Is an Island*, p. 16.

80. *New Seeds of Contemplation*, p. 22.

81. Ibid., p. 109.

82. *Thoughts in Solitude*, p. 68. Cf. *New Seeds of Contemplation*, p. 4.

83. *No Man Is an Island*, p. 95.

84. Karl Rahner, *The Christian Commitment* (New York: Sheed & Ward, 1963), p. 140.

85. Thomas Merton, "Day of a Stranger," *The Man*, Vol. I,

Collected Essays (Trappist, Ky.: Abbey of Gethsemani, n.d.), p. 193.

86. *No Man Is an Island*, p. 118.

87. SJ, p. 16.

88. *Thoughts in Solitude*, p. 104.

89. Ibid.

90. *No Man Is an Island*, p. 169.

91. Ibid., p. 94.

92. Ibid., pp. 116–17.

93. SJ, p. 262. Cf. *New Seeds of Contemplation*, pp. 52ff, 80.

94. *New Seeds of Contemplation*, p. 54.

95. *No Man Is an Island*, p. 183.

96. *Thoughts in Solitude*, p. 12.

97. *No Man Is an Island*, p. 85.

98. Thomas Merton, *The Strange Islands* (Trappist, Ky.: Abbey of Gethsemani, 1952), p. 85.

99. Ibid., p. 56. These same lines are included in "The Tower of Babel," *The Strange Islands*, pp. 56ff, where the idea is elaborated.

CHAPTER V

1. Thomas Merton, *The Sign of Jonas* (Garden City, N.Y.: Image Books, 1953), p. 59.

2. Thomas Merton, "Solitude," *Spiritual Life* 14:172 (1968).

3. Thomas Merton, *Contemplation in a World of Action* (Garden City, N.Y.: Doubleday & Company, 1971), pp. 154–55. Hereafter cited as CWA.

4. Thomas Merton, "Answers on Art and Freedom," *Raids on the Unspeakable* (New York: New Directions, 1960), p. 172. Hereafter cited as *Raids*. Cf. "Preface," *Nanal No Yama* (*The Seven Storey Mountain*), trans. Tadishi Kudo (Tokyo: Chuo Shuppansha, 1966); and Thomas P. McDonnell, "An Interview with Thomas Merton," *Motive* 28:31–32 (Oct. 1967).

5. Merton, CWA, pp. 143–44.

6. Thomas Merton, "First and Last Thoughts: An Author's Preface," *A Thomas Merton Reader*, ed. Thomas P. McDonnell (Garden City, N.Y.: Image Books, 1974), p. 16.

7. Ibid.

8. Ibid., pp. x–xi.

9. Thomas Merton, *Thoughts in Solitude* (Garden City, N.Y.: Image Books, 1956), p. 110.

10. See Thomas Merton, *Disputed Questions* (New York: Farrar, Straus & Cudahy, 1960), p. 171; "The Council and Religious Life," p. 9, and "The Council and Monasticism," p. 49, *The Impact of Vatican II*, ed. J. P. Dougherty (St. Louis: B. Herder Book Co., 1966).

11. John Howard Griffin (J.H.G.), from his notes on 1966.

12. Thomas Merton, unpublished journals, from J.H.G.'s notes. This complaint recurs frequently in his chronicle throughout the year.

13. On file at the Abbey.

14. Unpublished journals.

15. Ibid.

16. Naomi Burton Stone, "I Shall Miss Thomas Merton," *Cistercian Studies* 4:221 (1969).

17. John Eudes Bamberger, "The Cistercian," *Continuum* 7:229 (1969). Cf. Charles Dumont, "A Contemplative at the Heart of the World," *Lumen Vitae* 24:633–46 (1969).

18. Thomas Merton, *Life and Holiness* (Garden City, N.Y.: Image Books, 1964), p. 78.

19. Ibid., p. 8.

20. Ibid., p. 103.

21. Thomas Merton, *The Secular Journal of Thomas Merton* (Garden City, N.Y.: Image Books, 1969), p. 41. On "Peace," see p. 114.

22. Thomas Merton, *The Seven Storey Mountain* (New York: Harcourt, Brace & Company, 1948), p. 306. Failure of the physical examination for military service precluded his having to render any service.

23. Thomas Merton, *The Behavior of Titans* (New York: New Directions, 1961), pp. 65, 71.

24. Jean Leclercq, "Introduction," CWA, p. xiv.

25. Ibid.

26. Thomas Merton, *Zen and the Birds of Appetite* (New York: New Directions, 1968), p. 29.

27. Thomas Merton, *Conjectures of a Guilty Bystander* (Garden City, N.Y.: Image Books, 1968), p. 336. Hereafter cited as CGB.

28. Thomas Merton, *The Monk: Prophet to Modern Man*, Tape 9B, *The Thomas Merton Tapes*, ed. Norm Kramer (Chappaqua, New York: Electronic Paperbacks, 1972).

29. Thomas Merton, *Faith and Violence* (Notre Dame, Ind.:

University of Notre Dame Press, 1968), p. 145. Hereafter cited as *FV*.

30. "Prologue," *Raids*, p. 5. There is an allusion here to Berdyaev's *Dream and Reality*.

31. *CGB*, p. 124.

32. Ibid., p. 113.

33. "The Time of the End Is the Time of No Room," *Raids*, p. 75.

34. "Final Integration: Toward a 'Monastic Therapy,'" *Monastic Studies* 6:98 (All Saints 1968). Cf. "We Have to Make Ourselves Heard," *Catholic Worker* 23:5 (Jun, 1962).

35. Dumont, p. 634.

36. *Raids*, pp. 12–13.

37. Merton, *CGB*, p. 257.

38. *Thoughts in Solitude*, p. 22.

39. *CGB*, p. 222.

40. Ibid.

41. Frederic Joseph Kelly, S.J., *Man Before God: Thomas Merton on Social Responsibility* (Garden City, N.Y.: Doubleday & Company, 1974), p. 233–34.

42. Thomas Merton, *New Seeds of Contemplation* (New York: New Directions, 1961), pp. 86–87.

43. Gordon C. Zahn discussed Merton, King, and Gandhi as a triumvirate. "In Martin Luther King, the charismatic activist, and Merton, the cloistered contemplative, we find two thoroughly committed Christians who found inspiration in the life and acts of Gandhi; and they were alike, too, in their determination to make Gandhi's way relevant to the American scene and situation. In both we find the same sensitivity to the underlying unity that made what appeared to be two separate social issues, racial justice and world peace, really one. King's nonviolent struggle against discrimination and poverty forced him into open opposition to the war in Vietnam against the wishes and advice of many who felt that such opposition might split or weaken the movement he headed. Merton, of course, had no problem. With no activist movement dependent upon him for leadership, he was free to give equal weight to the search for peace and for justice to all men in his exposition of the fullness of Christian witness and responsibilities." Gordon C. Zahn, "Introduction," in Thomas Merton, *Thomas Merton on Peace* (New York: The McCall Publishing Company, 1962), p. xxi.

44. Thomas Merton, *Seeds of Destruction* (New York: Farrar, Straus & Giroux, 1961), p. 43.

45. *CGB*, p. 112.

46. *FV*, pp. 134–35.

47. Thomas Merton, "Neither Caliban nor Uncle Tom," *Liberation* 8:20 (Jun. 1963).

48. Eldridge Cleaver, *Soul on Ice* (New York: Dell, 1970), p. 42. Cf. E. Glenn Hinson, "Merton's Many Faces," *Religion and Life* 42:157 (1973).

49. Merton, *FV*, p. 3.

50. *CGB*, p. 33. Merton's analysis is very similar to that of W. J. Cash's pioneer sociological vivisection of the South, *The Mind of the South* (New York: Random House, 1941). However, this writer could find no evidence to indicate that he was familiar with the work.

51. *FV*, p. 141.

52. *New Seeds of Contemplation*, p. 54.

53. *FV*, p. 138.

54. Merton was awarded the Pax Medal in 1963. Pre-Vietnam discourses on peace may be found in the following: *Gandhi on Non-Violence*, ed., and "Introduction" (New York: New Directions, 1964); *Original Child Bomb* (New York: New Directions, 1962); *Seeds of Destruction*; "The Tower of Babel," *Jubilee* 3:20–35 (Oct. 1955).

55. *FV*, p. 87; *Thomas Merton on Peace*, p. 192.

56. Hinson, "Merton's Many Faces," p. 158. Merton seems almost always to have been a model monk in yielding to the authority of his superiors. He confided to several of his friends that the material disapproved was rash, too hurriedly put together, and not of good quality. The best of it did finally appear in his later published works on the subject. The censorship was most likely, he thought, providential.

57. Jim Forest, who, along with Philip Berrigan, merited Merton's dedication of *FV*, insists that the most important names in the movement, people like the Berrigans, John Howard Yoder, etc., viewed Merton as an important spiritual resource who served the movement best with his literary and prayer support from Gethsemani.

58. Thomas Merton, "Christian Culture Needs Oriental Wisdom," *Catholic World* 195:76 (May 1962).

59. *Thomas Merton on Peace*; he cites Mt. 5:9, 26:53, p. 13;

Ep. 2:14; Is. 9:6, 54:13; Ho. 2:18–20, p. 35. The Kingdom of God could not, he insisted, be brought in by force; Jn. 20:19; Ga. 5:22; Jn. 18:36; Rv. 11:15–18, 13:3–9, 17:6, 13:4ff, 19:3, pp. 36–37. Merton's works on this subject are replete with scriptural references; the above are cited only as examples.

60. Ibid., p. 13.

61. "We Have to Make Ourselves Heard," p. 5.

62. *Seeds of Destruction*, p. 138.

63. Origen, *Contra Celsum*, V, 33, in *Seeds of Destruction*, p. 139.

64. *Seeds of Destruction*, pp. 147–48.

65. *Thomas Merton on Peace*, p. 15. He cites as examples Hiroshima and Nagasaki. Cf. pp. 94ff.

66. FV, p. 7.

67. Ibid., p. 3.

68. *Thomas Merton on Peace*, p. 177. Cf. *Seeds of Destruction*, pp. 118ff.

69. Merton, FV, p. 14.

70. *Seeds of Destruction*, pp. 249–50.

71. FV, p. 112.

72. Merton quoted in E. Glenn Hinson, "The Catholicizing of Contemplation: Thomas Merton's Place in the Church's Prayer Life," *Perspectives in Religion* 1:18 (Summer 1973). Cf. Merton, "The Contemplative Life: Its Meaning and Necessity," FV, pp. 215–24; CWA, pp. 157–65, 334–84.

73. See his notes on Ailred and mystical transformation, Part I, *Monastic Orientation* (1950–52), Vol. XVI, *Collected Essays* (Trappist, Ky.: Abbey of Gethsemani, n.d.), p. 42.

74. Thomas Merton, *Mystics and Zen Masters* (New York: Farrar, Straus & Giroux, 1967), pp. 114–15.

75. Thomas Merton, *The Way of Chuang Tzu* (Trappist, Ky.: Abbey of Gethsemani, 1965), p. 17. Cf. *Disputed Questions*, pp. x ff.

76. Thomas Merton, "Notes on Christian Existentialism," *The Critic* 24:20 (Oct.–Nov. 1965). Cf. Thomas Merton, "Prayer, Personalism, and the Spirit," *Sisters Today* 42:129–36 (1970).

77. In his later years, because of his huge volume of correspondence, it became Merton's custom to circulate a Christmas letter among his many friends. This quotation was contained in his Christmas letter, December 1967.

78. "Prometheus: A Meditation," *Raids*, p. 84.

79. *Zen and the Birds of Appetite*, p. 31.

80. Quoted from *You Shall Be as Gods* (p. 88) in Thomas Merton, *Opening the Bible* (Collegeville, Minn.: Liturgical Press, 1970), p. 71.

81. "Christian Humanism," p. 233.

82. Julian of Norwich, *Revelations of Divine Love*, in F. C. Happold, *Mysticism: A Study and an Anthology* (Baltimore, Md.: Penguin Books, 1964), p. 292.

83. Merton, *Opening the Bible*, p. 74. Cf. Thomas Merton, "To Live Is to Love," *U. S. Catholic* 37:20 (Mar. 1972); "Christian Humanism," pp. 226, 230.

84. *Mystics and Zen Masters*, p. 118.

85. Unpublished material from original manuscript of *The Seven Storey Mountain*, *A Thomas Merton Reader* (Garden City, N.Y.: Image Books, 1974), p. 314. Cf. "Is the Contemplative Life Finished?," *Monastic Studies* 7:12 (Michaelmas 1969); Thomas Merton, *The New Man* (New York: Mentor-Omega Books, 1961), pp. 35, 85; *Ascent to Truth* (New York: Harcourt, Brace & Company, 1951), pp. 71, 260.

86. *FV*, p. 25. Cf. *New Seeds of Contemplation*, p. 32; "We Have to Make Ourselves Heard," p. 4.

87. Published under the title "As Man to Man," *Cistercian Studies* 4:93–94 (1969).

88. Brother Patrick Hart, who was Father Louis' secretary at the time of his death, says that the first draft was written in 1961. Merton apparently returned at intervals to the piece, periodically reworking it. Shortly before he left for Asia, Father Louis gave an annotated copy of his latest revision to Father Dan Walsh and asked him to comment on it. There are four different versions (some of the differences are slight) in the Ballarmine Collection. These comments are based on what appears to be the latest of the four. Father Louis' will forbids the publication of the work as a whole but permits its use by "qualified scholars." The Merton Legacy Trustees have been quite generous in the limits set for quotation. Because the work has not been published and most likely will never be published in its entirety, large portions of the work are included in the text and their location indicated in the same place.

89. Thomas Merton, "Merton [sic] View of Monasticism" (Calcutta: extemporaneous talk given to spiritual summit conference,

October 1968), p. 2. Cf. *CWA*, p. 14, and "Final Integration,"
p. 88.

90. *Contemplative Prayer*, p. 23.

91. *Mystics and Zen Masters*, p. 168.

92. Thomas Merton, "Extemporaneous Remarks," *The World of Religion Speaks on "The Relevance of Religion in the Modern World"* (The Hague: W. Junk N.V., 1970), p. 81.

93. "Extemporaneous Remarks," p. 75.

94. Ibid.

95. *CWA*, pp. 6–7.

96. "Is the Contemplative Life Finished?," pp. 12–13.

97. John Ruysbroeck, *The Adornment of the Spiritual Marriage*, in Happold, p. 254.

98. Merton, *New Seeds of Contemplation*, p. 39.

99. Bernard of Clairvaux, *Sermons on the Song of Songs*, in Happold, p. 206.

100. *Contemplative Prayer* (Garden City, N.Y.: Image Books, 1971), p. 33. The last phrase is from Augustine's *Confessions*.

101. *Contemplative Prayer*, p. 67.

102. Thomas Merton, "The Life that Unifies," ed. Naomi Burton Stone, *Sisters Today* 42:65 (1970). Cf. *FV*, p. 229, where he discusses Robinson's *Honest to God* and Tillich's idea of God as "pure ground of being." Merton had encountered a similar idea in his work on Blake at Columbia. "The knower and the thing known actually become identified. This identification of being and intelligence is also made by the Hindu, and it is implicit in Blake's remark, 'every eye sees differently. As the eye, such the object.'" Two sources are cited for support: *Transformation of Nature in Art* (Cambridge, Mass.: Harvard University Press, 1934), and William Blake, *Annotations to Reynolds*, p. 34 in *William Blake*, Vol. X, *Collected Essays*, p. 63.

103. *CWA*, pp. 100–1.

104. "Final Integration," pp. 88–89.

105. Ibid., p. 96.

106. *Spiritual Direction and Meditation*, p. 7.

107. *CGB*, p. 189.

108. "Merton View of Monasticism," p. 2.

109. *FV*, p. 67.

110. *Contemplative Prayer*, p. 25.

111. "The Inner Experience," p. 130. "The truth is that everyone would like to escape from the pressures, the anguish, the insecurity, and the peril of secular life: but that no one can do

without the benefits that are inseparably connected with these pressures. The paradox of the truly monastic vocation today is the paradox of a desire for peace that is strong enough to resist and break away from the conflicts of the world: for it is by conflict that the world holds us. And duty nowadays always seems to turn up on the side where there is the most conflict. One feels guilty in renouncing the struggles of secular life, as if one had some kind of obligation to go on accepting an existence in which the spirit is exhausted and frustrated: as if one could not in conscience allow himself to find real peace. And where the conflicts and contradictions of secular life find their way into a busy monastery, they suddenly by some miracle cease to be secular and become religious: business affairs and material preoccupations are now 'the cross' and to sidestep them is regarded as infidelity."

112. Ibid., pp. 132–36.
113. New Seeds of Contemplation, p. 150.
114. The New Man, p. 159.
115. Ibid., p. 160.
116. Ibid., p. 158.
117. New Seeds of Contemplation, p. 152.
118. Thomas Merton, The Asian Journal of Thomas Merton, ed. Naomi Burton, Brother Patrick Hart, and James Laughlin (New York: New Directions, 1973), p. 325.
119. CGB, p. 144. In another passage (pp. 89–90) he wrote: "How do I know what grace God can and does give to the sincere evangelical Christian who obeys the light of his conscience and follows Christ according to the faith and love he has received? I am persuaded that he would have greater security and clearer light if he were in my Church, but he does not see this as I do, and for this there are deeper and more complex reasons than either he or I can understand. Let us try to understand them, but meanwhile let us continue each in his own way, seeking the light with all sincerity."
120. New Seeds of Contemplation, p. 43. Cf. Ascent, p. 146.
121. "Is the Contemplative Life Finished?," p. 13.
122. CGB, p. 21. Cf. ibid., pp. 14–15, where he notes that the "ghetto mentality" is alien to both the spirit and the Rule of Benedict.
123. Aelred Graham quoted in Thomas Merton, "Zen: Sense and Sensibility," America 108:753 (May 25, 1963).
124. Mystics and Zen Masters, p. 207.

125. *The Way of Chuang Tzu*, p. 10. Contrast this with his stated position at the beginning of the decade (1961): "Where there may be some similarity in practices and even in vocabulary, and where all 'monks' whether Christian or otherwise may seem to be seeking the same kind of spiritual perfection, these similarities are merely external. They represent nothing more than a 'material convergence.' Resemblances which may be apparent to the uninitiated observer are in fact masks of realities that differ totally in their essence. Hence there can be no univocal concept of 'monk' which applies both to Christian and non-Christian monasticism." *Monastic Origins*, Vol. XVIII, *Collected Essays*, p. 1. Both exponents and critics have sometimes taken the position that mysticism is mysticism whatever nomenclature is attached to it, e.g., William James, *Varieties of Religious Experience* (rev. ed.; New Hyde Park, N.Y.: University Books, 1963), p. 419: "In Hinduism, in neoplatonism, in Sufism, in Christian mysticism, in Whitmanism, we find the same recurring note, so that there is about mystical utterances an eternal unanimity which ought to make a critic stop and think, and which brings it about that the mystical classics have, as has been said, neither birthday nor native land. Perpetually telling of the unity of man with God, their speech antedates languages and they do not grow old."

126. "Nhat Hanh Is My Brother," *Thomas Merton on Peace*, pp. 262–63. He wrote of Nhat Hanh, ". . . he has shown us that Zen is not an esoteric and world-denying cult of inner illumination, but that it has its rare and unique sense of responsibility in the modern world. . . . We are both monks . . . both poets, both existentialists." Ibid., p. 263.

127. James, p. 195.

128. Merton points out in his Foreword to Sally Donelly, "Marcel and Buddha: A Metaphysics of Enlightenment," *The Journal of Religious Thought* 24, 1:51 (1967–68) that in spite of this protest, "the basic insights of Buddhism are philosophical and metaphysical." Merton investigated all the Eastern religions whose literature and practice were familiar or available to him, but his greatest affinity (and, for that matter, access to information) was for Buddhism, particularly Zen.

129. *Mystics and Zen Masters*, p. 252.

130. Ibid., p. 241. Merton detected a special problem for his Catholic brothers who had been trained in Scholastic theology and Aristotelian logic. That such men should be aggressively hos-

tile to Zen, with its stress on nonlogical being and contemplation, should surprise no one. Ibid., pp. 8–9.

131. Ibid., p. 245.

132. Ibid., p. 245.

133. "Zen: Sense and Sensibility," p. 753. Cf. *Zen and the Birds of Appetite*, p. 69. Here he cites similar language in John of the Cross.

134. *Mystics and Zen Masters*, p. 17.

135. "Final Integration," p. 89.

136. From the Dhammapada, in D. T. Suzuki, "Knowledge and Innocence," *Zen and the Birds of Appetite*, p. 107.

137. Meister Eckhart, Sermon, "Blessed Are the Poor," in Blakney, p. 231, in ibid., p. 9. Merton also calls on the witness of his old friend John of the Cross. "St. John of the Cross compares man to a window through which the light of God is shining. If the windowpane [sic] is clean of every stain, it is completely transparent, we do not see it at all: it is 'empty' and nothing is seen but the light. But if a man bears in himself the stains of spiritual egotism and preoccupation with his illusory and exterior self, even in 'good things,' then the windowpane itself is clearly seen by reason of the stains that are on it." Merton, *Zen and the Birds of Appetite*, p. 119.

138. *Zen and the Birds of Appetite*, pp. 55–56.

139. *Mystics and Zen Masters*, p. 41. Merton correlates this with John of the Cross's attitude toward the flesh and finds no conflict. "This reminds us of St. John of the Cross and his teaching that the 'Spiritual Way' is falsely conceived if it is thought to be a denial of flesh, sense, and vision in order to arrive at higher spiritual experience. On the contrary, the 'dark night of sense' which sets the house of flesh at rest is at best a serious beginning. The true dark night is that of the spirit, where the 'subject' of all higher forms of vision and intelligence is itself darkened and left in emptiness: not as a mirror, pure of all impressions, but as a void without knowledge and without any natural capacity to know the supernatural." Ibid., pp. 25–26. Merton operates in the context of Suzuki's position that Zen is basically an attitude of mind, a metaphysical intuition about life. "Zen: Sense and Sensibility," p. 752.

140. *Mystics and Zen Masters*, pp. 12, 74.

141. *Zen and the Birds of Appetite*, p. 38.

142. Thomas Merton, "Address to the Special General Chapter, Sisters of Loretto" (Aug. 1967), p. 7. Merton continues to as-

sert that this concept of spiritual direction is implicit in Benedict's writings.

143. "To Live Is to Love," p. 23.

144. Foreword to "Marcel and Buddha," pp. 52–56.

145. *Mystics and Zen Masters*, p. 16.

146. Eckhart, in Blakney, in *Zen and the Birds of Appetite*, p. 10. The next sentence after Merton ends his excerpt. Eckhart says ". . . there is something in the soul so closely akin to God that it is already one with him and need never be united to him." It is not difficult to see why Suzuki felt an affinity with Eckhart. Even the language in which Eckhart cast his mysticism has the flavor of the East. Compare the following passage from Eckhart with the one below it taken from the *Bhagavad-Gita*. "There is in the soul something which is above the soul, Divine, simple, a pure nothing; rather nameless than named, rather unknown than known. . . . Sometimes I have called it a power, sometimes an uncreated light, and sometimes a Divine spark." In William R. Inge, *Studies of English Mystics* (Freeport, N.Y.: Books for Libraries Press, n.d.), pp. 157–58.

> See!
> Steadfast a lamp burns sheltered from the wind;
> Such is the likeness of the Yogi's mind
> Shut from sense storms and burning bright to heaven.
> When the mind broods placid, soothed with holy wont,
> When Self contemplates self, and in itself
> Hath comfort; when it knows the nameless joy
> Beyond all scope of sense, revealed to soul—
> Only to soul, and knowing wavers not
> True to the farther Truth . . .
>   Call that state "peace"
> That happy severance "yoga." (Bk. VI)

147. John Tauler, quoted in *Contemplative Prayer*, p. 82.

148. John Ruysbroeck, *The Adornment of the Spiritual Marriage*, II, in *Contemplative Prayer*, p. 82.

149. David Steindl-Rast, "Recollections of Thomas Merton's Last Days in the West," *Monastic Studies* 7:10 (1969).

150. Merton, "Christian Culture Needs Oriental Wisdom," p. 78.

151. John of the Cross, *The Collected Works of St. John of the Cross*, trans. Kieran Kavanaugh and Otilio Rodriquez (Garden City, N.Y.: Doubleday & Company, 1964), p. 582.

152. Augustine, *Enarratio in Psalmum 41*, in Edward Cuthbert Butler, *Western Mysticism*, p. 22, in "The Inner Experience," p. 12.

153. Augustine, *Confessions*, vii, 16, in Butler, p. 31, in "The Inner Experience," p. 12. Also cited are two passages from John Tauler. Both texts, although from different works, are rich in mystical language and symbol. "Now man with all his faculties and also with his soul recollects himself and enters into the temple (his inner self) in which, in all truth, he finds God dwelling and at work. Man then comes to experience God not after the fashion of the senses and of reason, or like something that one understands or reads . . . but he tastes Him, and enjoys Him like something that springs up from the 'ground' of the soul as from its own source, or from a fountain, without having been brought there, for a fountain is better than a cistern, the water of cisterns gets stale and evaporates, but the spring flows, bursts out, swells: it is true, not borrowed. It is sweet." 'Sermon for Thursday before Palm Sunday' "The Inner Experience," p. 13. "After this, one should open the ground of the soul and the deep will to the sublimity of the glorious Godhead, and look upon Him with great and humble fear and denial of oneself. He who in this fashion casts down before God his shadowy and unhappy ignorance then begins to understand the words of Job who said: The spirit passed before me. From this passage of the Spirit is born a great tumult in the soul. And the more this passage has been clear, true and unmixed with natural impressions, all the more rapid, strong, prompt, true and pure will be the work which takes place in the soul, the thrust which overturns it; clearer also will be the knowledge that man has stopped on the path to perfection. The Lord then comes like a flash of lightning; he fills the ground of the soul with light and wills to establish Himself there as the Master Workman. As soon as one is conscious of the presence of the Master, one must, in all passivity, abandon the work to Him." (II Sermon for the Exaltation of the Holy Cross, No. 5) Ibid.

154. Thomas Merton, "The Self of Modern Man and the New Christian Consciousness," *R. M. Burke Memorial Society for the Study of Religious Experience Newsletter-Review*, Vol. II, No. 1 (Apr. 1967), p. 18.

155. Ibid.

156. See Thomas Merton, "Introduction and Commentary," Al-

bert Camus, *The Plague* (New York: The Seabury Press, 1968), and "Rain and the Rhinoceros," Thomas Merton, *Raids on the Unspeakable* (New York: New Directions, 1966), pp. 9–26.

157. *Zen and the Birds of Appetite*, p. 4.

158. Suzuki, *Introduction to Zen Buddhism*, p. 51, in *Zen and the Birds of Appetite*, p. 49.

159. FV, p. 269.

160. "An Apostle of Discretion," *The Cell of Self-Knowledge: Seven Old English Mystical Works*, ed. Edmund Gardner, in Evelyn Underhill, *Mysticism* (New York: E. P. Dutton & Co., 1961), p. 85.

161. Merton, "Herakleitos the Obscure," *The Behavior of Titans, A Thomas Merton Reader*, p. 263.

162. Eckhart, in Happold, p. 238. Cf. Underhill, p. 32. "When I stand empty *in* God's will and of all His works and of God Himself,' cries Eckhart with his usual violence of language, '*then* am I above all creatures and am neither God nor creature, but I am what I was and evermore shall be.'" ("*Schriften und Predigten aus dem Mittelhochdeutschen," ubersetzt und herausgegeben von Buttner*), p. lxxxvii.

163. Thomas Merton, "Song: If You Seek," *Emblems of a Season of Fury* (Trappist, Ky.: Abbey of Gethsemani, 1961), pp. 38–39.

164. In 1967, Merton responded to a request to rate his major works on the following scale: best, better, good, fair, poor, bad, awful. Inevitably, those works that can be characterized as dogmatic fall into the lowest range. *What Are These Wounds?* (1950) enjoys the dubious distinction of the lowest assessment, being placed at the bottom of the "awful" range. *Exile Ends in Glory* (1949), a little-known spiritual biography, fared little better. *Season of Celebration* (1965), the last of his works marked by a degree of Catholic ghetto mentality, joins *Living Bread* (1956) and *Spiritual Direction and Meditation* (1960) on the "bad" line.

165. FV, p. 147.

166. *Asian Journal*, p. 296.

167. James, p. 380.

168. Ibid.

169. Ibid., p. 381.

170. Pseudo-Dionysius, *Mystical Theology*, in Thomas M. Gannon and George W. Traub, *The Desert and the City* (London: The Macmillan Company, 1969), p. 45.

171. James, pp. 420–21.
172. Luke Flaherty, "Thomas Merton's Cables to the Ace: A Critical Study," Renascence XXIV (Autumn 1971).
173. Thomas Merton, Cables to the Ace; or Familiar Liturgies of Misunderstanding (New York: New Directions, 1968), p. 1.
174. Ibid., p. 7.
175. Ibid., p. 58. Cf. p. 27, where he advocates being "no man" "no where," life waiting to be born!
176. Ibid., p. 55.
177. Ibid., p. 27.
178. Thomas Merton, The Geography of Lograire (New York: New Directions, 1969), p. 1.
179. Ibid.
180. Ibid., p. 36.
181. Thomas Merton, The Strange Islands (New York: New Directions, 1957), p. 41.
182. Ibid., p. 42.

CHAPTER VI

1. John Howard Griffin (J.H.G.), Notes on 1965.
2. J.H.G., Notes on 1966.
3. Henri J. Nouwen, Pray to Live, trans. David Schlaver (Notre Dame, Ind.: Fides Press, 1972), p. 33. De Pinto alludes to this quality in his eulogy on Merton: ". . . there was something of Thomas Merton that remained hidden and secret; there were inmost depths of the man. . . ." Basil De Pinto, "In Memoriam: Thomas Merton, 1915–1968," The Cistercian Spirit: A Symposium in Memory of Thomas Merton, ed. M. Basil Pennington (Shannon, Ir.: Irish University Press, 1969), p. viii
4. Thomas Merton, Conjectures of a Guilty Bystander (Garden City, N.Y.: Image Books, 1968), p. 160.
5. Thomas Merton, "Who Is It That Has a Transcendent Experience?," R. M. Burke Memorial Society for the Study of Religious Experience Newsletter-Review, Vol. 1, No. 2 (Sept. 1966), p. 7.
6. Thomas Merton, Notes on Art and Worship, p. 18.
7. Merton, quoted in James Thomas Baker, Thomas Merton, Social Critic (Lexington: The University Press of Kentucky, 1971), p. 71.
8. Thomas Merton, No Man Is an Island (Garden City, N.Y.: Image Books, 1967), p. 109.

9. Baker, p. 145.

10. Merton, CGB, p. 91.

11. Thomas Merton, Thoughts in Solitude (Garden City, N.Y.: Image Books, 1956), p. 13.

12. Thomas Merton, Life and Holiness (Garden City, N.Y.: Image Books, 1964), p. 38.

13. No Man Is an Island, p. 9.

14. Thomas Merton, Faith and Violence (Notre Dame, Ind.: University of Notre Dame Press, 1968), p. 25.

15. Ibid., p. 213.

16. Jean Leclercq, "New Forms of Contemplation and of the Contemplative Life," Theological Studies 33:318 (June 1972).

17. Thomas Merton, "Final Integration: Toward a 'Monastic Therapy,'" Monastic Studies 6:93 (All Saints 1968).

18. Thomas Merton, "Two Comments for Forum," Art and Literature, Vol. IV, Collected Essays (Trappist, Ky.: Abbey of Gethsemani, n.d.), p. 8.

19. Thomas Merton, The Asian Journal of Thomas Merton, ed. Naomi Burton, Brother Patrick Hart, and James Laughlin (New York: New Directions, 1973), pp. 312–13.

20. Asian Journal, p. 154.

21. See Aelred Graham, "Thomas Merton: A Modern Man in Reverse," Atlantic Monthly 191:72 (1953); also Virgina M. Shaddy, "Thomas Merton and No Man Is an Island," Catholic World 184:54 (1956).

22. Casserley has written convincingly of Augustine's metaphysics of unity or philosophy of the singular. See J. V. Langmead Casserley, The Christian in Philosophy (London: Faber and Faber, 1946), pp. 40–47.

23. Thomas Merton, Mystics and Zen Masters (New York: Farrar, Straus & Giroux, 1967), p. 282.

24. "Who Is It That Has a Transcendent Experience?," p. 5.

25. Ibid.

26. Christian Duquoc, "Theology and Spirituality," Spirituality in the Secular City, ed. Christian Duquoc (Glenrock, N.J.: Paulist Press, 1966), p. 89.

27. William James, The Varieties of Religious Experience (rev. ed.; New Hyde Park, N.Y.: University Books, 1963), p. 388.

28. Paul Tillich, Systematic Theology, III (Chicago: University of Chicago Press, 1967), p. 83.

29. Thomas Merton, "Freedom and Spontaneity," Tape 60 (Louisville, Ky.: Thomas Merton Collection, Bellarmine College).

30. Thomas Merton, "To Live Is to Love," *U. S. Catholic* 37:23 (Mar. 1972).

31. Thomas Merton, Notebooks from J.H.G., Notes on 1966.

32. Raymond Panikkar, "The Theandric Vocation," *Monastic Studies* 8:71 (Spring 1972).

OTHER IMAGE BOOKS

OTHER IMAGE BOOKS

OTHER IMAGE BOOKS

OTHER IMAGE BOOKS

OTHER IMAGE BOOKS